Our increasing national reliance on the criminal justice system as the preferred means of dealing with a wide range of vexing social, economic, and personal problems has contributed to racial and social instability. The war on drugs, begun in the Reagan administration and still continuing, has created an explosion in the American prison population, with the number of prison inmates now threatening to exceed the number of students attending college. Whether or not by design, this increase has been accounted for by a severely disproportionate number of African-American males. In *Search and Destroy*, Jerome Miller demonstrates that an African-American male between the ages of 18 and 35 has an inordinate likelihood of encountering the criminal justice system at some point during those years.

Miller contends that the drug war's racial bias has exacerbated an already present prejudice throughout the criminal justice system. This bias makes it much more likely not only that young black males will encounter that system, but that they will begin to develop, on the basis of minor offenses more easily plea-bargained than contested, records that result in mandatory prison sentences for any subsequent encounters. The entire system, Miller argues, cascades from a greater likelihood of blacks' initial encounter with the justice system to an increased probability of incarceration for longer and longer periods.

In a wide-ranging survey, Miller describes widespread bias among police officers, probation officers, and courts, while social scientists, whose data form the basis for much public policy toward crime, and social workers, whose responsibility is allegedly to members of the underclass, have uncritically accepted the questionable assumptions of criminal justice processing. He warns that the sudden rekindling of interest in genetics and crime along with the creation of a massive crime control industry hold even greater danger for racial minorities in their encounters with the justice system.

Search and Destroy

Search and Destroy

African-American Males in the Criminal Justice System

JEROME G. MILLER

CAMBRIDGE
UNIVERSITY PRESS

PUBLISHED BY THE PRESS SYNDICATE OF THE UNIVERSITY OF CAMBRIDGE
The Pitt Building, Trumpington Street, Cambridge CB2 1RP, United Kingdom

CAMBRIDGE UNIVERSITY PRESS
The Edinburgh Building, Cambridge CB2 2RU, United Kingdom
40 West 20th Street, New York, NY 10011-4211, USA
10 Stamford Road, Oakleigh, Melbourne 3166, Australia

© Cambridge University Press 1996

First edition published 1996
Reprinted 1996 (twice)
First paperback edition 1997
Reprinted 1997

Printed in the United States of America

Typeset in Ehrhardt

A catalogue record for this book is available from the British Library

Library of Congress Cataloguing-in-Publication Data is available

ISBN 0-521-46021-2 hardback
ISBN 0-521-59858-3 paperback

Tables and Figures

Tables

Contents

To Patrick

He is telling a terrible story,
But it doesn't diminish his glory.
Gilbert & Sullivan,
Pirates of Penzance

Figures

Preface

I wrestled with this book for too long. From the beginning, it has been a work in progress that could have gone on indefinitely. The early rewrites too often arose from paltry attempts to find "consensual validation" where none was possible. Then, as matters of crime, race, and justice grew crazier across the country, I found myself rushing to make changes in the manuscript as my most dire predictions wound their way into national policy – all before I could get the book to press. It is an oddly disorienting experience to mouth "Aha!" as one's nightmares keep coming true.

The errors are my own. However, I take some refuge in the traditions of St. Thomas Aquinas, who held that while sins of the intellect may be great, those of passion are more easily forgiven. Try as I might, I can't excise passion from my work or my writing. However, I do not see this as inappropriate to intellectual discovery. Having labored in the criminal justice field as a researcher, teacher, administrator, and clinician, I've been privileged to see it from many vantage points. To paraphrase Jacques Barzun,[1] when one is moved by a rich cluster of feelings, experiences, and ideas, one comes to see reality as a series of postulates with history as the court of appeals.

For the better part of a century and a half, most observers had seen the criminal justice system as highly influenced by race and occasionally suffused with racism. Recently, however, as relations between blacks and whites deteriorated and as the gap between rich and poor widened, something quite remarkable happened simultaneously. Researchers and policymakers were suggesting that racism had been largely excised if not totally eliminated from the criminal justice system in the United States. This conclusion seemed wrongheaded to many of us who were involved in the daily rituals of criminal justice processing. However, the social prestige accorded these new policy commentators was so compelling, and the mathematical models developed by their researchers so dazzling, as to silence any naysayers lest they appear unsophisticated. I hope that this book will give some small voice to that dwindling number of brave souls in the criminological community who have not yet jettisoned their critical sense and denied their own experience in pursuit of a fashionable and (despite its positivistic pretensions) a highly ideological kind of validation.

The auxiliary thesis of this book is that criminal justice processing, in and of itself (arrest, jailing, convicting, imprisonment), is an alienating and socially destabilizing exercise that usually creates more problems than it solves. Though this view has its roots in the works of respected observers and theorists like George Herbert Mead and Erving Goffman, it is conditioned by three decades of direct clinical work with too many young offenders whose identities have been assaulted and whose families have been irrevocably crippled by the ministrations of juvenile or criminal justice. The national attempt to deal with a wide array of economic, social, and personal problems through criminal justice processing has brought social disaster to our cities. If we are to make progress, we will need a new paradigm. It will be possible only when we begin handling most "criminalizable" incidents outside the criminal justice system altogether.

I must first thank Alex Holzman, my editor at Cambridge University Press, who, despite our occasional differences over content, and Alex's greater concerns over my at times too combative style (he called it "ranting"), turned out to be correct. The book is much the better for Alex's intransigence. As a result of his advice, I retreated from some themes. But stubborn as I am, I've occasionally managed to disguise them and slip them in anyway.

I'd still be pounding out redrafts had it not been for the timely intervention of Cynthia Ayers, whose iron-fisted editing always came in a velvet glove. As a result of Cynthia's efforts, the manuscript was shortened by a third. Her approach forced me to focus while her manner allowed me to save face – afflicted as I am with the virus of obsessively treasuring phrases, meanderings, and what I vainly perceive at times to be monumental insights.

I wish as well to thank Barbara Folsom, whose copyediting brought the manuscript to the point where it began to look like a legitimate book in record time. Her unsolicited comments on the content were much welcomed at a particularly critical time. Likewise, the timely efforts of production editor Helen Wheeler assured that the manuscript, after so much delay, moved onto the fast track to publication.

Particular thanks to Alice ("Sunshine") Boring, who bore the brunt of having to deal with a dozen or so rewrites as I worked in my responses to constantly changing events. Her skills at layout, charting, and graphs are unparalleled and she displayed a patience well beyond what one could legitimately expect.

The staff of the National Center on Institutions and Alternatives also helped with much of the research, bringing matters to my attention, finding obscure citations, assisting in rewrites, alternately criticizing and offering suggestions. I wish to thank Herb Hoelter, cofounder of NCIA, who came into my life two decades ago as a student intern, and over the ensuing years has become an irreplaceable colleague and trusted mentor in good times and bad. Thanks also to Mary Cate Rush, a friend of 30 years (since she was a child), for her assistance and patience in running down particularly elusive data and for offering her critical sense as this book took shape. Likewise, I wish to thank T. J. Ambrosio, Eric Lotke, and John

Irvin, each of whom assisted in the research and offered many constructive ideas and comments.

I was fortunate to have the counsel of friends and colleagues who I'd come to trust over the years for their critical assessments. They include Jim Vorenberg, former Dean of Harvard University Law School; John McKnight, Co-Director of Northwestern University's Center for Urban Affairs; Professor Andrew Rutherford, Professor of Law at Southampton University, England; Dr. Gisela Konopka, Professor Emeritus at the University of Minnesota School of Social Work; Michael Tonry, University of Minnesota Law School; Professor Rosemary Sarri of the Department of Sociology and Social Work at the University of Michigan; Simon Dinitz, Professor Emeritus in Sociology at The Ohio State University; Ira Schwartz, Dean of the University of Pennsylvania School of Social Work; Professor Leon Kamin of Northeastern University; Dr. Barry Krisberg, Director of the National Council on Crime and Delinquency; Professor John Hagan at the University of Toronto; Professor Alfred Blumstein, Dean of the Department of Sociology at Carnegie Mellon University; Professor John Laub at Northeastern University; and former Chairman of the District of Columbia City Council, the late John Wilson.

Finally, I must thank my wife, Charlene, for her inexhaustible patience and abiding support during my recurring bouts of irascibility and depression as we watched so many tragic events regarding crime and race unfold across the nation. Through it all, she still found time to prepare the index to this book.

Introduction

Amid two decades of economic growth and social neglect, the white majority in America presented its inner cities with an expensive gift – a new and improved criminal justice system. It would, the government promised, bring domestic tranquility – with particular relevance to African-Americans. No expense was spared in crafting and delivering it inside the city gates. In reality the gift was a Trojan Horse.

While neoconservative commentators like Charles Murray argued that welfare had undermined family stability and sabotaged work incentives, the real value of Aid to Families with Dependent Children (AFDC) and food-stamp payments to the poor had been steadily declining.[1] Not so with criminal justice. In a society obsessed with single mothers on welfare, more money ($31 billion) was being spent in 1993 at local, state, and federal levels on a failed drug war (mostly directed at African-American and Latino citizens) than on AFDC, that much vaunted symbol of liberal largesse ($25 billion).[2] The politics of crime and welfare came with a decidedly racial cast.[3]

As governmental investment in social and employment programs in the inner city was held stable or reduced, the criminal justice system was ratcheted up to fill the void. The citizenry was told the reason was an explosion of crime – particularly, violent crime. However, a closer look would show this to be a highly questionable premise.[4] Meanwhile, federal, state, and local funding of the justice system literally exploded in the 1980s. Average direct federal, state, and local expenditures for police increased 416%; for courts, 585%; for prosecution and legal services, 1,019%; for public legal defense, 1,255%; and for corrections, 990%. Federal spending for justice grew by 668%, county spending increased 711%, and state spending surged 848%. By 1990, the country was spending at least $75 billion annually in direct costs to apprehend and lock up offenders.[5] However, even these figures were grossly understated.[6] With the passage of federal crime legislation and the rush to enact similar measures across the nation, the United States was spending in excess of $200 billion annually on the crime-control industry by the mid-1990s.

To the inner cities, all this criminal justice activity brought a war mentality, destructive strategies, and vicious tactics, which exacerbated the violence and fueled social disorganization far beyond whatever negative effects might hitherto have been attributed to single-parent homes, welfare dependency, or the putative loss of family values. The white majority embraced the draconian measures with enthusiasm, particularly as it became clear that they were falling heaviest on minorities in general, and on African-American males in particular.

Although crime had occasionally surfaced as a lesser concern in polls taken over the previous three decades, only in the mid-1990s did it show up as a major, if not *the* major concern of the public. Why, then, all the divisive politics and frenetic activity surrounding crime? Some insight might have been culled from a seminal paper written by the respected "symbolic interactionist" sociologist Herbert Blumer a quarter-century earlier. Blumer had observed that what we decide to label as social problems "are fundamentally products of a process of collective definition" and do not exist "as a set of objective social arrangements with an intrinsic makeup."[7]

Blumer's insight is at the center of the contemporary sociological debate over what constitutes a "social problem." "Objectivists" saw our social problems as resulting from an objective set of conditions. "Constructionists" studied the emergence of these crises in terms of "claims-making" and "typification" – that is, how a set of conditions comes to be defined and typified as a "social problem" (e.g., through demonstrations, marketing "think tank" reports, publicizing books, journalistic investigative reports, and political initiatives) – and thereby made eligible for anything from public curiosity to public obsession. As the constructionist sociologist Joel Best commented: "Any social condition is a potential subject for claims-making, or rather for several kinds of claims-making. Each social condition can be constructed as many social problems."[8] In his compilation of articles on how some contemporary "social problems" were constructed and "typified," Best cited studies with the following titles:

- "Horror Stories and the Construction of Child Abuse";
- "Dark Figures and Child Victims: Statistical Claims about Missing Children";
- "Learning Disabilities, Dyslexia, and the Medicalization of the Classroom";
- " 'Violence' Is 'Violence' . . . or Is It?"
- "The Social Construction of 'Wife Abuse' and Public Policy";
- " 'A Greater Threat than the Soviet Union': Mexican Immigration as a Social Problem."

With the marriage of electronic news to entertainment consummated in the early 1990s, no set of social conditions better lent itself to manipulation by claims-makers than crime. Crime became a political game of bait and switch. The bait was violent crime – more money and resources were necessary to fight it. The switch occurred when the newly acquired criminal justice armamentaria were brought to bear. Because relatively few violent offenders could be found among the millions of underclass citizens of color who received the brunt of the newly energized justice system – from police to prosecutors – the definitions of dangerousness were twisted and stretched to include as many among them as possible, as often as possible.

It was perhaps not so ironic, therefore, that the incident which plunged Los Angeles into civil disorder in 1992 involved the police beating a convicted felon. It was a phenomenon of the same genre as that which occurred when Americans were polled about whether, after viewing the most publicized murder trial of the century, they thought the African-American sports hero and actor O. J. Simpson was guilty or innocent. The responses to the poll fell along clearly divided racial lines, over 80% of whites seeing Simpson as guilty whereas a similar percentage of blacks felt he was probably innocent.

In the contemporary American scene, though a white suburban jury might buy the sharp difference between the criminal and the law-abiding, such neat distinctions have limited force in communities where most have seen a father, son, brother, or close friend hauled away and labeled as "criminal." The phenomenon was not confined to Los Angeles. Polls have consistently shown that African-Americans and Hispanics view the police in often diametrically opposed ways from how whites do. For example, 43% of all respondents to a 1994 *New York Times* poll believed that corruption was widespread in the city police force. When broken down by race, however, 58% of blacks polled and 51% of Hispanic respondents viewed the police as corrupt, compared to only 32% of white respondents.[9]

How Many Enemies Are There?

In the early stages of the rioting, when Los Angeles city prosecutors ran background checks on the first 1,000 arrestees charged with misdemeanors (most having to do with curfew violations), they discovered that 6 out of 10 had criminal records and nearly a third were on probation or parole. From this important bit of information, the deputy city attorney drew the kind of flawed conclusion that has shaped justice policy in the inner city for most of the past two decades: "This was not an instantaneous 'good guy rage' kind of thing," said deputy city attorney John Wilson. "This was a 'bad guy' taking advantage of a situation out of control."[10] Wilson's statement was, at best, misinformed.

Indeed, a 1991 study of the Los Angeles County Adult Detention Center revealed that *nearly one-third of all the young black men (ages 20–29) living in Los Angeles County had already been jailed at least once in that same year.*[11] At this point, good-guy versus bad-guy analyses begin to falter. The figures suggested that the absolute majority of young black males in Los Angeles could expect to be dragged into one or another of the county's jails, detention centers, camps, or prisons as they traversed the years between adolescence and age 30. Similar patterns were showing up in other large cities.[12]

What the city attorney seemed not to realize was that, had he stopped 1,000 inner-city African-American young men at random in 1992, rioting or not, at least 500 to 600 would have been found to have criminal records. What he should have considered was the *kind* of records they had. The Los Angeles County deputy public defender cited the case of one of his clients, a 50-year-old man arrested during the riots. His criminal record consisted of a single drunk-driving arrest 20 years earlier.[13]

The social disaster that is now overtaking black males in the United States has been brewing for a long time. In 1967, the socioeconometrician Alfred Blumstein noted that if then current patterns continued, the chances of a black male city resident's being arrested at some time in his life for a nontraffic offense was as high as 90%, with 51% being charged with a felony.[14] In their 1970 birth cohort study of Philadelphia boys who had been born in 1945, University of Pennsylvania criminologists Marvin Wolfgang,

Robert Figlio, and Thorsten Sellin discovered that 52% of non-white boys and 29% of white boys had been arrested by age 18.[15]

Blumstein and Elizabeth Graddy examined 1968–1972 arrest statistics from the country's 56 largest cities.[16] Looking only at felony arrests, they found that one out of every four males living in a large city could expect to be arrested for a felony at some point in his life. When broken down by race, however, they found that *a nonwhite male was three and a half times more likely to have a felony arrest than a white male.* Whereas 14% of white males would be arrested, *51% of nonwhite males could anticipate being arrested for a felony at some time during their lives.*[17]

Misdemeanors, which make up the largest share of arrests and bookings into jails, were not included in Blumstein and Graddy's calculations. Had they been, the percentage of nonwhite males who could expect to be arrested and jailed at least briefly would have reached Blumstein's original 90% prediction. As appalling as Blumstein's numbers seemed, they were confirmed by others over the ensuing decades.

In 1987, Robert Tillman, a criminologist assigned to the California Attorney General's Office, found a similar pattern in arrests of nonwhite males in California, not over a lifetime but in the short 12-year span between ages 18 and 30. Drawing upon a 1974 "cohort" of 18-year-old males of all races, Tillman traced their arrest records between 1974 and 1986, when they turned 30. At least one out of three had been arrested. When he broke the percentages down by race, however, he discovered that *two-thirds of the nonwhite adult males had been arrested and jailed before completing their 29th year (41% for a felony).*[18] Tillman did not include juvenile arrests or arrests after age 30. Had he done so, the lifetime risk of arrest would likely have surpassed 85%. Moreover, Tillman's cohort of 18-year-olds was drawn from across the whole state of California, including both rural and urban youth, not exclusively city populations as in the Blumstein–Graddy study. Had he confined his sample to inner-city minority youth, the number arrested before completing their 29th year would have approached 80%.

A 1990 Rand Corporation study of the economics of the drug trade in the District of Columbia found that one-third of *all* the African-American young men between the ages of 18 and 21 who lived in the district had been arrested and charged with a criminal offense. Moreover, the Rand researchers noted that the fraction of one-third for black males aged 19 did not "decline noticeably over the age range 20–29, as other studies of crime rates in the general population have suggested."[19] The Rand researchers did not include juvenile arrests; had they done so, other research suggests they would have found that close to half of the District of Columbia's young men had been arrested and jailed or detained before reaching legal adulthood.[20]

Also in 1990, the nonprofit Washington, D.C.–based Sentencing Project released the results of a survey revealing that *on an average day in the United States, one in every four African-American men ages 20–29 was either in prison, jail, or on probation/parole.*[21] The study caused a brief flurry in the media, but the next logical question went unasked by the press. If one in four young African-American males are under correctional supervision on any given day, what percentage *have been, or will be* drawn into the justice system? As it turned out, the Sentencing Project's figures pointed to a social disaster.

In 1992, the National Center on Institutions and Alternatives (NCIA) conducted a survey of young African-American males in Washington, D.C.'s justice system. It found that *on an average day in 1991, more than four in ten (42%) of all the 18–35-year-old African-American males who lived in the District of Columbia were in jail, in prison, on probation/parole, out on bond, or being sought on arrest warrants.* On the basis of this "one-day" count, it was estimated that approximately 75% of all the 18-year-old African-American males in the city could look forward to being arrested and jailed at least once before reaching age 35. The lifetime risk probably hovered somewhere between 80% and 90%.[22]

Three months later, NCIA completed a similar survey in Baltimore, Maryland. It proved even more disturbing. Of 60,715 African-American males aged 18–35 living in Baltimore, 34,025 were under justice supervision of some sort. *This meant that on an average day in Baltimore, 56% of all its young African-American males were in prison, jail, on probation/parole, on bail, or being sought on arrest warrants.*

In Baltimore, the rationale given by police and prosecutors for the high arrest rates among young black men was fear of violence arising from the so-called war on drugs. However, fewer than 1 in 10 arrests in Baltimore were for violent crimes. Most young black men who were being arrested and jailed were charged with lesser felonies and misdemeanors. The racial disparities were most alarming when drug arrests were isolated. African-Americans of all ages were being arrested for drug offenses in Baltimore at six times the rate of whites, and over 90% of these arrests were for "possession."[23]

Preliminary results of a 1993 study by the California State Assembly's Commission on the Status of African-American Males revealed that one-sixth (104,000) of California's 625,000 black men 16 and older are arrested *each year,* "thereby creating police records which hinder later job prospects." The researchers found that 64% of the drug arrests of whites and 81% of Latinos were also not sustainable. Perhaps the most startling finding was that *92% of the black men arrested by police on drug charges were subsequently released for lack of evidence or inadmissible evidence.* Black men, who made up only 3% of California's population, accounted for 40% of those entering state prisons.[24]

The Limits of "Them" versus "Us" Paradigms

All of these studies challenged what Tillman referred to as the "two assumptions [that] underlie most popular discussion of crime": (1) The world is made up of two types of people, those who commit crimes and those who do not; and (2) Criminals form a very small portion of the total population.

Tillman noted that, if being arrested and possessing a criminal record are the prime criteria for being classified as a member of the criminal population, the number of criminals in our midst is much larger than we recognize. He concluded that the fact that such large numbers of young men are being arrested is related less to criminal behavior than to " 'social-structural' conditions, that is, political, economic, and social institutions that adversely affect large numbers of young adult males, particularly those within certain strata of society."[25] Nationally, at least 4 to 5 million adults acquire a "criminal record" annually.

In fact, most of the frenetic law enforcement in the black community had nothing to do with violent crime. When the justice juggernaut is wheeled into the streets, it tends to crush those more easily identifiable by race and socioeconomic status than by their violent or serious criminal behavior. Sustained and increasingly technologically sophisticated law-enforcement intrusion into the homes and lives of urban African-American families for mostly minor reasons has left the inner cities with a classic situation of social iatrogenesis – a "treatment" that maims those it touches and exacerbates the very pathologies which lie at the root of crime. It suggests that the criminal justice system itself has been a major contributor to breakdown in the inner cities. Along the way, it has spawned an industry fully capable of producing sufficient numbers of new clientele to validate the need for its existence and justify its growth, demanding more police, arrests, prosecutions, and prisons.

I

Is It Violent Crime?

Most of the frenetic criminal justice handling in the country is concerned with minor incidents, many of which could be dealt with in a manner far short of arrest and jailing. Often, this has less to do with the seriousness of the behavior or the dangerousness of the alleged perpetrator than it has to do with some other vague point like "upholding the integrity of the system." In Duval County (Jacksonville), Florida, this was the common rationale used to explain the large numbers of individuals brought to the jail on warrants for such things as not making court dates, driving with suspended licenses, and being in "technical" violation of conditions of misdemeanor probation. The fact that there were a host of alternative strategies and tactics immediately to hand by which defendants could be encouraged to fulfill these legal obligations seemed not to matter. It mattered even less as the potentially arrestable moved down the socioeconomic ladder.

Lest the reader think I exaggerate, I offer in Table 1 one day's list of unserved arrest warrants I chanced upon one day in the jail.

The police expected to arrest and jail these individuals. This particular batch of warrants had been issued for offenders who had failed to appear in court. For most, the question was not whether

Table 1. *"Failure to Appear" Arrest Warrants*

Simple assault	2
Breach of peace	10
Consumption of alcohol on vendors' premises	3
Consumption of alcohol on city property	10
Damage to public lands	1
Disorderly intoxication	1
Dog at large	1
Dog running loose without leash	1
Dogs prohibited on beach	3
Drinking in public	25
Driving on prohibited ocean front dune within 1000′	1
Driving other than where vehicles are permitted	1
Employee in license premises	1
Failure to transfer title/registration	1
Fishing without a license	4
Harvest of redfish in closed season (oversize redfish)	1
Harvesting shellfish prohibited area	1
Illegal dumping	1
Lewd and lascivious behavior	2
Loitering/prowling	6
Molestation of nesting birds	1
Offering for lewdness	1
Open containers in vehicle	1
Operation of unnumbered or unregistered vessel	1
Operating a wrecker without registering with sheriff	1
Opposing police officer	1
Petit theft (mostly shoplifting)	44
Possession of firearm with altered serial number	1
Possession of alcoholic beverages by person under 21	12
Possession of alcohol in city park	5
Possession of controlled substance	1
Possession of drug paraphernalia	5

Table 1. *(cont.)*

Registration not properly displayed	1
Retail theft	2
Resisting arrest without violence	2
Saltwater harvesting without license	1
Sale of alcoholic beverages to a person under 21	3
Soliciting for prostitution	5
Trespassing	4
Trespassing on school property	1
Truancy	2
Violation of adult entertainment	3
No inoculation, registration, city tags (dog)	1

Source: Duval County, Florida Sheriff's Office.

society had a right to expect accountability of them, but whether arrest and jailing were the only means to that end or whether it might not compound the problem.[1]

None of this was new. A quarter-century earlier, President Lyndon Johnson's Commission on Law Enforcement and the Administration of Justice had noted that almost half of all the arrests in the U.S.A. had to do with lesser offenses (excluding traffic offenses). That pattern has not changed in 30 years. As Peter McWilliams noted in 1994: "Roughly half of the arrests and court cases in the United States each year involve consensual crimes – actions that are against the law, but directly harm no one's person or property except, possibly, the 'criminal's.' "[2] Approximately 24 million Americans used illicit drugs in 1993. Virtually all of them, under current law, would be subject to imprisonment or fines or both. The 781,800 persons arrested that year for possessing illicit drugs made up only 3% of those who broke the drugs laws that year by possessing and using illicit drugs.[3]

In his recent book, *Overcoming Law*, the conservative/libertarian law scholar Richard Posner, now chief judge of the U.S. Court of Appeals for the 7th Circuit, described the phenomenon: "Our statute books," he wrote, "overflow with vicious exploitive, inane, ineffectual and extravagantly costly laws." As proof, Posner pointed to our exploding prison populations and the severe penalties imposed "for intrinsically minor, esoteric, archaic or victimless crimes."[4]

Debate in the 1960s and 1970s over crime control had been couched in terms of so-called victimless crime and the policy of "radical non-intervention" originally advanced by criminologist Edwin Schur.[5] Although the policy was much discussed in criminological circles, it was not implemented – except perhaps with reference to such matters as possession of small amounts of marijuana among middle-class white college students. Meanwhile, the absolute numbers of persons being arrested and jailed for these and other kinds of lesser offenses increased dramatically. By 1990, at least 4 million people were being arrested annually for "consensual" crimes, with minorities again grossly overrepresented.

Rabble Management

Having been appointed by the federal court of the Middle District of Florida to monitor jail overcrowding in Duval County from 1989 to 1994, I had unusual access to the written police summaries of each arrest, as well as to the individual criminal histories of those who were being jailed. The stories that emerged from reading files, counting heads, and interviewing those who sat in jail challenged the stereotypes of the predatory and violent black man as typical of those who people the justice system. That system seemed to be disproportionately concentrating its considerable power on African-Americans charged with relatively minor offenses. The best face one could put on these patterns was that the criminal justice system was being inappropriately applied to the wide range of personal and social problems that afflict the cantankerous poor and minorities. It all gave validity to sociologist John Irwin's unhappy characterization of jails as places of "rabble management."[6]

Far more important to the thesis of this book than the approximately three million annual arrests for index offenses are the 11.5 million arrests for *nonindex* offenses. In 1991, there were an estimated 14,211,900 arrests in the United States.[7] Only one in five of these arrests was for an index (i.e., serious) crime. About six million of these arrests were "new admissions" – meaning the arrestee was a first-time offender in that jurisdiction.[8] In 1991, for example, offenses included everything from forgery (103,700), to public drunkenness (881,100), to curfew and loitering (93,400), to "runaways" (177,300). The largest single category was a vague "other," making up more than one in five (3,240,000) of all arrests in that year. (These involved lesser charges not subsumed under the "index" serious crime categories as set forth in the nomenclature of the FBI Uniform Crime Reports.)[9] Only 5% of these arrests were for violent offenses. Moreover, a substantial percentage of these ostensibly more serious felony arrests did not warrant an appearance in court beyond the initial "morning-after" hearing. What does all this tell us about serious crime in America? Unfortunately, not much.

An interesting glimpse of what was happening emerged in Michigan. In 1993, the Michigan Council on Crime and Delinquency (MCCD) issued a report on arrest trends in that state. It found that although arrests for index crimes had actually *decreased* by 12% between 1981 and 1991, the total number of arrests had increased substantially, mostly concentrated on lesser offenses. *Nonindex* offenses accounted for 78% of all the arrests in the state during 1991. Arrests for these lesser "nonindex" crimes increased 46% between 1981 and 1991.[10] Of reported index crimes in Michigan, a relatively small percentage were violent (12.5% in 1991).

But what about the differences in serious and felonious crime between rural/suburban areas and urban (predominantly black) areas? When the Michigan researchers compared reported index crimes from rural areas of the state with those from Wayne County (Detroit), there were some differences. However, given the economic disasters in the city, they were not all that striking. For example, larceny accounted for 60% of reported crimes in rural areas and 44% in the city. Burglary accounted for 26% of reported rural crimes and 20% in the city. Aggravated assault made up 6% of the reported rural crimes and 8% in the city. Reports of rape (2%), robbery (.6%), and homicide (.1%) totaled about 3% of all crime reports in rural areas. These same offenses accounted for about 10% of crimes in the city: rape (1%), robbery (7.8%), and homicide (.3%).[11] The most telling difference between urban- and rural-area crimes involved robberies. Nevertheless, 90% of rural arrests and 82% of city arrests had little or nothing to do with violent crime.

Researchers from Pennsylvania State University's Center for the Study of Law and Society for the Pennsylvania Sentencing Commission compared "offender processing" in 1980 with 1990 and found similar patterns.[12] While there was a negligible 2% increase in convictions for violent crime in the decade between 1980 and 1990, there was a concomitant 20% *drop* in those being processed into the prison system for violent offenses. This suggested that the circumstances involved in the incidents were not so serious as the formal charge had indicated. Meanwhile those brought into the state's prisons for property crimes increased by 72%.

Similar patterns prevailed among drug offenders. Whereas there had been a negligible 8% increase in the number of those *charged* with drug sales in the decade between 1980 and 1990, there was a 500% increase in those charged with possession; and while there was a 112% increase in those *convicted* of drug sales, there was an 863% increase in convictions for possession. This was consistent with national statistics on admissions to state prisons (Figure 1). The percentage of individuals being sent to prison for violent crimes fell progressively from 1980 to 1990.[13]

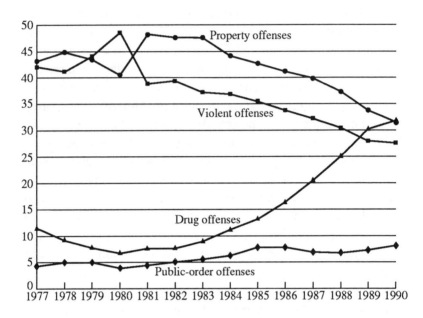

Figure 1. Percentage of new court commitments to state prisons, by type of offense, 1977–1990. *Source:* National Prisoner Statistics and National Corrections Reporter.

Among inmates who made up the daily population of state prisons (as distinct from new admissions), there was also a substantial (21%) *drop* between 1980 and 1990 in the percentage who originally had been convicted of violent crimes.[14] Though the *daily inmate populations* contained high percentages of inmates convicted of violent crimes (46.6%),[15] only slightly more than one in four of new *admissions* to prisons, were for violent crimes (27%). This is because violent offenders generally serve longer sentences and accumulate in the system. Here, for example, are the charges for which individuals had been arrested and booked into the Duval County Jail during three months in 1991 (Table 2). The reader should recognize that these were charges, not convictions. For

Table 2. *Bookings by Charge, July–August–September 1991*

Offense	Number
Homicide: Murder	23
Homicide: Justified	0
Negligent manslaughter	4
Kidnapping	16
Forcible rape	118
Forcible sodomy	6
Forcible molesting	65
Robbery	153
Robbery (outdoors)	64
Assault, aggravated	**680**
Assault, simple	**670**
Assault, intimidation	3
Arson	19
Extortion/blackmail	3
Burglary, residential	**328**
Burglary, nonresidential	200
Theft (petit) – Pickpocketing	20
Theft (petit) – Purse snatching	4
Theft (petit) – e.g., shoplifting	**1,266**
Theft (petit) – Building	12
Theft (petit) – Coin device	3
Theft (petit) – from motor vehicle	71
Theft (petit) – Any other	139
Theft (grand) – Picckpocketing	4
Theft (grand) – Purse snatching	2
Theft (grand) – Shoplifting	79
Theft (grand) – Building	19
Theft (grand) – Coin device	3
Theft (grand) – Motor vehicle	32
Theft (grand) – Any other	125
Motor vehicle theft	267

Table 2. *(cont.)*

Counterfeit/forgery	135
Fraud – Swindle/false	49
Fraud – ATM/credit card	9
Fraud – Impersonation	4
Fraud – Welfare fraud	1
Fraud – Wire/computer	0
Embezzlement	61
Stolen property – Buy/sell	49
Criminal mischief	80
Drugs – Sell/buy/transport	**973**
Drugs – Paraphernalia	166
Nonforcible sex	48
Obscenity – Phone/porn	4
Gambling	6
Sex – Commerce/prostitute	251
Liquor violations	248
Weapons violation	251
Traffic (not including DUI)	**2,505**
Driving under the influence	**783**
Breach of peace	141
Disorderly intoxication	**469**
Worthless checks	**317**
Other offenses	**2,666**
Unknown UCR code	139
Total	13,756

Note: Ten most frequent offenses are in bold type.

example, as many as half of the felony charges (including 87% of the charges for "aggravated assault") were not sustained.[16]

Feeding Alligators

The ten most frequent charges for which individuals were jailed that same year in Duval County were "other" (18.4%); traffic, excluding drunk driving (16.3%); shoplifting (9.1%); driving under the influence (7%); simple assault (6.6%); drug sale/purchase (6%); aggravated assault (5%); disorderly intoxication (3%); worthless checks (3%); and burglary (3%). When one considers the fact that "simple assault" usually consists of a misdemeanor with no physical injury whatsoever to the assaulted, and that the majority of arrests for "aggravated assault" are either dismissed or reduced to "simple assault" before the arrestee's first court hearing, one comes away with the perception that little of this police activity concerned violent or serious crime. However, in press conferences and interviews, local law-enforcement officials had aggressively cultivated the perception that violent crime was out of control, demanding bigger jails, more police, more armamentaria (e.g., sophisticated computerization, criminal-history retrieval, computerized fingerprint scanners, and helicopters). As we shall see, the figures did not bear out these presentations.

Take, for example, the 31% increase in crime noted in Duval County between 1988 and 1991 (while the county was in the throes of a massive jail-building program). When arrests were broken down by offense in these years, an interesting pattern emerged. It is true that 3,273 more persons were arrested from July through September in 1991 than during the same three months in 1988. However, 85% of the increase fell under two categories: "traffic" (excluding drunk driving) and "other," a loosely defined category that included such crimes as "feeding of alligator or crocodile," "resisting without violence," "trespassing," "nonsupport," "feeding unsterilized garbage to animals," "contempt," "impersonating a massage license holder," and 2,990 others.

Here are a few examples:

- A young African-American man suffering from asthma and pneumonia was in jail for 22 days on $1,500 bond. He had been jailed on a "capias" (violation of probation) for not paying $35 in court costs on a four-month-old petit theft (shoplifting) charge. While in jail he lost his job as a truck driver.
- An unemployed 25-year-old African-American male was jailed for "petit theft" and kept there for want of $353 bond. The police arrest report stated: "Investigation revealed that suspect walked into Woolworths then suspect went to the candy isle [*sic*] and picked up two Snickers valued at $1.58. Suspect was observed by store security placing the items in bag without paying for the merchandise. Suspect was apprehended by store security and held for police. Suspect had to be physical [*sic*] restrained by store security since suspect was uncooperative."
- A 38-year-old African-American electronic engineer – well-dressed, middle-class – was jailed for "allowing an unauthorized operator to drive." As the arrest summary put it: "The suspect who owns the listed vehicle, allowed the co-defendant to drive his car. She did not have a driver's license and NCIC advised that her license was suspended for failing to pay traffic fines. He was arrested."
- A 21-year-old African-American woman student was arrested for "driving with license suspended," "violation of right of way," "no proof of license," "failure to use seat belts," and "failure to yield at an intersection." Her license had been suspended for failure to pay traffic fines. When he arrested her, the officer noted that she had two children with her, ages one and three "not in restraints," and a child age four "not in a seat belt." No note was made of what happened to the children when the woman was taken to jail.
- A frail 81-year-old African-American man was arrested for "gambling" (playing cards for money with friends on his front porch).
- A mentally disordered 59-year-old African-American man was ar-

rested for "breach of peace" at the main gate of a nearby naval base. He had tried to enter the base and refused to leave.

- A 30-year-old man was jailed after having been released from a Florida state prison two weeks earlier where he had served six years. He was out for three days and, as per the law, went to the police station to inform them that he was back in town. He was arrested on the spot. He had not paid a four-year-old traffic fine. He was in state prison when the warrant had been issued and was unaware of it.

- An 18-year-old African-American was sentenced to 45 days for "petit theft," having been charged with taking one cigarette out of a pack on a store shelf, smoking it, and returning the pack to the shelf. While he awaited sentencing, his bond had been set at $1,503 or $150 cash. He was unable to come up with the $150 and sat in the jail until his trial two months later.

And what about those African-American adults who had been duly convicted and sentenced to serve jail time?

- A 32-year-old homeless African-American man was sentenced to one year for burglary, having taken two clocks from a rescue mission. He was caught running away with the clocks and charged with a third-degree felony.

- A 31-year-old African-American man was sentenced to four months in jail for taking a pair of sunglasses from a store. He was originally charged with petit theft, but the charge was amended to a first-degree misdemeanor.

- A 37-year-old unemployed African-American man was sentenced to 150 days in jail for nonpayment of child support.

- A 32-year-old African-American man was sentenced to 60 days for shoplifting a package of lunch meat.

- A 29-year-old African-American man was sentenced to 60 days for petit theft from a gas-station convenience store, having put food items into his pants pocket.

- A 25-year-old African-American man was given 60 days in jail for walking out of a store wearing a pair of tennis shoes for which he had not paid.

- An 18-year-old African-American was sentenced to 60 days for selling fake "crack" to vice police for $20. After the sale, he rode off on his bike, but was later apprehended.
- A clearly psychotic 54-year-old African-American male was sentenced to 60 days for "trespassing" and "resisting arrest without violence." He had been harassing customers at a convenience store and refused to leave.
- A 65-year-old African-American man was sentenced to 60 days for "attaching a license tag not assigned" and "driving with a suspended license." (The license had been suspended for failure to pay a fine.)
- A 34-year-old African-American man was sentenced to 60 days for shoplifting a package of meat from a supermarket. Pending sentencing, he had been home, having paid the $150 cash bond. He returned to court for his sentencing and jailing.

Barring some unusual condition, in very few of these cases would a white person of moderate means with adequate legal representation expect to be jailed. The same could not be said of a black male, even one of moderate means.[17] This is not to suggest that some action should not have been taken in these testy situations. Whether confinement in an expensive maximum-security jail was ultimately the most productive approach is open to question.

The "End-of-Sentence" Phenomenon

One of every three arrestees brought to the Duval County Jail pled guilty and was released as having served his or her sentence. This "end-of-sentence" phenomenon was less a measure of guilt or innocence than a seductive ploy offered the poor and born of administrative necessity, often bordering on the surreal. Most of these "sentenced" inmates stayed in jail a relatively short time, as they were convicted of minor offenses. A guilty plea was usually the only means by which impoverished detainees could avoid a long stay in jail. After pleading guilty at their first or second hearing, they were immediately sentenced to "time served" and released. The guilty plea added a conviction to their criminal record. The matter of actual guilt was beside the point and often open to question.

Unable to raise even the nominal amount required for a 10% bail (usually $200 or less) and lacking property as collateral, the poor were unlikely to find an accommodating bondsman. Although a defendant might initially deny the charges, the message is clear that pleading "not guilty" would entail a relatively long stay in jail until legal counsel could be appointed and a court date scheduled – conceivably weeks or months later. (This was usually referred to as "doing state's attorney's time.") On the other hand, pleading "guilty" usually meant that one would be sentenced to "time served" and shortly be released from the jail – albeit as a convicted misdemeanant or lesser felon. Most took the quicker exit. It made its own kind of odd sense.

About 40% of all the individuals released from the Duval jail left with a new conviction on their record after having served such sentences – namely, "end-of-sentence" releases. Most served less than a week in jail. The charges included such offenses as "loitering," "disorderly intoxication," "theft of a single pack of cigarettes," "theft of a pencil and mascara worth less than $5.00," "driving with a suspended license," "no driver's license and making threats," "possession of marijuana cigarette," "eluding and public drinking on a bicycle," "driving with a suspended license" (for having an expired tag), "playing a radio too loudly," "ordering a steak in a restaurant without money" – ("I tried to leave because I knew I didn't have any money"), "trespassing" (a young man had refused to leave the apartment of the man he had been living with), and "allowing dog to run at large."[18] A three-day sample of releases taken from 1991 is shown in Figure 2.

These patterns suggested that (allowing for repeat offenders) at least 15,000 county residents had convictions attached to their criminal records each year as a result of pleading guilty and being released with "time served." (A plea of "no contest" was consid-

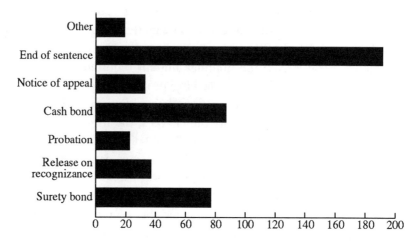

Figure 2. Releases from Duval County Jail, 1991. *Source:* Duval County Sheriff's Office.

ered to be the same as "guilty.") The bureaucratic procedures put in place to handle these matters often seemed only remotely related to the alleged offense or to the actual guilt or innocence of the individual defendant. The process was a quasi-judicial response to administrative backlogs and management problems. It was applied primarily to the black and poor of the community.

Overkill

In those rare cases where black men were allowed an "alternative" to incarceration, overreaction seemed to abound. In the home detention alternative, for example, an electronic bracelet is attached to a person's ankle, making it impossible for him or her to leave home without an alarm being sent to a central computer system. Leaving home without preapproval leads to a new charge of "escape" and consequent prosecution. Here are some of the African-

Americans who were sentenced to "home detention" in lieu of jailing:

- A 72-year-old man given a one-year sentence for "driving under the influence" on his moped. He was sentenced to home detention due to his age and poor health (arthritis). Unable to work, he was placed on 24-hour curfew. He lived alone with his dog.
- A 43-year-old man sentenced to four months for "resisting arrest without violence." He was a first offender and a practicing attorney. While on home detention he lived with a friend and maintained dual custody of his five-year-old daughter.
- A 22-year-old placed on home detention and charged with sale and possession of crack cocaine. He was placed on the program due to a handicap. He had been shot and totally blinded. He was recovering from eye surgery while in home detention. He lived with and was cared for by his girlfriend and their two children.
- A 25-year-old sentenced to 30 days for "petit theft" and "resisting and opposing" a police officer. He was in the advanced stages of Hodgkin's disease and while on home detention had to be rushed to a hospital emergency room on two occasions to be resuscitated. The young man died one week prior to the expiration of his 30-day sentence.

Were these anomalies confined to one southern jail? Unfortunately they were not. An extensive study, made by Rutgers criminologist Todd Clear and his associates, of over 7,000 probationers in six jurisdictions found precisely the same patterns. Many of those who were in "technical" violation of the conditions of probation (e.g., missed appointments, broke curfew, failed to maintain employment) were placed in electronic monitoring programs. The authors noted that the minor nature of most of these violations did not justify the use of "controlling strategies" like electronic monitoring. They concluded that such programs seemed "excessive" for these populations and would be better used for the "higher risk felons diverted from prison – for whom they were intended."[19] Similar patterns of overkill appeared in jurisdictions as disparate as Rochester, New York,[20] and Los Angeles.[21]

An Old Tradition

The practice of arresting massive numbers of minorities for petty public-order charges has a long tradition. Citing the studies of H. Donaldson on the Negro migration of 1916–1918,[22] University of Michigan criminologist Shirley Brown notes that many blacks had migrated to the North during these years because of their resentment of the arrest tactics of southern police. Indeed, law-enforcement officials were paid by the head for every man arrested. With what amounted to a "bounty" for arrests, large numbers of black men found themselves in jail as a result of roundups for petty infractions like littering and disorderly conduct. "Heavy fines were often levied for such small violations and . . . those who could not pay them were imprisoned."[23] As sociologist Mark Carlton discovered at the turn of the century, black men tended to be picked up in states like Louisiana when the labor market was in short supply or workers were needed for county roadwork.[24]

Many of these practices followed black men to the North. In Pittsburgh arrests of blacks for petty offenses (disorderly conduct, drunkenness, and the crime of "suspicion") nearly doubled between one seven-month period in 1914–1915 and the same period in 1916–1917.[25] Perhaps the most telling arrest statistic, however, was the charge of "suspicion." A contemporary Department of Labor study in Cleveland revealed that in 1916–1917, extraordinarily large numbers of black men were being sent to prison on this charge.[26] Brown commented, "It was this type of action by police that accounted for much of the 'Negro Crime' reported during this period in the United States."[27]

Measuring Crime Rates

For the past 20 years, crime trends have been measured in two ways: (1) FBI Uniform Crime Reports (UCR), gathered from index arrest statistics reported by state and local police departments; and (2) The National Crime Survey (NCS), based on interviews with 100,000 people from scientifically selected samples of American households regarding crimes committed against members of their households.

The UCR figures are derived from victim reports of crime, from "officers who discover infractions," and from the all-encompassing "other sources."[28] The UCR reports have always been highly subject to police practices and policies, and are as prone to reflect the local politics of crime as much as actual reported crime. Because police do not make most arrests on the basis of citizen complaints, arrest patterns are highly susceptible to local police tactics, prosecutorial policies, media interests, and politics (drug sweeps, sting operations, increased serving of outstanding warrants, etc.).[29] The UCR statistics routinely masked police overcharging and omitted such crucial narrative information as arrest summaries, victim statements, and other observational indicators that might place these data in context.[30] Whereas most European nations were reporting their crime statistics on the basis of convictions, the United States, through the U.S. Justice Department, inflated both the numbers and the seriousness of American crime by including complaints and arrests. Most reporters and policymakers seemed not to notice that of every 100 individuals arrested for a felony, 43 were either not prosecuted or their cases were dismissed outright at the first court appearance.[31]

In an attempt to mitigate these problems, the National Crime Surveys were established in 1972. It was felt that a large amount of crime, particularly violent crime, was not being reported to police and consequently not showing up in the UCR statistics. Indeed, NCS data from 1973 to 1989 revealed that only about half of robberies and aggravated assaults appeared in the UCR statistics. In 1973, for example, only about one-half of reports of aggravated assault were recorded by police. By 1988, however, it was estimated that 97% of the reports of aggravated assault were being recorded. In fact, in the early 1990s police began recording rates for some kinds of offenses (e.g., rape) which *exceeded* 100%.[32] This was probably a reflection of how local political demands can influence official crime reporting by the police.

However, though the National Crime Survey consistently recorded more crime than the FBI's "Uniform Crime Reports," some argued that it still understated the number of incidents of serious crime, as it consistently ignored the transient, the homeless, and prisoner populations in conducting its surveys. It was precisely among these populations, said some critics, that more crime was likely to occur.[33] In addition, it was hypothesized that many of the respondents in the NCS probably failed to report attempted crimes or minimized offenses committed by people they might happen to know. However, from another point of view it could also be argued that many of the offenses uncovered in the NCS interviews, though they might have formally and legally warranted legal action, were dealt with in other ways – within the family, among friends, employers, and so on. The decision not to involve the police was not necessarily a flawed decision in all or most cases.

The American sociologist William Chambliss saw the national perception of out-of-control crime rates as the result of a political process not unlike that described 30 years earlier by Blumer. Chambliss notes that in the 1980s and 1990s, a coalition of interests ("conservative legislators, law enforcement agencies, the media and social scientists") had brought on something of a "moral panic" about crime in the U.S.A. The most obvious result was the transfer of public expenditures at every level from social problems into crime control.[34] There is considerable evidence to support Chambliss's conclusion. The raw numbers generated by UCR reports and periodically released to the press by the FBI regularly suggest rises in both violent and nonviolent crime from year to year. When these same reports are broken down by "crimes per 100,000 population," and are "age-adjusted" to take into account the number of those in the age categories most at risk, however, it appears that serious crime has either been stable or dropping for more than a decade.

Rates per 100,000 population

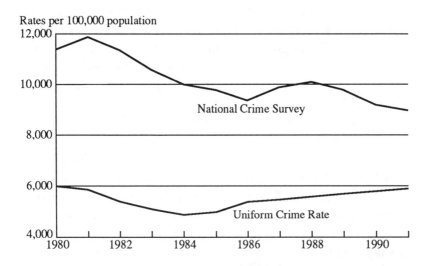

Figure 3. Crime rates, 1980–1991. *Source:* U.S. Department of Justice, *The Economist*, November 12, 1993; UCR and NCS crime reports, 1980–1990.

University of Michigan researchers John Bounds and Scott Boggess reanalyzed national crime reports (both UCR and NCS) spanning the years 1979 through 1991. They concluded that the UCR reports indeed demonstrated that index crime had fallen by 2%, while the NCS registered a 27% drop in "crimes against persons" and a 31% drop in "property" offenses during those years (Figure 3). As they summarized their findings: "[Despite] the widely held belief that there was a significant increase in the level of criminal activity during the 1980s, in general, we find that neither data source depicts increasing levels of crime over this period."[35]

Occasional rises and falls in homicide rates are nothing new. The record year for homicides in 1991 approximated the levels reached in 1981 and a near-decade earlier in 1973. After each of these peaks, homicides tended to return to the relatively stable rate of approximately 10 per 100,000 – a rate which, though lamentable, had obtained for more than two decades.

Even conservative commentators have had difficulty with the

crime statistics being churned out by the Justice Department. "Crime is an area where it is difficult to know what to make of the data," states Charles Murray. "One of the most solid crime statistics is the number of homicides, and it shows that homicide victimization among blacks dropped in the '80s and the gap with whites closed modestly. On the other hand, arrests of blacks rose during the '80s after remaining flat during the '70s, and the public perception that crime has gotten worse seems universal."[36]

Murray's observations echoed those of James Q. Wilson and John DiIulio, Jr., who concluded in 1989 that, "for most people, crime has gone down." They noted that between 1980 and 1987, burglary was down 27% and robbery down 21%. "Despite what we hear," they commented, "3,000 fewer murders were committed in 1987 than in 1980. Even in some big cities that are in the news for the frequency with which their residents kill each other, the homicide rate has decreased. Take Los Angeles: despite freeway shootings and gang warfare, there were 261 fewer murders in 1987 than in 1980, a drop of more than 20 percent."[37]

A Long History

Violent crime in the United States comes with a long history of regional differences, many of them related to earlier patterns and folkways of European and British immigrants. British criminologist Michael Levi has noted that, though the theme of social deterioration is an important one – for example, "in the good old days when we had the death penalty and corporal punishment there was less violence" – in fact, the homicide rate in mid-17th-century Great Britain was double what it is today. Levi also notes that the patterns of homicide appear to have changed dramatically since then, *with more intrafamilial homicide now than then* – though, clearly, the amount of violence fell during the Victorian period – "at least outside the home."[38]

The cultural historian David Hackett Fischer traces the sources of regional differences in American violence to the markedly different "folkways" of the four large waves of English-speaking immigrants who settled in New England, Virginia, Appalachia, and the Delaware Valley between 1629 and 1775 – each with distinct cultural traditions regarding violence. Fischer suggests that these early traditions have persisted over the ensuing 300 years and are still roughly reflected in regional differences in rates of violence.[39] He concludes that despite the changes in ethnic makeup that came with later waves of continental and Mediterranean immigrants to various parts of the country, contemporary regional differences in violent crime continue to show "remarkably strong linkages with the distant colonial past."

Although the murder rate in the United States as a whole has been at about 9 or 10 per 100,000 for the past two decades, rates have always differed from one region to another. The northern tier from New England to the Pacific Northwest historically has had the lowest rates of homicide, whereas the middle states had moderately higher rates, but still well below the national average. However, homicide rates have always been much higher in the upper coastal South, with the southern Atlantic states averaging 10.9 murders per 100,000, the west south-central states having a rate of 14.7, and Texas a rate of 16.1.

Fischer notes that homicide rates have always been high in northern cities with large percentages of southern immigrants, both black and white. On the other hand, southern neighborhoods with large numbers of northern immigrants tended to have lower homicide rates. He concludes that homicide rates can be more easily correlated with what he calls "cultural regions of origin than with urbanization, poverty, or any material factor."[40] Fischer dismisses the comparative wealth of some New England states as accounting for these differences in homicide rates, noting that "many a hardscrabble Yankee hill town is poor and orderly, and more than a few southwestern communities are rich and violent." He also rejects the hypothesis that southern violence is a legacy of racial diversity: "some of the most violent communities in the southern highlands have no black residents at all, and are in ethnic terms among the most homogeneous in the nation."[41]

From the beginning, New Englanders gave little latitude to violence. Town schools taught children not to use violence to solve social problems. Town meetings condemned violence and town elites taught each other, by example, "that violence is not an acceptable form of behavior. It simply 'wasn't done.' " In contrast, in the South and Southwest the tradition was precisely the opposite. "Texas is entertained by . . . violence. Massachusetts is not amused. . . . In short, violence simply *is* done in Texas and the southern highlands, and always has been . . . since before the Civil War and slavery and even the frontier – just as it had been done in the borderlands of North Britain before emigration."[42] As Richard Harwood succinctly summed up this phenomenon: "That is the way of the South. An eye for an eye, a tooth for a tooth. If you offend a man's sense of honor – 'dissing' is the street term – he responds with fists, guns or knives. A pickup truck with a rear-window gun rack is a mobile symbol of the male passage from adolescence. Lynching . . . was a regional sport for more than 50 years."[43]

But if regional patterns in violent crime have not changed all that much in the past 200 years, surely the incidence of violent crime in our cities has changed dramatically in recent years. This is not necessarily true either. As Manhattan District Attorney Robert M. Morgenthau noted in opposing the reintroduction of the death penalty in New York, the number of homicides in that borough dropped by half between 1975 (648 homicides) and 1994, when there were 330 homicides.[44] Indeed, there has always been a tendency toward more violence in cities.[45] This was just as true where blacks were a small minority in some urban areas. It is in the cities that the dramas of social inequity are acted out. In 1851, for example, when San Francisco had only 30,000 citizens (few of them black), there were 100 murders. By comparison, there were 75 murders in San Francisco in 1984 when the city's population was 716,000. It is estimated that there were 1,300 murders in Los Angeles in 1842 when the city had between 20,000 and 30,000 people.[46] As Lewis Lapham recently noted, in gathering research material for a book on the American condition in the 18th and 19th centuries, he discovered that "the incidence of crime in New York City in the 1870s or on the Texas frontier in the 1840s defined itself as a statistical ratio surpassing the percentages now being reported by the FBI."[47]

The Character of Violent Crime

Most people probably think that violent crimes as reported by the FBI involve a murder, a mugging, or a bloody assault. This is seldom true. In most cases, the violent crime consists of a threat or a perceived threat. In approximately 68% of crimes designated as violent, there is no physical injury of any kind to the victim. Slightly over half of those who sustain some physical injury are treated by themselves, friends, or relatives on the spot. About 8% of those who are injured are taken to a hospital emergency room.[48] Most of these injuries consist of bruises, black eyes, cuts, scratches, and swelling. Of the victims of all crime classified as "violent" nationally in 1991, slightly over 1% required a hospital stay of one day or more.[49] Of course, one might conclude that most murder victims do not require hospitalization. However, for example, reported homicides in 1992 (22,540) constituted only .003% of the violent crime incidents (as reported in victimization surveys) nationally (5,964,090).[50]

Even in those cases classified as *serious* violent crime (i.e., rape, robbery, and aggravated assault) the national victimization surveys showed that, although 36% of the adult and 35% of the juvenile victims of crime had an injury, about 3% of adult victims required a hospital stay of over two days and fewer than 1% of juveniles were similarly injured. Interestingly, the percentage of serious violent incidents that resulted in serious injury declined from 11% to 7% between 1987 and 1991 – though the difference was judged to be statistically insignificant.[51]

A 1987 study found that 38 out of every 100 felony arrests nationally are declined for prosecution or dismissed in court.[52] Similarly, a 1990 study by the San Francisco County Prosecutor's Office revealed that the complaint was denied and no charges filed in 41% of all the felony arrests in that county.[53] More significantly, in about 20% of all *violent* index arrests the prosecutor elected not to proceed, whereas another 32% were dismissed by the courts.[54]

Of 399,277 arrests for aggravated assault reported by the FBI in 1990, only 53,861 (13.4%) resulted in a felony conviction.[55] A national survey of adjudication outcomes for felony defendants in the 75 largest counties in the country that same year revealed a similar pattern. Among defendants charged with assault, half the charges were dismissed outright and most of the remainder were reduced to a misdemeanor.[56] Although conservative commentators use such figures to demonstrate the permissiveness of the courts, quite another phenomenon is at work. Law enforcement is exaggerating the extent of violent crime by routinely overcharging arrestees with violent crimes they did not commit. Most arrests for aggravated assault (the largest category of violent crime), for example, reflect at most *simple* assaults (often misdemeanors) that resulted in no physical injury to anyone.

In an interesting analysis, criminologist Michael Tonry notes that the putative doubling of the rate of "aggravated assaults" between 1970 and 1992 as suggested by the FBI's Uniform Crime Reports was actually a reflection of the public's increased willingness to report incidents. "That this is so for assaults can be seen by comparing the steadily increased rates for assault with the mild decline for homicide. A homicide is a lethally successful assault." Tonry concludes that, "given increased availability of ever-more-lethal firearms, the proportion of assaults proving fatal (that is, the ratio of homicides to assaults) should be increasing. To the contrary, it has steadily fallen. This suggests that much of the apparent increase in assault rates reflects higher reporting and recording, rather than a higher incidence of assault."[57]

It was one of a number of patterns I found in overseeing implementation of the federal court's orders relative to jail overcrowding in Duval County. Among the largest single category of arrests for "violent" crime – aggravated assault – only about 20% remained "aggravated" for more than a few hours. Approximately 80% of the arrests for this ostensibly serious violent crime were downgraded to "simple assault" or to a misdemeanor.[58] The evidence simply did not warrant the more serious charge and the prosecution opted not to proceed. Moreover, this consistent downgrading of charges occurred in a southern jurisdiction that was among the more punitive and harsh in the region in prosecuting violent offenders. A "profile-workload" report prepared by the state's attorney's office showed that in one out of every four felony cases brought by local prosecutors, the charges were reduced to misdemeanors. Another 20% were dismissed by the courts, and 5% were "diverted." In other words, even in those felony arrests in which it was decided to prosecute, fully half were either dismissed or reduced to a misdemeanor.[59]

Things were similar in the federal courts. In 1991, federal prosecutors declined to proceed in one in three cases (29.5%), almost a third of those involving individuals suspected of being, or under interrogation as, likely perpetrators of crimes of "violence," and in half (48.5%) of the cases involving property crimes.[60] Even in cases of alleged assault in which prosecutors did proceed, nearly one in three (32.8%) were dismissed outright by the federal courts.[61] Again, these patterns suggested that persons were being routinely overcharged and that very little of this police activity had to do with serious or violent crime. Not surprisingly, the group most hard-hit by this pandemic overcharging and most likely to garner a "felony arrest" criminal record are African-Americans.[62]

My own experience in hundreds of criminal cases over the past two decades leads me to conclude that the major actors in the criminal justice drama are increasingly eager to arrest on the highest charge possible, prosecute to the limits of the law, and demand the longest prison terms potentially available. It is now common policy to overstate the seriousness of most alleged incidents from the first moment the individual is seen as a potential arrestee and deemed a possibility for criminal justice handling. The fact that police and prosecutors cannot always accomplish their agenda of arrest and imprisonment is less a measure of permissiveness in the courts than an indication that some vestiges of due process have managed to survive the hysteria of the times. The merits of the inflated charges are not at issue. Rather, it is a poker game in which the charges are kept close to the vest for purposes of intimidation or bluff, with an eye to their potential for getting the defendant to fold – guilty or not.

One element which fed the perception that violent crime was increasing had to do with shifts in the race and affluence of the victims. A study conducted by the respected Vera Foundation found that although crime overall had fallen in New York City in 1993, it did so in a selective fashion. Whereas neighborhoods with high-income levels tended to have low levels of violent crime, a steep rise in the income level of a neighborhood was accompanied by sharp increases in violent crime (primarily robbery).

The Vera researchers compared two areas of New York City that had equally high incomes in 1990. One neighborhood (Bay Ridge), had been a stable high-income area for a number of years, while the other (Brooklyn's Carroll Gardens and Park Slope) had become "gentrified" as young professionals replaced working-class inhabitants, median household income growing at roughly two and a half times the rate in most of the city. Despite the roughly equivalent average income of the two neighborhoods, robbery (and homicide) soared in the newly affluent areas, while it dropped in the more stable affluent neighborhoods. All of this suggested that, though actual violent crime rates in New York City might be falling in the late 1980s and early 1990s, the race and socioeconomic status of victims in some neighborhoods was changing, with more victims likely to be affluent and white.[63] Often, as the victims of crime come from affluent groups, public and political concern over crime rises.[64]

A New Breed?

With rising concern over urban violence in the 1980s and 1990s came the recycling of the familiar "new breed" theory of young offenders – with the implicit focus on the young black male offender. For example, in early 1994 the *Los Angeles Times* interviewed Robert Dacy, an inmate serving a life term in the maximum security unit of the California state prison in Tehachapi. Dacy, described as "a gaunt old man, dressed in faded blues, suffering from emphysema after decades of chain-smoking hand-rolled cigarettes in his cell," was presented by the reporter as an expert of sorts on the "new breed" of criminal walking the streets. As Dacy put it, "in the old days, the professional criminal had some kind of code. We would never consider pulling the trigger just for the hell of it." It was only parenthetically remarked that Dacy, ostensibly a product of a less violent era, had an arrest record dating to 1947 and had been sentenced to prison for kidnapping a four-year-old boy for ransom. He was caught after leading police on a high-speed chase, along the way exchanging shots with the FBI and wounding an agent.

Michael Zona, a psychiatrist with the Los Angeles Police Department, told the reporter that "what psychiatrists call 'anti-social personality disorder,' a person who basically has no feeling," is more prevalent today than in the past.[65] Politicians and human-service professionals alike periodically call the public's attention to this ostensibly more unfeeling, cold, and dangerous young offender who now stalks our streets. One could make the argument with equal force that the more obvious example of a "new breed" can be found among the psychiatrists, psychologists, social workers, and counselors who work directly for, or on, the periphery of the criminal justice system (see Chapter 2).

One measure of the so-called new breed of young offender was contained in the supposed explosion of stranger-on-stranger violent crime in recent years. However, this premise is highly questionable. A 1993 study of murder in the largest urban counties of the nation revealed that approximately 80% of murder victims and their killers were acquainted with, or related to, each other. Fully half of all the murder victims had a social or romantic relationship with the murderer. *Among black victims, 87% were either acquainted with or related to the murderer.*[66] A later analysis of the data revealed that 16% of murder victims were members of the defendant's family, with children more than twice as likely to be killed by their parents than the reverse. Over half of the murder victims had criminal records.[67] If the patterns displayed in these statistics gathered from the 75 largest urban counties in the nation were to be replicated nationally, it would mean that, of the approximately 24,000 homicides reported in the 50 states in 1994, 19,000 involved altercations and confrontations between friends and relatives, while only about 5,000 were committed by persons unknown to the victim.

When it comes to interracial homicide, data on incidents involving lone victims and lone offenders reveal that about 9 out of 10 were murdered by someone of the same race.[68] Ninety-four percent of black homicide victims are killed by other blacks, and 83% of white homicide victims are murdered by other whites. Among juveniles, 92% of white homicide victims are killed by other whites, whereas 76% of black victims are murdered by other blacks.[69]

The character of the individual violent offender has probably not changed as much as each succeeding generation seems to think. In their influential study, *Delinquents and Criminals: Their Making and*

Table 3. *Chicago Series of Outcomes, Males: Known Homicides*

Age	Nativity of parents	Mentality	Circumstances
15	Irish	Feebleminded	Street holdup
15	U.S. (white-colored)	Normal	Burglary
17	Norway-Germany	Normal	Burglary
17	German	Normal	Robbery
18	Polish	Psychopathic	Robbery
18	German	Psychotic	Robbery
18	Finnish	Feebleminded	Burglary
18	Irish-German	Psychotic	Robbery
19	U.S.	Normal	Burglary
19	Polish	Normal	Burglary
20	German	Feebleminded	Jealousy
21	U.S.	Normal	Burglary
24	Italian	Normal	Holdup

Source: William Healy and Augusta F. Bronner, *Delinquents and Criminals: Their Making and Unmaking, Studies of Two American Cities* (New York: Macmillan, 1928), p. 246.

Unmaking, William Healy and Augusta Bronner followed the criminal careers of 920 Chicago male delinquents from 1909 to 1914. From this group, Healy and Bronner identified 420 as the "most serious" offenders. They found that 13 (3%) of the 420 boys were subsequently convicted of murder. Healy and Bronner diagnosed seven of these 13 young murderers as "normal mentally," two as "psychotic," one as "of psychopathic personality," and three as "mentally defective" (Table 3). In light of current concerns regarding violence among African-American youths, the ethnic background of these youthful murderers of the 1920s is of particular interest.

In their classic cohort analysis of 3,475 delinquent Philadelphia boys conducted in the late 1960s and early 1970s, Marvin Wolfgang, Robert Figlio, and Thorsten Sellin identified 627 "chronic offenders" who accounted for a disproportionate share of serious offenses – much the same as the 420 "serious" youthful offenders identified in the Healy and Bronner study. However, among Wolfgang et al.'s 627 offenders, only 10 youths (1.5%) were subsequently found to have been involved in homicide.[70] Again, this was half the percentage found among the serious offenders Healy and Bronner studied in the 1920s.

Similarly, researchers from The Ohio State University studying violent youthful offenders in the 1970s found that, in their cohort of 985 "most violent" offenders, 15 (1.5%) had been arrested for murder.[71] Again, this was precisely the same percentage found in the Wolfgang studies but half that found by Bronner and Healy. One factor which might alter the findings is the fact that by the 1960s modern medical shock-trauma procedures had significantly advanced, thereby increasing the chances of survival by a victim of an attack or assault. However, even this consideration might not eradicate the differences in murder rates between the 1920s and the 1970s – particularly in light of the research of William Doerner, which suggests that response time for ambulances in minority communities is demonstrably longer than for similar calls made for emergency assistance in white communities. As a result, more serious assaults are likely to end up as homicides among victims in need of prompt medical attention.

The Juvenile Crime "Explosion"

Burgeoning crime among adolescents is the perennial cry when it comes to hysteria on crime. Although juvenile crime has grown dramatically at times, many knowledgeable criminologists have seen little evidence of a profound difference in the rate of serious crime among adolescents over the past thirty years. Even during the period in which the so-called explosion of crime occurred (between 1960 and 1972), there is evidence that much of the rise could be attributed to differences in police practices and reporting procedures as well as the so-called baby boom.

For example, at the height of a putative 29% increase in arrests of juveniles between 1967 and 1972 as measured by UCR statistics (including a 326% increase in drug arrests), criminologists Martin Gold and David Reimer could find no actual increase in criminal behavior among teenagers. Notwithstanding the fact that the true offense rates of teenagers surpassed UCR arrest-rate figures by more than 15 times, Gold and Reimer discovered that the *frequency* of delinquency among juveniles had declined by 14% between 1967 and 1972, and the *seriousness* of the delinquent acts had also declined by 14%. The researchers asked the question, "What happened to the teenage crime wave?" Gold and Reimer found that media reports of the rise in juvenile crime were in response to highly unreliable data being released by the FBI crime reports and local law-enforcement agencies. Many of the putative rises in juvenile crime were attributable to record-keeping procedures, changes in local law-enforcement definitions, and policies regarding juvenile offenders, "including even deliberate distortion of the data for political purposes." Gold and Reimer concluded that "*Official data on delinquency are tied so loosely to the actual behavior of youth that they are more sensitive to the changes in the measurement procedures than they are to the object of measurement* . . . the data we have reported here . . . simply do not testify to rapidly rising rates of juvenile delinquency."[72]

From their inception in 1972, so-called victimization surveys consistently yielded results that supported the contentions of Gold and Reimer. These NCS data showed that, although the incidence of crime was greater than the UCR statistics revealed, the *rates* of serious crime were more stable than the political rhetoric had suggested. Indeed, when one moved past simple arrest statistics to those offenses which the police considered to have been "cleared" by the arrest, the scenario of burgeoning juvenile crime changed rather dramatically. (Police "clear" an offense when the arrested person is charged with the offense and turned over to the court for prosecution. It does not mean that the person is ultimately convicted of the offense.) Although juveniles accounted for 16% of all arrests and 17.5% of arrests for violent crime in 1992, they accounted for only about 12.5% of the violent crimes cleared by arrests in that year. This means that the proportion of violent crimes attributable to juveniles – when measured by those crimes *cleared* by the police – was actually lower than the percentage of juveniles in the U.S. population (see Figure 4).

In 1993, the National Center for Juvenile Justice completed an analysis of more than 1.4 million cases handled by juvenile courts in 10 selected states from 1985 through 1989.[73] Although the study found that juveniles charged with violent offenses (homicide, aggravated assault, violent sex offenses, and robbery) took up a disproportionate amount of time and effort in juvenile courts, the number actually charged for these violent crimes made up a relatively small part (7%) of the average juvenile court caseload. Even when it came to the ostensibly "violent" or "person" crimes, of the 239,700 cases processed, 105,700 (44%) were "nonpetitioned." Of the 134,000 formally handled cases, 58,700 (44%) were "nonadjudicated" and another 37,900 (28%) were dismissed outright.[74] This means that *of all the violent crimes brought to juvenile court from 1985 through 1989, fully 84% (202,300) were either handled informally, nonadjudicated, or dismissed.*

These findings were consistent with those of David Altschuler of the Center for the Study of Social Policy at Johns Hopkins University, who found serious differences with reference to simple "arrests" of juveniles versus "cleared" crimes (in the Hopkins study, a crime was considered cleared when police had identified a juvenile, charged him or her, and taken that youth into custody).[75] Arrest statistics focus on persons, whereas "clearance rates" have to do with crimes the police consider to be "solved." The Johns Hopkins researchers found (as had the NCCD) that clearance rates pro-

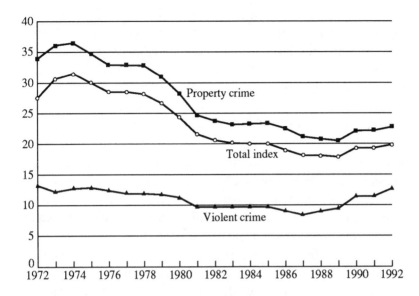

Figure 4. Percentage of offenses known to police that were cleared by arrest of persons under 18 years of age, United States, 1972–1992. *Source:* Michael A. Jones and Barry Krisberg, "Images and Reality: Juvenile Crime, Youth Violence and Public Policy." National Council on Crime and Delinquency, San Francisco, California. April 29, 1994, p. 11.

vided a more accurate measure of the extent of juvenile violent crime than did simple arrest rates. Furthermore, the arrest statistics tended to overstate the incidence of such crimes by juveniles because they made no allowance for cases in which individuals were later acquitted or charges were lowered or dropped. For example, in both the city of Baltimore and the state of Maryland, juveniles consistently accounted for a smaller proportion of crimes than the arrest figures had suggested.[76] Juveniles, unlike adults, are more prone to commit crimes in groups. As a result, arrest figures tend to overstate the actual number of crimes involving juveniles, as a single incident usually results in multiple arrests. The Hopkins researchers found that *although 13% of those arrested for homicide in*

Baltimore were juveniles, only 2 percent of Baltimore City murders in 1990 were in fact, solved (i.e., "cleared") by juvenile arrests."[77] Statewide in Maryland, juvenile arrests accounted for as many as 20% of homicides. However, only about 7% were "cleared" by arrest of the juvenile in question.

University of California researcher Franklin Zimring has called attention to the gross differences between simple-arrest statistics and arrests whereby the offense is "cleared." "[T]here are good reasons to doubt that trends in arrests reflect trends in crime commission rates when clearance rates change over time," he writes. "If a clearance rate by arrest per 100 crimes goes down, the change in arrest rate will be lower than any increase in rate of offenses attributable to young offenders. An increase in arrest to crime ratio will mean an increase in arrests will overstate any increase in crime."[78]

The implications of this kind of analysis for national arrest figures are quite startling. If the ratios found in Maryland were applied nationally, for example, only about 1,800 of the 25,000+ arrests for homicide would actually be "cleared" by a juvenile arrest. That would mean that about 1,200 to 1,500 juveniles would probably end up being indicted, whereas about 500 to 700 would be convicted of personally murdering another individual – an average of 10 to 12 per state (ignoring gross population differences state to state). If, on the other hand, arrest patterns in the city of Baltimore were replicated at the national level, of the 2,828 arrests of juveniles (under age 18) in 1992 for murder and nonnegligent manslaughter, only about 700 would result in a "cleared" case wherein the accused would proceed to the courts on a charge of murder or manslaughter – with guilt or innocence still to be established. The actual number of juveniles convicted annually of murder or manslaughter would probably be no more than 300. However, this figure seems too low and points up the dangers of extrapolation.

A different insight can be gained from a study published by the research arm of the National Council of Juvenile Court Judges, the National Center for Juvenile Justice.[79] This study of 1991 referrals to juvenile court in selected states, both rural and urban (representing 23% of the "at-risk" youth population),[80] revealed that 885 cases of murder/nonnegligent manslaughter were processed in juvenile courts. However, barely half (483) led to an adjudication in juvenile court or transfer to an adult court. Moreover, an adjudication did not necessarily mean that the juvenile was convicted of murder or manslaughter. The term *adjudicated* simply means "judged to be a delinquent or status offender," and in many cases, even though the person was found not to be involved in the alleged offense, other conditions or behaviors may have been revealed that in the court's opinion warranted involvement to curb what it saw as other delinquent behavior (e.g., ungovernable, runaway, truant, etc.).

If these ratios were to hold nationally, about 1,600 of the 24,000 annual arrests (adult and juvenile) for homicide would end in juveniles being "adjudicated" or transferred to adult court, about 32 per state (again not allowing for population differences). However, even this is too high a proportion relative to the approximately 3,000 juvenile annual arrests nationally for homicide/manslaughter.

The ratio of simple arrests to cleared arrests for violent crime in Baltimore is probably closer to the mark when it comes to arrests of African-American juveniles in cities. This is because city arrest patterns (as distinct from state patterns) are more likely to apply to the bulk of African-American juveniles arrested for violent crimes in inner cities nationally. The Johns Hopkins researchers also found that the number of arrests of juveniles for violent crimes grossly distorted and overstated the realities of juvenile crime. For example, there were 10,732 arrests of juveniles in 1990. The most common charge was motor-vehicle theft (1,791). The next largest number of arrests was for drug violations (mostly possession) (1,411), followed by larceny/theft (1,307) and "other" assaults (1,122) (as distinct from felonious or aggravated assaults). Crimes classified as violent accounted for about 10% of all juvenile arrests in Baltimore. However, the term *violent* covered a wide array of charges.[81]

The Ohio State University cohort study (mentioned earlier) found that 811 of the 50,000 youths studied compiled a record of at least one violent crime. However, 73% of these "violent" youths had neither threatened nor inflicted significant physical harm during the commission of their formally violent offenses. Only 22 youngsters committed two or more aggravated offenses in which physical harm was threatened or inflicted.[82]

In his 1978 report on violent crime in the U.S.A., researcher Paul Strasburg found similar patterns, commenting that in the course of his study he was "impressed by the number of acts resulting in arrests of juveniles (even those labeled as violent) that do not seem to fit the usual conception of what constitutes a crime." He noted that "schoolyard fights, children striking adults who threaten them, minor acts of extortion: all appear with high frequency in police and court records, particularly, it seems, with regard to poor and minority juveniles." Noting that his observations were consistent with the findings of another study of assaultive boys, Strasburg cited the comments of Boston research psychiatrists Donald Russell and G. P. Harper: "The forbidding legal names of their offenses (Armed Robbery, Assault and Battery with a Dangerous Weapon, Homicide) both represent these boys at their worst and may even over-represent that worst," they wrote. "The minor-league quality of most of what passes for 'assault' is the most striking finding."[83]

Franklin Zimring has called for new empirical studies of youth violence – studies that would once again touch upon the narrative. He notes that the "extreme heterogeneity of the robbery and assault categories in crime surveys and in police statistics" makes it difficult, if not impossible, to draw any conclusions regarding alleged changes in the quality of youth violence in recent years. He pointed to a need for a more complete description and analysis of the types of behavior that end up being classified as "aggravated";

how serious these incidents actually are when compared with other behaviors that are similarly labeled; and how those incidents classified as "assaults by youth" differ from those of older offenders.[84]

Although some streets of some of our large cities are more dangerous than they were 50 years ago (though not more than they were 100 years ago), this does not necessarily testify to the existence of another "new breed" of violent offender. In summarizing the research on youth violence, sociologist Delbert Elliott noted that, though today's youth are more frequently the victims of violence, about the same proportion of youth are committing serious violent offenses as in 1980, with approximately the same frequency of offending. However, one important dimension of youth violence has clearly changed: today's violent acts are more lethal. Elliott noted that this was "explained almost entirely by the increased use of handguns in these violent exchanges."[85]

Despite the fact that attributing mayhem in the streets to some new kind of young "psychopath" is a familiar response, and though this analysis may have some merit in individual cases, a better analytical model might be found by looking at the social antecedents that led an infantry company of remarkably ordinary American troops to rape, torture, and mutilate Vietnamese women and children at My Lai while some resisted doing so. The distortion of power relationships, the defining of the "enemy" as beneath contempt, the chronically threatening and paranoid world in which one lives, the inuring to violence and wearing down of sensitivity to others, and the impotence of one's condition – all these bespeak a social context that most survive but to which some succumb. A common defense of those most affected by that context is to assume a hyperaggressive stance, to "identify with an aggressor," as the Freudians would say, which is actualized in random acts of violence. It is a destructive way of avoiding further victimization.

2

Tracking Racial Bias

As jail monitor for the federal court in Duval County (Jacksonville), Florida, I learned that although African-American males made up only slightly more than 12% of the county's population, more than half of those brought to the jail each day were African-American. The criminal justice system had penetrated the black community of this predominantly white county deeply and widely. One in four of all the young African-American males (ages 18–34) who lived in the county were being jailed at least once each year.[1] Approximately 75% of all 18-year-old black youths living there could expect to be jailed before reaching age 35. Because African-American males tended to fall at the lower end of the socioeconomic scale, they were often unable to make even the most modest of bail bonds. As a result, even those arrested on minor offenses were more likely to be kept in jail longer (hundreds for want of $200 and a bondsman). Consequently, though African-Americans made up about half of the arrestees, they constituted three-fourths of the average daily population of the jail.

The juvenile figures were even more depressing. One-fourth of all black youngsters (ages 15–17) living in the county had been arrested during the last four months of 1991 alone.[2] In 1994, this one adult jail regularly held upward of 500 teenagers under eighteen, 85% of them African-American. The risk to an African-American male of eventually being jailed in this county approached the 90th percentile – just as Alfred Blumstein had suggested would happen nationally some 20 years earlier.[3]

I thought that all these figures on race and the local criminal justice system would shock the local authorities. However, few seemed concerned. Far from being an embarrassment, the depressing data was seen as a kind of badge of honor, demonstrating the fortitude of local law-enforcement authorities in getting tough on crime. The figures on juveniles, for example, were quoted in a letter the state's attorney circulated to the county's secondary schools as a warning to would-be errant teenagers.

The presumption – apparently shared by most of the nation – was that so many African-American youths and young adults were being dragged off to jail because, as one judge commented to me, "they're the ones committing the violent crimes." In the wake of this kind of analysis, the county had invested close to $100 million to build new jail complexes and was quite willing to spend approximately $150,000 per day to operate them. Although inner-city males committed a disproportionate share of violent crimes, particularly homicide and robbery, the absolute number of such crimes was insufficient to explain the thousands of young African-Americans being brought into the jail day after day. Something was gravely wrong with the premise. A relatively small percentage of these arrests had to do with serious crime. Most concerned misdemeanors, "public order" offenses, and lesser felonies.

The matter of who ends up in the criminal justice system of any country has always carried racial and ethnic implications. While those who are confined in a country's jails or prisons are a rough measure of the types of criminal activity at a given time, they provide a sharper picture of who is at the bottom of the socioeconomic heap or on the political outs at that given time. Visit Berlin's jails and count the Turks. Visit France's prisons and see the Algerians. Visit

Canadian prisons in the English-speaking provinces and count the French-speaking and the Native populations. Visit American prisons and jails and see the blacks and Hispanics. The patterns are far from new. They give validity to the discomfiting comment of California sociologist John Irvin that the nation's jails exist less for purposes of crime control than as places of "rabble management."

During the social tumult and exploding crime rates that accompanied the waves of Irish, Italian, Greek, Portuguese, and Eastern European immigrants to the United States, these ethnic groups disproportionately filled the nation's prisons and jails. First-generation European immigrants had higher crime rates than "native-born" whites and were also overrepresented in America's jails, prisons, and reform schools of the late 19th and early 20th centuries. The percentage of second- and third-generation immigrants in the nation's criminal justice system was even higher.

In *The Jack-Roller: A Delinquent Boy's Own Story*, a study of a young man's criminal career in Chicago of the 1920s, Clifford Shaw made note of the breadth of criminal justice system penetration in certain ethnic communities, revealing that in one large neighborhood of Chicago – the so-called Back of the Yards: "During the three-year period between 1924 and 1926, 28% of the young men from seventeen to twenty-one years of age were arrested and arraigned in the Boys' Court on charges of serious crime."[4] (This was a particularly interesting finding in light of similar statistics yielded in the 1990 Rand Corporation study of young African-American males in the District of Columbia, which found that approximately one-third of all the African-American males between the ages of 18 and 21 who lived in the district had been arrested and charged with a criminal offense.)[5] In Chicago's Back of the Yards neighborhood 17.6% of the boys between 10 and 17 had been charged as delinquents by the police in 1926 alone.[6]

Shaw attributed much of this to the changing ethnic patterns in the neighborhood: "In 1900 the population was 33.5% Irish; 20.4% Czechoslovakian; 14.6% German; 9.2% Scandinavian;

7.8% Polish; and 4.7% Lithuanian. By 1920, 45.2% was Polish; 28.5% Russian; 11.9% Lithuanian; only 5.6% Czechoslovakian, 1.5% Irish, 1.7% German; and there were practically no Scandinavians."[7] As Shaw concluded, "[S]uch marked changes in the cultural composition of the neighborhood have undoubtedly entailed considerable disorganization and confusion of moral standards."[8]

African-Americans: A Special Case

Although the disproportionate number of immigrants involved in crime moderated as immigrant families were assimilated into American culture,[9] things were always different for African-Americans. As a group, they stood on the bottom rung – even when substantial percentages of first- and second-generation European ethnic populations were themselves very low on the socioeconomic ladder. Blacks were never assimilated in the ways primarily European whites had been. And when it came to blacks who had been labeled as "criminals," the differential treatment came with its own brutal history and vicious traditions. As "Stanley," the young white "Jack-Roller" of Shaw's study, described the situation during his last stint in prison in the mid-1920s: "Niggers out there were no better than brutes. Here they were given the hardest work, the worst cells, and subjected to the most brutal punishment. Everybody, especially the guards, are prejudiced against them."[10]

As sociologist Shirley Ann Vining-Brown noted: "In the South, both the facilities and the philosophy of prisons were tailor-made for Black convicts in the post-Civil War period . . . the crime problem in the South became equated with the 'Negro Problem' as Black prisoners began to outnumber White prisoners in all Southern prisons. . . . The sudden change in the racial composition of Southern prisons produced changes in various penal practices." Brown goes on to note that the most notable of these changes was the "prisoner lease system," whereby mostly black inmates were leased to local farmers and plantation owners as a way of making profit for the penal system and avoiding the costs of maintenance for the inmates. As one southerner of the times put it, "Before the war we owned the Negroes. . . . But these convicts we don't own 'em. One dies, get another." Brown concludes that "once a Black man was convicted in the South, he was viewed as incorrigible and any attempt to rehabilitate him was considered wasted money."[11]

In its 1918 report *Negro Population: 1790–1915*,[12] the Bureau of the Census noted that while blacks made up about 11% of the general population they constituted about one-fifth (21.9%) of the inmates in the prisons, penitentiaries, jails, reform schools, and workhouses of the states. They represented 56% of those held for "grave homicide" and about half of those held for "lesser homicide," and contributed slightly less than one-third of the commitments for robbery, burglary, and larceny. On the other hand, only about 16% of those held for drunkenness, disorderly conduct, or vagrancy were black.[13] The authors of the 1918 report then posed the questions in terms that would be entirely familiar today:

While these figures . . . will probably be generally accepted as indicating that there is more criminality and law breaking among Negroes than among whites and while that conclusion is probably justified by the facts, . . . [i]t is a question whether the difference . . . may not be to some extent the result of discrimination in the treatment of white and Negro offenders on the part of the community and the courts. It must always be borne in mind that the amount of crime punished in different classes or communities may not bear a fixed or unvarying ratio to the amount of crime committed.[14]

These comments on race and the justice system from nearly three-quarters of a century ago seem more measured than many contemporary assessments. Significantly, the report's relatively civil discussion of racial differences in reported crime and the possibility of discrimination makes no mention of the fact that, in the 30 years leading up to its publication, a black man was being lynched somewhere in the country on an average of every two or three days – public events often attended by hundreds and, in some cases, thousands of white citizens and frequently involving local law-enforcement officers – with the perpetrators virtually always listed as "unknown" and going unprosecuted.[15] In the "informal" justice system in the United States, the most extreme punishments and unjust procedures for blacks were never beyond tacit support of a substantial proportion of the white population well into this century. Castration, lynching, and other vigilante-type actions were characteristically reserved for citizens of color and provided the backdrop and collective memory against which the formal criminal justice system functioned when it came to blacks.

These incidents numbered 3,224 (of those recorded) between 1889 and 1918.[16] Although a few whites were lynched, the practice was virtually exclusively focused on young black males. As historian Richard Maxwell Brown noted, for a lynching to have the "maximum intimidative effect" on the black population of the surrounding area, ample notice had to be given.[17] Indeed, railroads ran special trains and frequently assigned extra cars to regular trains to accommodate the demands of lynch-minded white crowds numbering as many as 15,000. The "macabre ritual" was less likely to be a hanging than one in which "the doomed victim was burned at the stake – a process that was prolonged for several hours, often as the black male was subjected to the excruciating pain of torture and mutilation . . . climaxed, ordinarily, by the hideous act euphemistically described as 'surgery below the belt.' " "Souvenirs" taken from the mutilated body were passed out, picture postcards of the proceedings were sold by enterprising photographers, and the leading participants were written up in the local newspapers. Yet the coroner's report inevitably concluded with a finding that the death of the victim was caused by "persons unknown."[18]

Although it is not surprising that census researchers in 1918 would vacillate over whether racial discrimination existed in the justice system, the fact that the problem remains as mysterious to

contemporary criminologists and sociologists is troubling. In his
1940s classic study of race, *An American Dilemma*, the Swedish
anthropologist Gunnar Myrdal presented a devastating picture of
what happened to black males in southern courts of that time.[19]
Historically, there was little argument that blacks had been handled
differently from other minorities in the justice systems of most
majority white nations.[20] Indeed, until the late 1970s, most criminologists accepted the proposition that racial bias was an important
element to be considered in studying the justice system.[21] The
prevailing view was perhaps best summarized by the journalist Haywood Burns: "The likelihood of the legal process being entirely
uncontaminated by bias in any given case is small. Individual
Blacks can and do win civil suits, and Individual Blacks can [be]
and are acquitted of criminal charges, but in an institutional sense
in almost all instances the law functions in a discriminatory and
unfair manner when Blacks (and poor people) are involved."[22]

While there was every reason to rejoice in the civil rights progress that African-Americans had made in the United States in the
1960s and 1970s, something else was quietly but inexorably building in the criminal justice system. Though the percentage of
African-Americans in the national population had not grown appreciably over the past half-century (from 12% to 13%), the percentage of African-Americans going into state and federal prisons was
steadily increasing, with the largest surge occurring simultaneously
with the war on drugs (see Table 4). In 1991, for example, the
national incarceration rate in state and federal prisons was 310 per
100,000. For white males it was 352 per 100,000. For black males
ages 25–29 it stood at an incredible 6,301.[23]

The Question of Racial Bias

The questions asked in 1918 by the U.S. Census Bureau statisti-
cians remain unanswered today. Do these high rates of arrest and

Table 4. *Race of Admissions to State and Federal Prisons, 1926–1993*

Year	White (%)	Black (%)	Other (%)
1926	79	21	1
1930	77	22	1
1935	74	25	1
1940	71	28	1
1945	68	31	1
1950	69	30	1
1960	66	32	2
1964	65	33	2
1974	59	38	3
1978	58	41	1
1981	57	42	2
1986[a]	40	45	15
1993[b]	27	55	18

[a]When Hispanic inmates were broken down in 1986, the percentage of "white" inmates dropped precipitously.

[b]Estimated – a 1990 survey of 267,394 "New Court Commitments to Prisons in 35 States" (states that accounted for nearly 90% of all prison admissions nationwide during 1990) indicated that 54.0% were black and 45.2% were white. However, those of "Hispanic origin" who made up 18.3% of these new commitments were not broken down by race. These trends suggest that the total minority percentage of new court commitments to prisons nationally probably reached 73% by 1993, of which approximately 55% were black.

Sources: Andrew Hacker. *Two Nations: Black and White, Separate, Hostile, Unequal,* Chas. Scribners, New York, 1992, p. 197; and U.S. Department of Justice, Bureau of Justice Statistics, *National Corrections Reporting Program,* 1990, NCJ-141879 (Washington, D.C.: U.S. Department of Justice, 1993), p. 15.

imprisonment of African-American males reflect racial bias or do
they simply demonstrate that African-American males commit
more crime? The answer to both questions is a qualified yes. Although there has always been more crime in the cities (whatever
the race of the majority), discrimination clearly plays a major role in
who gets a criminal record, who stays in jail, and who goes to
prison. In the 1980s and 1990s, the discussion shifted. A number
of researchers reached the conclusion that more blacks were in
prisons simply because they committed most of the crimes. Concomitant with these developments, we saw the reintroduction of the
proposition that genetic racial differences might be a major contributor to criminal behavior.[24] It was a quick and somewhat unexpected shift in focus and appears to be as attributable, in large part,
to the sea change in the national mood as well as in the research
methodologies that came to characterize American criminological
research.

Grounding Research in Tainted Sources

The poststructuralist historians George Lakoff and Mark Johnson
have pointed to the familiar dilemma that plagues historians who
depend upon official records as their primary sources. "Whether in
national politics or in everyday interaction," they noted, "people in
power get to impose their metaphors."[25] In much of contemporary
criminal justice research the same principle applies a fortiori. As
criminologists increasingly immersed themselves in a world of binaries, they became quite comfortable dealing with individuals in bits
and pieces. Coincidentally, their methodology fit neatly with the
onerous demands of an ever more formal criminal justice procedure.

In discussing narrative research, Clifford Shaw, the respected
sociologist of the Chicago School of the 1930s, put his finger on
the dilemma plaguing the many modern-day researchers of crime
and punishment: "The validity and value of the personal docu-

ment," he states, "are not dependent upon its objectivity or veracity." Rather, "rationalizations, fabrications, prejudices, exaggerations are quite as valuable as objective descriptions, provided, of course, that these reactions be properly identified and classified."[26] Shaw then quotes W. I. Thomas, who first postulated the concept of the "self-fulfilling prophecy." "There may be, and is," wrote Thomas, "doubt as to the objectivity and veracity of the record. But even the highly subjective record has a value. . . . For his immediate behavior is closely related to his definition of the situation, which may be in terms of objective reality, or in terms of a subjective appreciation – 'as if' it were so. *Very often it is the wide discrepancy between the situation as it seems to others and the situation as it seems to the individual that brings about the overt behavior. . . . If men define situations as real, they are real in their consequences.*"[27]

Even when memory is grounded in unassailable realities, the ways in which it is carried by each individual may vary greatly – particularly when the memory is of harrowing realities. In looking at Holocaust survivors, for example, Lawrence Langer distinguishes "chronological memory," with its narrative form of a beginning, middle, and end (which dims with the passage of time) from "durational memory," which results from having experienced events so horrific and threatening that the memories defy time and suffuse one's total life experience thereafter.[28] Such considerations are impossible for the criminal justice system to absorb.

Therefore, the researcher might be best advised to consider a criminal justice record as a written apologia at each stage of criminal justice processing for what was about to happen at the next stage. In his 1987 presidential address to the American Criminological Society, John Hagan warned that "One of the clearest things these [studies on racial bias in the criminal justice system] tell us is that criminal justice records are potentially problematic not only for the etiological study of criminal behavior, but also for the study of reactions to this behavior in the form of processing decisions. These problems involve sample selection biases in the sifting of cases from stage to stage, and incomplete social background information on the offenders involved."[29]

Hagan was correct. The records by which the justice system memorializes itself – from arrest summaries, to charges brought by prosecutors, to pleading the "facts" of a case by frequently uninterested or incompetent lawyers, to acquittal or conviction, to sentencing based on inadequate and often incorrect information – present truncated and highly distorted versions of reality. Even apparently objective data, such as that generated for statistical reports of criminal justice agencies, cannot be taken at face value. The annual report of a sheriff in pursuit of having a new jail built will present a highly different statistical picture of who will reside therein than that of a sheriff who is satisfied with his jail's present capacity. A police department looking for more staff and equipment will present a different profile of crime locally than one in a "no growth" stance. A politically appointed state corrections administrator who feels unable to question nary a speech or proposal generated by a governor's or legislative committee chairman's posturing on crime will present a different view of his population and needs than one who assesses his situation on the basis of facts.

In recent years, records have left crucial realities unaddressed through the adoption of "mandatory" sentencing laws and so-called sentencing guidelines. These dicta all but ensure that the major participants in the criminal justice drama will remain blissfully ignorant and official files be kept unsullied by any sense of narrative or meaning. What in any other field would be seen as essential to the minimal understanding of human behavior (personal and family history), or crucial to intelligently addressing a bona fide social problem, is marginalized in formal criminal justice procedure.

A police arrest report may or may not be an accurate summary of the facts. A charge may be overdrawn by a prosecutor with an eye toward its potential for later bargaining. Even a record of conviction carries no guarantee that it mirrors either a complete or honest appraisal of what actually happened. A conviction for "aggravated assault," for example, may not necessarily mean that a victim was touched or required medical attention. Likewise, probation reports upon which the courts base their sentencing decisions may not be either fair or complete. Modern probation officers are sometimes apologists for harsh sentencing and long-term incarceration. Their reports are written in such a way as to validate this ideological stance. In reading hundreds of presentence reports prepared by probation officers, I have noticed a clear disposition to revel in exaggerating the putative dangerousness of their charges, while investing themselves with a heroic mantle for managing so threatening and disreputable a lot.

Finding No Bias

In comparing reported crime rates with national arrest rates, Carnegie-Mellon socioeconometrist Alfred Blumstein concluded that "the arrest process whose demographics we can observe, is reasonably representative of the crime process for at least . . . serious crime types" (i.e., homicide, aggravated assault, and robbery).[30] Blumstein's conclusion that there was little evidence of racial bias in criminal justice processing was generally accepted within the scholarly community and is still regularly used as a basis for many other analyses of crime in urban areas, including those of the respected African-American sociologist William Julius Wilson and Christopher Jencks.[31] Although Blumstein acknowledged that racial disparities increased when it came to less serious crimes, he nevertheless concluded that "even if relatively large racial differences in handling these [lesser] offenses were totally eliminated, [they] would not result in a major shift in the racial mix of prison populations." While accepting Blumstein's analysis to a large degree, criminologist Michael Tonry also noted that arrest patterns by race had not changed appreciably from 1976 through 1992. Gener-

ally, 50% to 54% of arrests for violent crime were of whites, and
44% to 47% were of blacks. In recent years, the percentage of
blacks arrested for violent crime had actually dropped (from 47.5%
in 1976 to 44.8% in 1992). Tonry concluded that something else
might be going on as well. If arrests for serious violent crimes were
the principal determinant of incarceration, the percentage of blacks
in prisons and jails should have remained stable throughout the
1970s, 1980s, and early 1990s. However, while arrest patterns did
not change, the percentage of black males being admitted to federal
and state prisons relative to whites increased from 35% to 55% in
1993.[32]

Studies by researchers from the Rand Corporation have landed
on both sides of the bias argument, one concluding that sentences
were generally racially equitable when such factors as criminal
records were included, and another finding evidence of bias.[33] In
their study finding no bias, the Rand researchers added a somewhat odd disclaimer: "We did not find widespread, *conscious* prejudice against certain racial groups. Rather, when we found racial
disparities . . . they seem to have developed because the system
adopted procedures without analyzing their possible effects on different racial groups" (emphasis added). Whether racial disparities
are the result of conscious or unconscious motives is probably of
minimal interest to those who are subject to them.

U.S. Justice Department researcher Patrick Langan found even
less likelihood than Blumstein that the disproportionate number of
blacks in state prisons had anything to do with racial bias. Using
National Crime Survey data rather than the FBI's Uniform Crime
Reports to compute expected imprisonment rates of black males,
Langan concluded that in fully 84% of the cases of black men sent
to prison, the disparity with white incarceration rates could be
explained by differential crime rates alone. He concluded that racial bias could possibly be at work in at most 16% of the cases.[34]

Although Blumstein's and Langan's conclusion that racial bias
in the criminal justice system was probably negligible gained credi-

bility among policymakers and some criminologists, it was not so easily accepted by others. Indeed, to many it flew in the face of their own experience in the criminal justice system. Not surprisingly, whether the public at large believed the criminal justice system to be racially biased was itself conditioned by race. For example, a 1994 poll showed that when respondents were presented with the statement "Blacks are treated more harshly than whites in the U.S. criminal system," 74% of blacks agreed whereas 65% of whites disagreed.[35]

A 1989 survey of 169 superior court judges and 113 court managers, commissioned by the New Jersey State Supreme Court, revealed that fully 98% of the respondents saw bias against minorities in the justice system.[36] Half saw "small increments of discrimination against minorities at each step of the justice process" (arrest, setting bail, jury verdicts, prosecutorial decisions regarding charges to be brought, and sentencing). Equally interesting was the fact that this study was shelved for over two years. Only as the result of a news "leak" did it appear in the *New Jersey Law Journal,* and subsequently in the *New York Times.*

In February 1993, a frustrated African-American federal district judge gave a black defendant a lesser sentence on a drug charge than that called for by the sentencing guidelines. Commenting that prosecutors routinely asked the federal courts to impose sentences below the guideline when white defendants agreed to cooperate in other drug prosecutions – the so-called snitch motion – the judge noted that no such motion had been made in the case of the young African-American defendant before him. Although the judge admitted he found it hard to pin down, he nevertheless concluded that "racism of the present, unlike racism of the past, has been highly sophisticated and covert, by acts that are hidden and very difficult to ferret out."[37] The open racial bias that characterized so many courtrooms 30 years ago had been exiled to chambers and courthouse offices. Ferreting it out would take more than a little work. This federal judge who felt but could not pin down the racial discrimination in the courts was right. Racial bias in the criminal justice system had come to haunt that "gray area" between the obvious and the ambiguous – precisely the position in which most young black men find themselves when they first encounter the police or are brought before the courts. It is a bias that speaks directly to the issue of later criminal convictions and deeper penetration of the criminal justice system.

A Question of Methodology

In researching bias, it is crucial to know how the local social context influences decision making in courts and law-enforcement agencies – to examine such matters as patterns of punishment as well as the differences in social and economic equality. In 1994, criminologists Robert Crutchfield, George Bridges, and Susan Pitchford took a second look at some of the modern research on bias and concluded that its methodological limitations made it all but impossible to draw any conclusions regarding the existence or nonexistence of racial bias in the criminal justice system.[38] Faulting Blumstein and Langan (who found little or no evidence of racial bias in the criminal justice system) for limiting the foci of their analysis to single decision points in the system (e.g., imprisonment) and for aggregating data in such a manner as to mask racial disparities, Crutchfield et al. found large variations between the states in the degree to which actual levels of criminal involvement were reflected in black imprisonment rates (Table 5). Blumstein and Langan's static methodology did not allow for taking regional or local racial disparities into account. After disaggregating the data for regions and states, rather than aggregating them on a national level, Crutchfield et al. discovered that the rate of imprisonment of blacks reflecting actual differences in criminal behavior dropped precipitously: "nearly 40% of the states explain less of their observed Black imprisonment via differential Black involve-

Table 5. *Black Observed Imprisonment, 1982, and Black Expected Imprisonment (Based on Index Arrests, 1981)*

State/Region	Black imprisonment observed	Black imprisonment expected	% of black observed imprisonment explained by expected[a]
National	155,924	103,552	66.41
Northeast	26,650	16,505	61.93
Maine	15	56	39.45
New Hampshire	5	1	28.81
Massachusetts	1,329	408	30.71
Rhode Island	246	145	85.89
Connecticut	2,105	1,247	59.26
New York	13,407	9,721	72.50
New Jersey	4,455	1,974	44.30
Pennsylvania	5,088	3,003	59.03
North Central	33,813	22,900	67.73
Ohio	7,229	3,866	53.47
Indiana	2,795	2,677	95.78
Illinois	8,217	5,639	68.63
Michigan	8,515	5,715	67.12
Wisconsin	1,689	950	56.26
Minnesota	421	196	46.64
North Dakota	2	31	42.98
South Dakota	14	11	75.54
Nebraska	533	276	51.79
Kansas	934	609	65.16
South	81,065	54,645	67.41
Delaware	1,021	792	77.57
Maryland	6,671	3,387	50.09
Virginia	5,376	3,401	63.27
West Virginia	218	180	82.66
North Carolina	8,380	7,477	89.23
South Carolina	4,972	4,238	85.24

Table 5. *(cont.)*

State/Region	Black imprisonment observed	Black imprisonment expected	% of black observed imprisonment explained by expected[a]
Georgia	7,313	6,081	83.15
Florida	11,351	7,205	63.48
Kentucky	1,171	882	75.35
Tennessee	3,346	2,519	75.28
Alabama	4,718	2,883	61.11
Mississippi	2,829	2,816	99.54
Arkansas	1,632	1,292	79.19
Louisiana	6,763	3,879	57.36
Oklahoma	1,482	1,178	79.47
Texas	12,732	6,433	46.84
West	14,396	9,502	66.00
Idaho	26	10	38.32
Wyoming	25	17	67.35
Colorado	579	282	48.69
New Mexico	160	–	–
Arizona	1,009	561	55.56
Utah	107	54	50.74
Nevada	591	615	104.14
Washington	1,106	213	19.26
Oregon	340	281	82.65
California	10,270	7,350	71.57
Alaska	139	856	.99
Hawaii	44	34	78.00

[a]The percentage of observed imprisonment that is explained by the black expected imprisonment was calculated prior to rounding of the expected values.

Source: Crutchfield et al., "Analytical and Aggregation Biases in Analyses of Imprisonment: Reconciling Discrepancies in Studies of Racial Disparity," *Journal of Research in Crime and Delinquency* 31, no. 2 (May 1994): 178.

ment in serious crime than can be explained for the aggregated national observed Black imprisonment rate."[39] They concluded that a new "growing body of evidence suggests that justice is by no means guaranteed for some groups facing criminal processing."[40]

Crutchfield et al. summarized their concerns in this way: "Until scholars fully identify the nature of these macrolevel processes, analyses that ignore the varying contexts of law will contribute little to debate over inequality in the imposition of punishment. Further, the analyses will be vulnerable to biases that undermine their validity and importance to the field."[41]

A 1991 analysis of 800 cases by the 8th Circuit Federal Court of Appeals concluded that racial disparities increased significantly under the new federal reform "sentencing guidelines," which were designed to minimize bias in the federal courts. Under these guidelines, federal judges were stripped of their power to fashion sentences to fit the particularities of the crime and the individual offender and were made to follow a set of rules ostensibly designed to make sentences more equitable and uniform. The effect of the sentencing guidelines, however, was quite something else: it transferred decision-making power over the sentence from judges to politically driven prosecutors. In the wake of this sentencing reform, a more virulent kind of bias emerged to replace the previous alleged bias of judges. Federal prosecutors began routinely charging more African-American men with offenses that called for mandatory sentences. They were less disposed to offer a black defendant a "plea bargain" than a white defendant. The average sentence for comparable crimes rose 55% for blacks and only 7% for whites after Congress's "reforms," and blacks got sentences 49% longer than whites convicted of similar offenses. This represented a retrenchment from previous years. In 1983, blacks had received sentences "only" 28% longer than whites sentenced on similar offenses.[42]

Other studies found bias as well. After analyzing 1,165 criminal cases from 1990 and comparing them to nearly 60,000 cases involving mandatory sentences dating back to 1984, researchers for the

U.S. Sentencing Commission observed that "the difference (in length of sentences) found across races seems to have increased since 1984." During 1990, the study revealed that 68% of African-American defendants were chosen for "mandatory" sentences, whereas only 54% of whites and 57% of Hispanics were similarly sentenced, though the report noted that mandatory sentences were not being universally applied, and that it was up to prosecutors to decide whether the defendant would be charged under a statute which required mandatory sentences. It was also noted that a defendant could win a shorter term by turning in accomplices to the prosecutor.[43]

Similar things were happening at the state level. A study conducted by the Florida Department of Corrections and Florida State University revealed a long-standing bias in the handling of African-American defendants in pretrial status.[44] Researchers also found that defendants arrested on felony charges who did not have prior arrests were less likely to be incarcerated than those arrested for misdemeanors who had prior arrests (usually for misdemeanors). However, minorities were incarcerated more often than whites in all the counties surveyed for 14 of 21 felony arrest charges and 11 of 13 misdemeanor charges. Most significantly, for the purposes of this discussion, the racial disparities were greatest among those arrested for misdemeanors. An employed African-American male found guilty of drug crimes was six times more likely to be sentenced to incarceration than similarly situated whites.[45] When it came to imposing enhanced sentences on those offenders labeled as the "most serious," the racial bias was even more obvious and clear.

Another Florida legislative study found that county prosecutors across the state were using the "habitual offender" statute in grossly biased ways.[46] Under this statute (an early version of what would later come to be known as "three strikes" legislation) prosecutors could seek enhanced sentences for offenders with two or more prior convictions for felonies, or for one previous conviction for a violent offense. For a first-degree felony, the defendant could be sentenced to life imprisonment; for a second-degree felony, up to 30 years; and for a third-degree felony, up to 10 years. The researchers found that black offenders were more likely to be sentenced as habitual offenders than white offenders, even after taking into consideration differences in criminal history and current offenses. The bias was anything but subtle. Black offenders whose offenses were at the lowest level of seriousness were almost three times (2.73) more likely to be habitualized than similarly situated nonblack offenders. At the most serious offense levels, black offenders were 50 percent more likely to be habitualized than nonblack offenders.

A journalistic investigation of over 650,000 criminal cases prosecuted between 1981 and 1990 in California confirmed these patterns. It showed that at virtually every stage of pretrial negotiations, whites got better deals than nonwhites. A significantly higher percentage of whites arrested on felony charges ended up convicted only of misdemeanors, and a higher proportion of those whites who were charged had the charges reduced or dismissed. Of 71,000 adults with no prior record arrested on felony charges, one-third of whites had charges reduced, compared with one-fourth of blacks and Hispanics. Whites also received more lenient sentences and were less likely to go to prison. Looking at one of the more "liberal" jurisdictions – San Francisco County – the investigators found that whereas 4% of first-time white defendants were sentenced to state prison, 7% of first-time African-American defendants were sent into the state-prison system. The only group that fared worse were the Latino first-timers, 11% of whom were sentenced to state prison.[47]

Deciphering the Code

A good example of how easily evidence of racial bias can elude the researcher was found in an analysis of 223 adult offenders sentenced in Florida courts in the early 1980s. Initially, criminologists James Unnever and Larry Hembroff had relied upon a methodology they described as "linear and additive." The research design was premised on the assumption that judges determined the length of sentence by considering characteristics of *the defendant* (employment status, race, etc.), *the case* (seriousness of offense, number of arrest charges, etc.), and *the defendant's prior record* (seriousness and number of prior arrests and convictions), assigning a "uniform weight" to these factors and then adding them up. This research method required that it be proven that race or ethnicity "linearly and additively" influenced the judge's sentencing decision. "With such a model," said the authors, "detecting racial/ethnic sentencing differentials requires that blacks and/or ethnic minorities receive uniformly more severe sentences than whites whenever they have identical court cases."[48] The study revealed no such evidence and the researchers concluded that in those *obvious* cases where either a term of prison or probation would clearly be imposed and the probation officer and judge were in substantial agreement, "race/ethnicity [did] not linearly and additively influence judicial decision-making."[49]

However, when Unnever and Hembroff dropped their "linear and additive" design and broke down that large middle span of cases where matters were less clear and in which the defendant might just as easily be granted probation as sent to prison, race emerged as a very real issue. When the probation officer recommended incarceration but the judge disagreed and placed the defendant on probation, whites were significantly more likely to be put on probation whereas blacks were routinely sent off to prison. Unnever and Hembroff cited the interesting research of Spohn, Gruhl, and Welch as illustrative of the distortions that go unrecognized with static methodologies. Using a 93-point "sentencing scale," Spohn et al. found that blacks were actually receiving *lighter* sentences than whites on many of the more serious offenses. This finding was so unexpected that the researchers reexamined their sentencing scale. They discovered, as had Unnever and Hembroff, that in those "borderline" cases wherein the judge could either impose a lengthy probation sentence or a short prison sentence, judges tended to sentence whites to probation and blacks to prison.[50]

This is precisely the pattern that has emerged in the administration of the so-called three strikes and you're out legislation in California enacted in March 1994, wherein conviction for a third felony carries a sentence of "life without parole." Within less than 90 days of its enactment, several hundred defendants had already been charged under the statute. Significantly, half of the affected defendants were charged with what had come to be known as the "wobbler" offense. These are incidents such as petty theft and second-degree burglary that can be prosecuted either as misdemeanors or felonies. The California attorney general moved to limit judicial discretion in order to ensure that more of those charged with so-called wobbler offenses would be tried as felons – subjecting them to life without parole.[51] The wobbler offenses present precisely the situation where racial bias is most likely to enter the scene.

Unfortunately, most of the multivariate models of analysis now common in criminological research – devoid of fieldwork – make little allowance for these crucial kinds of considerations. The methodology dictates that such traditional approaches as "labeling theory" and the potential for the unanticipated consequences of criminal justice handling in stimulating and sustaining criminal careers are overlooked. Research models that at first glance appear highly sophisticated at best provide snapshots of changing events.

Racial Disparities in Handling Juveniles

After identifying more than a thousand citations from the research literature dating back to 1969 on the processing of minority youth in the juvenile justice system, Carl Pope and Richard Feyerherm selected the 46 "most relevant" articles for analysis. In two-thirds of these studies, "race effects" were found at some stages of processing and not at others. One-third of the studies found no evidence of racial disparity.[52] Those studies which found bias were no less sophisticated methodologically than those which did not.

Pope and Feyerherm concluded that many of the studies that found no evidence of racial disparity "used control variables in a multivariate analysis" that were misleading. "Legally relevant" variables such as prior arrests, for example, were not necessarily racially neutral. Indeed, racial differences accumulated and appeared to grow more pronounced as minority youths moved from the earliest to later stages of the juvenile justice system.[53] Research methods that do not allow for a close look at each of the discrete levels in juvenile justice processing are not likely to demonstrate racial bias. "Race effects at any one stage . . . may be canceled out or enhanced at later stages. Only by examination of multiple decision points can we gain a more complete picture of the way in which minority status does or does not influence outcome decisions."[54]

For example, if police decisions are biased, as the "gatekeepers controlling who is funneled into the juvenile courts" they place minority youth at greater risk in the later sentencing and correctional stages of processing.[55] Pope and Feyerherm found that bias can appear at any stage of juvenile justice processing. They noted, for example, that relatively few large-scale studies examined police decisions made *after* the decision to do *something.* Typically, studies of police handling looked at whether the police took a youth to a detention facility or let him remain free pending a court appearance. Thus, racial bias at the earliest stage, when police are making the decision whether or not to arrest the youth, can remain hidden.[56]

In addition, bias is more difficult to detect if the researcher does not know something about the family of the juvenile: "youth from single-parent homes, especially if female-based, often face more severe dispositions than those from intact homes." Pope and Feyerherm note that studies often control for "family stability," which acknowledges the fact that a judge is less likely to incarcerate a youth from an intact family. But often "family situation" is a code phrase for "race."[57]

To a large extent, the inability of researchers to discern bias in recent years rests with their use of control variables in multivariate analysis methodology. In her review of studies on racial bias in the juvenile justice system, University of Missouri criminologist Kimberly L. Kempf found race to be a good predictor of what would happen to the young offender in the juvenile justice system, even when such relevant criteria as prior record, severity of offense, type and level of injury or damage were taken into account. Kempf concluded that the fact that some researchers found little or no evidence of racial bias probably resulted from methodological problems: "The reviewed research has revealed the need to examine multiple stages, the possible interdependence of juvenile justice decisions, and adopt a more process-oriented approach in recognition that decisions at earlier stages may affect those that occur subsequently."[58]

Pope and Feyerherm suggest that certain factors had to be addressed for research on racial bias to be valid. Researchers must:

- Pay more attention to the fact that race effects may be masked when information is combined on a statewide or county basis;
- Examine each stage of processing;
- Incorporate field and observational studies;
- Target police encounters as well as court and correctional processing;
- Employ techniques that can detect direct as well as indirect race effects;
- Be attentive to organizational structure and environmental influences;
- Focus on all minorities;
- Include information on family characteristics;
- Study rural, suburban, and metropolitan areas;
- Take changes in sample size into account as cases are processed through the system.[59]

In her study of juvenile justice processing in 14 urban and rural counties in Pennsylvania, Kempf described how racial disparities in handling build stage by stage, often ending in more grossly racially biased outcomes: "Juvenile justice outcomes were influenced by race at every stage except adjudication. . . . harsher outcomes at early stages, in the form of more formal intervention for minorities, retained minorities in the system at a higher rate and affected eventual case outcomes."[60]

When were racial disparities likely to crop up? They were most obvious at the very earliest and latest stages of juvenile justice processing. Black teenagers were more likely to be detained, to be handled formally, to be waived to adult court, and to be adjudicated delinquent. If removed from their homes by the court, they were less likely to be placed in the better-staffed and better-run private-group home facilities and more likely to be sent into state reform schools. An interesting exception was found at the middle stages of adjudication: black youths were more than three times as likely to have the charges against them dismissed than were white youths. Although this could be taken as a sign that some black juveniles were being let off more lightly by judges, it more than likely supported the overall conclusion that black youths were being overcharged by police and had been brought into the early formal stages of juvenile justice processing (including detention) more readily than white youths. Kempf's findings were similar to those of Edmund McGarrell, who studied "racial disproportionality" in juvenile court processing. McGarrell found that nonwhite youths were more likely to be referred or petitioned to court, detained, and placed outside the home.[61]

For the most part, juvenile records still display a narrative stance. As a result, they lend themselves to the kinds of research that might uncover racial bias. When it comes to identifying racial disparities, lack of contextual information can grossly distort the findings. For example, criminologists David Huizinga and Delbert Elliott found that the differences in the amount of criminal behavior between white and black juveniles all but disappeared when the study groups were controlled for social class. There was an enormous potential for small instances of bias at each stage of criminal justice processing to have cumulative effects later.[62] Noting that African-American youths were being incarcerated at two to four times the rate of white youths, they asked the same question as Blumstein: "the obvious question is whether this reflects differences in individual behavior or official responses to behavior (or both)?"[63] However, they came up with a notably different answer.

Basing their study on data taken from the National Youth Survey, Huizinga and Elliott selected a representative sample of 11–17-year-old adolescents for annual confidential, personal (face-to-face) self-report interviews regarding individual delinquent behavior covering the period from 1976 to 1983.[64] A search of police records for each respondent was completed in each location where the youth lived between 1976–1979 and 1976–1983. The record searches extended beyond the immediate city in which the youth lived to include every police/sheriff's jurisdiction within a 10-mile radius of the youth's home. The data revealed the youths' self-reports to be relatively accurate, often revealing more delinquent acts than official records showed. Huizinga and Elliott also found "few if any substantial and consistent differences" in the rates of delinquent activity of different racial groups. However, "among minority offenders the 'risk' of being apprehended and charged with an Index [felony] offense [was] substantially and significantly higher than it [was] for Whites who report involvement in the same kinds of offenses."[65] Although the higher arrest rates of minority youth for more serious offenses accounted for some of the disparities in incarceration rates, the bias often occurred when the decision was made over which charge to use at the time of the arrest. "Minorities appear to be at greater risk for being charged with more serious offenses than whites involved in comparable levels of delinquent behavior, a factor which may eventually result in higher incarceration rates among minorities."[66]

Class also appeared to be at work. As many as 75% of the minority youth came from the lower socioeconomic classes. As Huizinga and Elliott put it: "Social class and social conditions may affect the ability to avoid apprehension, the ability to avoid arrest if apprehended, the presence of parental and legal support at both arrest and court processing stages, and general demeanor at points of contact with the juvenile justice system."[67]

To address some of these concerns, Elliott later followed the 1976 sample of teenagers into the early 1990s when they reached their thirties. This afforded another opportunity to relate self-reports of delinquency to actual arrest data over those years during which a young man is more likely to develop a criminal "career." It turned out that black and white teenagers committed serious offenses at about the same rates. The ratio of black-to-white offending at ages 11 and 12 was 1:1. In their adolescent years, the black-to-white ratio of offending increased slightly to 1.5:1. However, by the time these adolescents moved into manhood and were in their late twenties, the ratio had soared to 4:1. Significantly, though the percentages of those who had committed a crime at some time in their lives was approximately the same for blacks and whites, the black youths tended to commit their crimes at younger ages and continued to do so, whereas the white subjects stopped as they moved into their twenties.[68] These findings were eerily similar to an earlier well-known comparison study of black and white delinquents done 40 years earlier.

Psychologists William McCord and J. Sanchez compared the subsequent criminal careers of 1950s alumni of two institutions set up to deal with delinquent boys sent them by juvenile courts – Massachusetts's infamous "Lyman [Reform] School" and a private, intensive treatment-oriented facility, the "Wiltwyck School." The majority of the Lyman School inmates were white, whereas most of the Wiltwyck residents were black. Five years after their release from Wiltwyck, only 9% of the predominantly black graduates had been convicted of a felony. However, 67% of the mostly white Lyman boys had been convicted of a felony during the same five years following release. Looking at the most serious offenders from both groups, McCord and Sanchez concluded: "Wiltwyck seemed to have a dramatic impact upon the youngsters diagnosed as psychopathic (judged potentially dangerous or violent). During the first five years after their release, only 11% of the psychopathic men from Wiltwyck committed grave offenses – murder, rape, armed robbery – compared with 79% of Lyman's psychopathic inmates." But after another five years, the pattern changed. The Wiltwyck boys grew progressively worse, while the Lyman graduates improved. By age twenty-five, recidivism lines had crossed; and by the time the men had reached their mid-thirties, 32 percent of the Wiltwyck alumni were getting into trouble as opposed to only 8 percent of the men from Lyman.

At this point, one overwhelming difference emerged – race and ethnicity. Virtually all the recidivists from Wiltwyck were black and Hispanic, and even among the fewer Lyman recidivists a disproportionate number were black or of French Canadian descent. McCord and Sanchez concluded that the therapeutic effects of Wiltwyck had grown less relevant as its mostly inner-city alumni moved into adulthood and ran up against discrimination in education, employment, and housing, and as they lived out their lives in increasingly socially disorganized communities. As the researchers put it, in a particularly poignant passage: "The ex-Wiltwyck men we interviewed remembered the school fondly – in one sense, perhaps too fondly. For most of these young men Wiltwyck offered a welcome relief from the 'real world.' "[69] In effect, the "real world" had undone the rehabilitation.

"Perverse, Systemic Racism"

Even well-meant reforms of the juvenile justice system have often made matters worse for African-American juveniles. For example, the initiative undertaken by the federal Office of Juvenile Justice and Delinquency Prevention in the 1970s and 1980s to stop the incarceration of "status offenders" (juveniles charged with offenses that would not be crimes were they adults – "running away," "incorrigibility," "truancy") backfired in a distinctly racial fashion.

As sociologists Katherine Hunt Federle and Meda Chesney-Lind noted, while this reform benefited white teenagers it placed black youths at a greater risk. Whereas the percentage of white arrests for curfew violations and running away fell by 72.8% and 81.1% respectively, arrests of minority youths actually *increased* during the same period. In 1978, 206,518 white children and 28,363 African-American children were arrested for all status offense violations. By 1989, the number of white children arrested for these offenses had declined to 152,385, a 26 percent decrease. During this same period arrests of African-American youths increased by 27 percent to 36,147.[70]

Meanwhile, ever larger numbers of African-American juveniles were being sequestered in public detention centers and reform schools. In 1977, 57% of youths in public detention facilities were white, 29.9% African-American, 11.2% Hispanic, and 1.7% Native American or Asian. By 1987, the percentage of whites had declined by almost 13%, whereas the percentage of black youths being held in detention had climbed to approximately 50%. Minority admissions to state reform schools grew from 46.7% in 1977 to 56.3% in 1987. By 1989, they had reached 60%, and by 1993 over two-thirds of admissions were minority.

A 1994 study of juvenile detention decisions found that African-American and Hispanic youths were more likely to be detained at each decision point, even after controlling for the influence of offense seriousness and social factors (e.g., single-parent home). Decisions by both police and the courts to detain a youngster were highly influenced by race, independent of other factors:

The consequences of having a system which places youth in secure confinement based on factors other than legal issues is far reaching. These findings indicate that race was a significant factor in locking up youth, whether at the police or court level. Not only were there direct effects of race, but indirectly, socioeconomic status was related to detention, thus putting youth of color again at risk for differential treatment. . . . The devastating repercussions of a justice system in which a young person's physical liberty is in part determined by his or her race are intolerable.[71]

Federle and Chesney-Lind effectively torpedoed the view that these high rates of incarceration were a reliable indicator of the involvement of black juveniles in violent crime. They noted that the "obvious explanation" (that more minority children were institutionalized because they committed more serious delinquencies) was not supported by the data. Perhaps surprisingly to many, arrest rates for serious crimes among white and minority youths between 1978 and 1989 had been relatively stable. White youth accounted for 67% of all arrests for homicide, forcible rape, robbery, aggravated assault, burglary, theft, arson, and motor-vehicle theft. Although minority youths made up 60% of all institutionalized youth by 1989, the percentage of African-Americans arrested for serious crimes had been rising by only 0.1% to 30.5%.

Even when Chesney-Lind and Federle isolated the violent crime rates, they could "find no persuasive explanation for the increasing rate of institutionalization among children of color. Although more African-American youths were arrested for the most serious violent crimes than white youths, there were not enough such arrests to account for the numbers of black youths being institutionalized. Only 15% of the youth incarcerated in public juvenile facilities in 1989 were being held for the most serious violent crimes.[72] While admitting that "a stable, but higher rate of arrest for violent crime, coupled with an increasing arrest rate for drug violations, may justify some slight increase in the incarceration rates for minority youth," the authors concluded that these factors alone could not explain why minority populations made up the majority of institutionalized youth.

These conclusions were entirely consistent with those of Huizinga and Elliott, who concluded that the high rate of incarceration of black youths in the 1970s could not be attributed to higher rates of offending among these juveniles. As they put it: "If differences in delinquent behavior do not explain the differential in incarceration rates, then differences in official responses to offenders/offenses (i.e., arrest rates, rates of referral to juvenile court, and court processing) would seem likely candidates to explore as major determinants of the differential in incarceration rates."[73] Federle and Chesney-Lind summarized it more succinctly: "The growth of the institutionalized minority population in the juvenile justice system can be explained only in terms of a pervasive, systemic racism."[74]

My experience as head of the Massachusetts youth corrections system confirmed these conclusions. I learned very early on that when we got a black youth, virtually everything – from arrest summaries, to family history, to rap sheets, to psychiatric exams, to "waiver" hearings as to whether or not he would be tried as an adult, to final sentencing – was skewed. If a middle-class white youth was sent to us as "dangerous," he was more likely actually to be so than the black teenager given the same label. The white teenager was more likely to have been afforded competent legal counsel and appropriate psychiatric and psychological testing, tried in a variety of privately funded options, and dealt with more sensitively and individually at every stage of the juvenile justice processing. For him to be labeled "dangerous," he had to have done something very serious indeed. By contrast, the black teenager was more likely to be dealt with as a stereotype from the moment the handcuffs were first put on – easily and quickly relegated to the "more dangerous" end of the "violent–nonviolent" spectrum, albeit accompanied by an official record meant to validate each of a biased series of decisions.

This is not to deny that adults and juveniles at the "deep end" of the criminal justice system (those sentenced to state prisons and reform schools) are more likely to have been involved in more serious crimes than those released on probation. However, it would be a mistake to sever the thread that joins those more serious convictions to those for lesser offenses over time. Knowing the final disposition may not be as significant as knowing in detail what occurred at each of the earlier stages of justice processing.

Feeding Stereotypes

It is probably no coincidence that as criminological research has grown more positivistic the stereotype of the African-American youth as "criminal" has grown more ubiquitous. This is not simply attributable to increased crime among black youths. Contemporary researchers also respond to the demands of their law-enforcement–oriented funders. Not surprisingly, when it comes to the problems of middle-class white youths, personal narrative (in the form of the psychiatric case record) continues to be the research modality of choice. As a result, very few white youths of means are subjected to the rigid categorizations demanded by the justice system. Even the bona fide delinquents among them are usually channeled into private psychiatric clinics and substance-abuse programs.

"Criminal behavior," says Washington University psychiatrist C. Robert Cloninger, "is essentially a disease."[75] Dr. Cloninger's comment is but another example of the fact that the labels we choose to attach to those we define as social deviants are less likely to be born of scientific research than constructed to rationalize prevailing ideologies and consider social class. The researcher who intrudes upon this scene should therefore realize that he or she is there to provide what the late British psychiatrist Ronald Laing called a "social prescription" – a label that can be used to validate what we are already disposed to do for a host of reasons other than scientific.

Labeling becomes especially dicey when particular racial or ethnic groups find themselves unusually eligible for such diagnoses. The labels change with the times – from the late-19th-century "moral imbecile," to the "constitutional psychopathic inferior" of the 1920s, the "psychopath" of the 1930s and 1940s, the "sociopath" or "person unresponsive to verbal conditioning" of the 1960s and 1970s – all attributions barely one step removed from a more atavistic nomenclature – "savages," "animals," and "monsters" – and, likewise, prescriptions for social neglect. Such labels are peculiarly "user-friendly" to the criminal justice system, in that they are mostly static, dichotomous categories that ignore individual, familial, social, and cultural history, minimize developmental conceptions of human behavior, and leave little room for nuance or individuality. They also lend a gloss of validity to racially charged decisions. The modern psychiatric diagnostic equivalent of the "insensible" criminal, the "antisocial personality" or "sociopath," is in fact suffused with racism.

Consequently, destructive terms like *psychopath* or *sociopath* are for the most part reserved for the poor and minorities.[76] Unable to afford a more benign label, they fill youth detention centers and reform schools in inverse proportion to those troubled and troubling middle-class youths who occupy a surfeit of private mental hospitals, schools, and specialized treatment programs that guarantee a less debilitating diagnosis, while softening the woes and enhancing the social survival of those with sufficient insurance to substitute interminable therapy for long-term incarceration. Although some poorer white youths also end up in the justice system, they are usually afforded a disproportionate share of the meager "alternative" programs available under juvenile correctional auspices, particularly in those states in which professionally staffed private agencies care for delinquent youngsters.

The War on Drugs: Race Falls Out of the Closet

The "drug war" was a disaster-in-waiting for African-Americans from the day of its conception. Despite the fact that drug usage among various racial and ethnic groups in the 1970s and 1980s remained roughly equivalent to their representation in the society, from the first shot fired in the drug war African-Americans were targeted, arrested, and imprisoned in wildly disproportionate numbers. There was historical precedent for what happened. As the African-American writer Clarence Lusane has noted, although there was no evidence of disproportionate opiate use among blacks in the 19th and early 20th centuries (with studies in Florida and

Tennessee at the time of World War I showing less opiate use proportionately among blacks than whites), law-enforcement agencies and the press at the time claimed that blacks were using cocaine at alarming levels. A *New York Times* article, entitled "Negro Cocaine Fiends Are a New Southern Menace," noted that southern sheriffs had switched from .32-caliber guns to .38 caliber pistols to protect themselves from drug-empowered blacks.[77]

Although the first "war on drugs" was declared by President Nixon in 1970, federal and state budgets for this conflict grew slowly until the late 1980s. Then, in the wake of University of Maryland African-American basketball star Len Bias's death from cocaine overdose, President and Mrs. Reagan defined drug abuse as the major problem facing the nation and the "war" began in earnest. By 1992, the country was spending over $30 billion annually on the drug war. Though this war had been a failure in its own terms, it had inadvertently exposed the depth of racial bias in the justice system, making hitherto subtle discrimination boldly obvious. While African-Americans and Hispanics made up the bulk of those being arrested, convicted, and sentenced to prison for drug offenses, in 1992, the U.S. Public Health Service's Substance Abuse and Mental Health Services Administration estimated that 76% of the illicit drug users in the United States were white, 14% were black, and 8% were Hispanic.[78] Patterns of cocaine use were only slightly different: two-thirds of cocaine users were white, 17.6% were black, and 15.9% Hispanic.[79] Studies of those who consumed all illicit drugs showed slightly lower percentages of blacks and Latinos than whites in every age category.[80] There was no evidence that the arresting patterns relative to African-Americans and Hispanics had stemmed cocaine use among these groups. The fact that drug dealing in the city, unlike that in the suburbs, often goes on in public areas guaranteed that law-enforcement efforts would be directed at young black and Hispanic men.

In Baltimore, Maryland, 11,107 of the 12,965 persons arrested for "drug abuse violations" in 1991 were African-Americans.[81] In Columbus, Ohio, where African-American males made up less than 11% of the population, they comprised over 90% of the drug arrests and were being arrested at 18 times the rate of whites.[82] In Jacksonville, Florida, 87% of those arrested on drug charges were African-American males, even though they comprised only 12% of that county's population.[83] In Minneapolis (where a state court held that the punishments mandated by the legislature for possession or sale of crack cocaine were racist in their effect), though black men made up only about 7% of the population, they were being arrested at a ratio of approximately 20:1 white males. These patterns were repeated in cities across the nation.

Penalties followed the same trends. In 1991, 90% percent of the "crack" arrests nationally were of minorities, whereas three-fourths of the arrests for powder cocaine were of whites. However, sentences for possession of crack were usually three to four times harsher than those for possession of the same amount of powder cocaine. Blacks were sent to prison in unprecedented numbers and were kept there longer than whites. Ninety-two percent (92%) of all drug possession offenders sentenced to prison in New York were either black or Hispanic, and 71% in California.[84]

In December 1990, a Minnesota judge, an African-American woman, declared unconstitutional that state's drug law, which in effect punished the possession of crack cocaine more severely (maximum sentence of 20 years) than possession of an equal amount of powder cocaine (maximum sentence of five years). Over 95% of those arrested for possession of crack cocaine were black (in this virtually all-white state), whereas 80% of those arrested for powder cocaine were white.

Although expert witnesses brought in from the Addictions Research Center of the National Institute of Drug Abuse testified that they "suspected" that crack cocaine led to addiction more quickly than powder cocaine, they were unable to produce a single study to support that claim. Nor was there any evidence that an addiction to crack was harder to break than an addiction to powder cocaine. The only testimony elicited was anecdotal – primarily from police, drug agents, and prosecutors. In upholding the lower court's decision, one state supreme court justice saw "a plausible case for the proposition that the statute evidenced intentional discrimination against blacks."

Despite this state court decision, the discriminatory distinction continued in the federal courts. Under the Congress's reform "sentencing guidelines," possession for personal use of five grams of crack cocaine carried a five-year mandatory minimum sentence, while possession of the same amount of powder cocaine or any other drug was a misdemeanor punishable by a maximum of one year. These guidelines were upheld by the U.S. Supreme Court even though the racial effect was evident in the burgeoning percentages of minorities entering the federal prison populations. As one long-time federal judge, taking note of the Minnesota court's decision, commented to me in 1992, "The Constitution is no longer as important to the Supreme Court as it is to state courts."[85]

By 1992, the Office of National Drug Control Policy was predicting that by 1996 sentenced drug offenders would comprise more than two-thirds of all inmates in the Federal Bureau of Prisons, but did not mention that the overwhelming majority of them would be black and Latino. A 1991 survey of racial rates of incarceration in Texas provided a graphic illustration of where things were headed (Table 6). Most of these gross racial disparities occurred between 1985 and 1991 and were directly related to the drug war.[86]

The racial discrimination endemic to the drug war wound its way through every stage of the processing – arrest, jailing, conviction, and sentencing. Among those sent to prison for drug offenses, African-Americans were less likely to be assigned to treatment programs than whites. In California, for example, whereas 70% of inmates sentenced for drug offenses were black, two-thirds of the drug-treatment slots went to whites. The situation was no different on the East Coast. A study done by a committee of the Monroe

Table 6. *Prison Incarceration Rates per 100,000 Adults in Each Racial Group for the Seven Largest Counties in Texas*

	All	White	Black	Hispanic
Statewide	337	167	1,415	293
Harris County	542	209	1,851	353
Dallas County	536	245	1,772	282
Travis County	360	149	1,534	516
El Paso	178	90	389	206
Tarrant	385	208	1,696	292
Bexar	229	81	701	308
Nueces	288	165	825	359

County (Rochester, New York) Bar Association revealed that, although drug use among ethnic and racial groups was roughly proportionate to their percentages in the general population, African-Americans were being arrested at 18 times the rate of whites. However, 75% of those who were afforded the few drug-treatment slots available were white.[87]

With these kinds of figures emerging, even Blumstein, who previously had found no evidence of racial bias in imprisonment rates, acknowledged possible racial disparities in the "dramatic, exponential growth in arrest rates for blacks compared to whites" related to the drug war.[88] In testimony in early 1994 before the Pittsburgh Commission on Human Relations, he argued that the war on drugs was victimizing black people. As he put it, "The approaches we are taking are clearly, in my mind, making matters appreciably worse."[89]

Nowhere were the racial disparities of the drug war more obvious than in its treatment of African-American juveniles. In 1980, the national rate of drug arrests for white and black juveniles was approximately the same – about 400 per 100,000. During the early 1980s, the drug-arrest rate for white youths declined by 33%, while the arrest rates among black youths remained relatively sta-

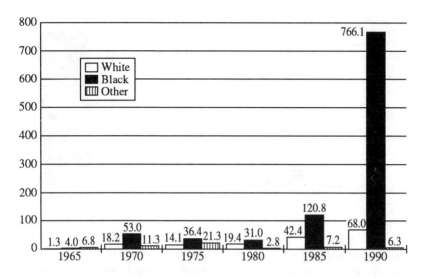

Figure 5. Juvenile heroin/cocaine arrest rates: United States, 1965–1990 (by race). *Source:* Uniform Crime Report, 1991.

ble. However, as the drug war expanded, arrests of black youths surged from 683 per 100,000 in 1985 to 1,200 per 100,000 – nearly five times the white rate – by 1989. By 1991, the rates of arrest for black juveniles was at 1,415 per 100,000.[90] The above graph (Figure 5) illustrates this pattern.

The effects of the drug war on juveniles in some cities was even more devastating. One of the most disturbing findings in the Baltimore study conducted by the National Center on Institutions and Alternatives can be seen in the following graph (Figure 6).

It reveals that a total of 18 white juveniles were arrested in the city of Baltimore in 1980 and charged with drug sales; by 1990, that number had actually dropped to 13 such arrests. However, whereas 86 black juveniles were arrested in Baltimore in 1980 for drug sales, by 1990, with the drug war in full swing, 1,304 black juveniles were being arrested annually on that charge. *Black juveniles in Baltimore were being arrested for drugs at roughly 100 times the*

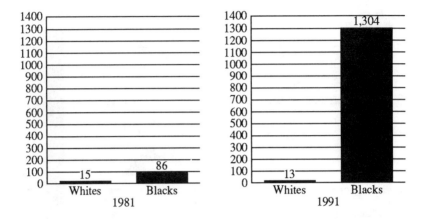

Figure 6. Historical comparison of juvenile drug arrests, 1981–1991, sale/
manufacture of drugs. *Source:* "Hobbling a Generation: Young African American
Males in the Criminal Justice System of America's Cities: Baltimore, Maryland."
Alexandria, VA: National Center on Institutions and Alternatives, September
1992.

arrest rate for whites of the same age.[91] A 1990 Johns Hopkins University study of the same population yielded similar results, with 97%
of the juvenile arrests for drug possession/selling in Baltimore
being black youths. Incredibly, statewide in Maryland, 90.5% of
the drug arrests were of black youngsters.[92] The national increase
in arrests of black youths for drug offenses, coupled with more
severe sentences in drug cases, was a primary factor contributing to
the disproportionate referral of African-American teenagers to
state reform schools and detention centers.[93] While the number of
white juveniles brought into the juvenile court system increased by
only 1% between 1987 and 1988, the number of nonwhite juveniles being processed in juvenile courts increased at 42 times that
rate.[94] Moreover, as youngsters were caught up in the earliest
stages of the juvenile justice system, one could anticipate that the
cumulative effect of bias would increase the probability of their
eventually being sentenced to jail or prison.

Off the Record

Having served in justice roles on the cabinets or personal staffs of governors of three major states – Massachusetts, Illinois, and Pennsylvania – I find it incredible that so many in the government and the judiciary deny the racism which is so much a part of the conversation and informal life of so many in the system. This was brought home to me while I was monitoring jail overcrowding for a federal court. I was taken aback, early in my tenure while sitting with the chief judge of the criminal court, to be told by him that the major reason for crime in the city was "Lyndon Johnson's Civil Rights Act." The judge then went on to explicate his embarrassing personal biases on black men and crime. When I mentioned the conversation later to other officials, the only response I got was, "Did he really say that?" – and the conversation turned quickly to other subjects. Meanwhile, hundreds of black males continued to have their cases heard in this judge's court. The same judge later "acquitted" himself with a local reporter (though the interview was not published for a number of months), by saying that the problems with blacks were not entirely their fault: "It's the fault of their mothers and their daddies and their ancestors and our fault. We have been too good to them." As a result, he concluded that "black youths have a tendency to fight and form gangs and have difficulty competing in public school where they molest teachers and commit rapes. . . . I would not date a black girl. I would not take one home. My mother would kill me. I wouldn't mistreat one. I would not want my children to marry a black or Asian or Chinese or a Puerto Rican."

The chief judge in Florida had committed the faux pas of speaking his mind. Unfortunately, what he said, in my opinion, was probably uncomfortably close to the quietly held attitudes that define the "social context" of justice for most young African-American males entering that judicial system. How else can we explain our increased reliance on imprisonment and harsher sentences as the skin color of arrestees and defendants grows ever darker?

This process, in turn, has had other unsavory effects. As the African-American sociologist Troy Duster put it: "If we are ignorant of recent history, and do not know that the incarceration rate and the coloring of our prisons is a function of dramatic changes in the last half century, we are far more vulnerable to the seduction of the genetic explanation . . . [the] astonishing pattern of incarceration rates by race . . . should give pause to anyone who would try to explain these incarcerated. . . . The gene pool among humans takes many centuries to change, but since 1933, the incarceration of African-Americans in relation to whites has gone up in a striking manner. In 1933, blacks were incarcerated as a race approximately three times the rate of incarceration for whites. In 1950, the ratio had increased to approximately 4 to 1; in 1960, it was 5 to 1, in 1970, it was 6 to 1, and in 1989, it was 7 to 1."[95] Initially, the trends led to calls for new, higher levels of harsh punishment, which were to have their own set of unanticipated consequences. Ultimately, they set the political stage for resurrecting the genetic theories regarding the black criminal that had obsessed white criminologists 75 years earlier.

3

Unanticipated Consequences
of the Justice System

When the United States was coming out of the brief depression following World War I, George Herbert Mead challenged those who would use the justice system to negotiate what he referred to as the "social settlement." "We assume," he said, "that we can detect, pursue, indict, prosecute, and punish the criminal and still retain toward him the attitude of reinstating him in the community as soon as he indicates a change in social attitude himself, that we can at the same time watch for the definite transgression of the statute to catch and overwhelm the offender, and comprehend the situation out of which the offense grows." In Mead's view, this was a false assumption. Indeed, he held that "the two attitudes, that of control of crime by the hostile procedure of the law and that of control through comprehension of social and psychological conditions, *cannot* be combined." He then summarized the dilemma: "To understand is to forgive and the social procedure seems to deny the very responsibility which the law affirms, and on the other hand, the pursuit by justice inevitably awakens the hostile attitude in the offender and renders the attitude of mutual comprehension practically impossible." [1]

Mead hoped that the newly invented juvenile court would breach

the wall of ignorance that characterized adult criminal justice procedure. In juvenile court, judges would, for the first time, consider
issues that were dismissed as irrelevant to strict criminal court
procedure. Issues associated with delinquency and crime – such as
unemployment, health problems, emotional disturbance, disorganized communities, socially debilitating environments, poor education, family disorganization, and socioeconomic pressures – would
all be fair game. Some thirty years later, Harvard law professor
Roscoe Pound commented that the founding of the juvenile court
was as potentially significant an event in the history of Western
jurisprudence as the signing of the Magna Carta. In the end,
Mead's hopes were never realized and Pound's assessment fell
short of the mark.

Unfortunately, from the beginning the juvenile court mimicked
adult justice procedure. It was eventually described by the U.S.
Supreme Court as embodying the worst of both worlds – punishment masquerading as "treatment," with few of the rights one
would have in formal adult courts.[2] In recognizing the potential
that lay dormant in the conception of the juvenile court, however,
Mead and Pound had been on to something. Indeed, the juvenile
court rarely, but occasionally, provides a glimpse of its original
promise. For this reason, it continues to represent a threat to the
legal system. It is why we still hear a constant drumbeat from
prosecutors and other politicians for its abolition. So long as the
juvenile court exists there is always the remote possibility that,
phoenix-like, it might one day rise from the ashes and overwhelm
us all with reason and decency. Meanwhile, the formal criminal
justice model continues apace, with the rules growing ever more
rigid and, if you will, legalistic. Whether this has lowered the
incidence of crime is highly questionable. It has, however, quietly
spawned a crime-control industry of political influence and power
unequaled in our history.

Foremost among the "unanticipated consequences" of increased
criminal justice activity has been the criminalization of the majority

of young African-American males. The marauding gangs of Los
Angeles provide a singular demonstration of the fact that "justice"
as practiced in the inner city was decidedly more successful at
alienating and arming the community than it was at stopping crime.
In 1992, the Los Angeles County District Attorney's Office estimated that there were 150,000 gang members in the county. Nearly
half of all black men ages 21–24 living in Los Angeles County were
labeled as gang members – an ominous prospect in any society.

However, a strong case could be made for the view that most of
L.A.'s violent gangs were themselves a response to heavy-handed
criminal justice approaches to complex problems rooted in poverty, unemployment, and family breakdown – birthed and nurtured in county and state-run juvenile halls, camps, detention
centers, reform schools and prisons with gang leadership routinely
confirmed in the same facilities. All these factors have fed a
culture of violence on the streets of California's cities and towns,
wherein the ethics of the street among certain minority groups is
indistinguishable from the rules of survival in a maximum-security
correctional institution.

The so-called war on drugs provides ample evidence that criminal justice procedures have intensified violence in the inner cities.
It was in the service of the anti-drug crusade that law-enforcement
activity in the inner city was stepped up. Ironically, the drug war
was begun in earnest at precisely the time when violence among
African-American males had either stabilized or was subsiding.
The number of African-American male victims of homicide per
100,000 had dropped from 70.1 in 1972 to 40.9 in 1983 (the all-
time black male victimization rate to that date having been set in
1934, at 74.2 per 100,000). Although homicides had risen nationally in 1981, most of the increase was attributable to a surge in
homicide by whites. The homicide rates among young black men
continued to decline for two more years until 1983. But by 1991,
homicide rates among young black men were surpassing the record
levels of 1934 and 1972. The trends suggested that aggressive

war on drugs in the inner cities was not making the communities safer.

Rain Dances

Nearly a half-century ago, the sociologist Robert Merton pointed to the crucial distinction between the manifest and latent functions of a social action. Using the Hopi rain dance as an example, Merton noted that although the *manifest* purpose of such a ritual may be to make rain, its *latent* purpose has to do with quite something else.[3] The rain ceremony brings together the scattered members of the group to engage in a common activity: reinforcing group unity during a time of stress. Indeed, Merton's analysis, drawn from the earlier work of Mead, Durkheim, Sumner, MacIver, and Thomas and Znaniecki, provides an apt characterization of contemporary justice policy in the inner city.[4]

Unfortunately, unlike the Hopi rituals that strengthened tribal unity, justice rites seldom have such felicitous effects on the minority, having no more direct impact on lowering crime rates in the inner city than Hopi rain dances had on the annual rainfall. All the chanting and dancing is really about something else. Although lowering crime rates may be the manifest purpose of the efforts, the latent purpose can be seen only in the results. Viewed in this context, the criminal justice rite (arrest, booking, jailing, trying, convicting, sentencing), along with the informal biases that shape each step, may exist not so much to lower crime as to reassure the larger society that its metaphors regarding offenders in general, and the black male offender in particular, are sustained. Cutting actual crime seems beside the point.

An example of the metaphor for this was contained in the notorious 1994 Florida cases involving the killing of tourists by juveniles. The murder that received the most attention from the press was that of a British visitor to Monticello, Florida. Among those charged with homicide was a 13-year-old black juvenile who local authorities said had 56 previous arrests beginning at age seven. Claiming confidentiality, the authorities declined to reveal the boy's specific offenses and family history. On the basis of the information passed on at the press conferences by local authorities, one might have concluded that an incipient psychopath had been aborning for a number of years in Monticello. A more salient question would have been how it came to be that a seven-year-old child was brought into the justice system in the first place. Why was he "arrested"? Why was a "rap sheet" started? Had he been white, and from a family of means, would he have been taken to court at that early age? One can surmise that many, probably most, of this young boy's arrests represented a substitution of the criminal justice response for profound issues of neglect and family dysfunction. Given the dismal record of that response to personal and social problems, it is hardly surprising that this youngster's offenses would escalate as the years went by.

Crucial to the criminal justice response is a well-fashioned objectification, if not demonization, of the offender – a reaction within easy reach of the majority when it comes to the African-American male. Knowing the family and personal history of a defendant tends to dilute the hostility that drives the criminal justice system. But in recent years we have been willing to ignore upsetting realities about the accused. Social and personal concomitants of crime are met with contempt. Such important elements as family breakdown, retardation, a life history of physical or sexual abuse, or childhood exposure to violence have become marginalized in courtrooms.

Deterrence

Does deterrence work? In respect to draconian measures, there is precious little evidence that either the threat of longer sentences or the death penalty have had any measurable effect on violent behavior in contemporary America. Indeed, some studies suggest an *inverse* relationship between the use of the death penalty and the rise in homicide, official violence encouraging an increase in unofficial violence.[5]

First, it should be noted that the studies and commentaries on deterrence in the United States justice system posit the continuance of a democratic society. If we were willing to scrap many of the tenets upon which this nation is founded, deterrence would probably "work" quite well. If, for example, we were willing to execute all first-time burglars on the spot without benefit of trial it would probably lower the burglary rate. However, for deterrence to work in this way, the punishment must be so extreme that a substantial number of citizens themselves fall victim to it – guilty or not.

However, there is less disposition on the part of the majority to fear the many law-enforcement tactics now routinely applied in the inner city, the effect of which is to nurture alienation, foment violence, and undermine democratic principles. As Michael Tidwell described the results of the crackdown on drugs in Washington, D.C., in 1992, "All the crackdown does is tear up turf and reshuffle turf and introduce additional chaos to the street, which leads to additional – and essentially gratuitous – violence sanctioned by a society ostensibly dedicated to bringing violence down."[6]

There is little evidence that deterrence produces the desired results in democratic societies (particularly among those individuals who have little or no stake in the society). However, there are considerably more indications that rehabilitative programs work substantially better. As Canadian researcher Paul Gendreau concludes: "Even though the anti-rehabilitation 'nothing works' rhetoric took firm hold in the United States for a variety of sociopolitical reasons, dedicated clinicians and researchers have continued to generate data on the effectiveness of offender rehabilitation programs."[7]

As the Clinton administration began, even researchers at the conservative Rand Corporation spoke out on the dismal results of justice policies based primarily in deterrence. In a critical 1993 Rand paper on drugs, Robert J. MacCoun commented that "defenders of existing drug laws and enforcement policies need to recognize that their faith in severity-based deterrence is largely misguided and often counterproductive."[8] MacCoun noted that the debate rested as much on core values as upon empirical questions:

It would be naive to assume that attitudes toward existing drug policies are based solely on implicit or explicit behavioral theories. For example, the retributive doctrine of punishment is strongly endorsed by the American public and policy elite (Grasmick, Davenport, Chamlin, and Bursik, 1992; Jacoby, 1983) and may play a subtle role in support for punitive drug laws. Attitudes toward the death penalty are particularly instructive. Attitude research indicates that many citizens overtly endorse a deterrence rationale for the death penalty that actually masks a deeper retributive motive (Bohm, Clark, and Aveni, 1991; Ellsworth and Ross, 1983; Tyler and Weber, 1982). As a result, support for capital punishment is relatively impervious to evidence that execution provides no marginal deterrence effect beyond that of life imprisonment. Many people may hold similarly hermetic attitudes toward drug policy.[9]

As it usually plays out in the streets however, deterrence has less to do with sanctions than with frequent police contacts, which for the poor easily degenerate into harassment, name-calling, occasional beatings, bookings into jails, mug shots, lineups, dishonest and manipulative interrogations, bond hearings, court arraignments, and sporadic stays in jails and juvenile detention centers on minor charges.

The Roots of "Oppositional Culture"

In his study of inner-city violence and poverty, University of Pennsylvania social scientist Elijah Anderson refers to the "oppositional culture" that has assumed major importance in the inner city. At the heart of such a culture lies the issue of *respect*, "loosely defined

as being treated 'right,' or granted the deference one deserves."
Anderson describes it as "an almost external entity" that must be
constantly guarded. The young man with respect must avoid showing any signs that he can be "bothered" in public, because that
might place him in physical jeopardy as someone who has been
disgraced or "dissed." Although such small things as maintaining
eye contact for too long might seem petty to middle-class people, to
those invested in the street code such actions reveal another's
intentions and "serve as warnings of imminent physical confrontation."[10] If others show no respect for a person's manhood, his life
may be in jeopardy. Anderson described that part of the code which
provides the backdrop to much of the so-called senseless violence
in the inner city:

True nerve exposes a lack of fear of dying. . . . among the hard-core
street-oriented, the clear risk of violent death may be preferable to being
"dissed" by another. . . . Not to be afraid to die is the quid pro quo of
being able to take somebody else's life – for the right reasons. . . . The
difference between the decent and the street-oriented youth is often that
the decent youth makes a conscious decision to appear tough and manly;
in another setting – with teachers, say, or at his part-time job – he can be
polite and deferential. The street-oriented youth, on the other hand, has
made the concept of manhood a part of his very identity; he has difficulty
manipulating it – it often controls him.[11]

Anderson attributes the oppositional code of the streets to the
absence of alternative ways for an inner-city black youth to gain
respect and a reputation. He sees the attitudes of the wider society
as deeply implicated in the street code. Moreover, the dynamic
does not rest with the "hard core" alone. As Anderson notes:

Many less alienated young blacks have assumed a street-oriented demeanor as a way of expressing their blackness while really embracing a
much more moderate way of life. . . . These decent people are trying hard
to be part of the mainstream culture, but the racism, real and perceived,
that they encounter helps to legitimate the oppositional culture. . . . In

fact, depending on the demands of the situation, many people in the community slip back and forth between decent and street behavior.[12]

Anderson concludes that a vicious cycle has been put in place, whereby "the hopelessness and alienation many young inner-city black men . . . feel, largely as a result of endemic joblessness and persistent racism, fuels the violence they engage in." Furthermore, he notes that the violence confirms the negative feelings many whites and some middle-class blacks harbor toward the ghetto poor. This serves to legitimate the code of the streets "in the eyes of many poor young blacks." Unless this cycle is broken, Anderson predicts that "attitudes on both sides will become increasingly entrenched, and the violence, which claims victims black and white, poor and affluent, will only escalate."

Although Anderson's conclusion that white society is greatly implicated in the formation of the "code of the streets" is correct, simply indicting racism is not enough. In fact, white racism has done more than restrict employment opportunities for inner-city youths. Increasing reliance on the criminal justice system as the preferred means of addressing the social problems of young black men has itself defined and shaped the "culture of opposition."

Rites of Passage

So many young black males are now routinely socialized to the routines of arrest, booking, jailing, detention, and imprisonment that it should come as no surprise that they bring back into the streets the violent ethics of survival which characterize these procedures. They have become, in their own way, peculiar rites of passage. Anderson's fearsome "code of the streets," for example, is indistinguishable from the violent codes that obtain in most of the nation's jails, prisons, reform schools, and detention centers.

Ron Hampton, executive director of the National Black Police

Association, characterized the process in these terms: "The way you police in an affluent white community is not the way you police in a poor black community." Describing a young black police officer who was in training in a predominantly black neighborhood (the same in which the officer had been raised) Hampton noted: "I asked him a few questions about his assignment. He said he was assigned to Georgetown, which is about ninety percent white, but he'd been training in a ninety-nine percent black community. He said, 'I'm disappointed. I don't want to go to Georgetown.' He said he wanted to work where the police tell the people what to do, not where the people tell the police. That kid wouldn't have said that before he went into the police academy. Now he's calling the people he grew up with trash; he's calling them scum."

One observer described one ritual in which the police go looking "for where the action is." It consists of looking for suspects. As sociologist William Chambliss put it: "they are not hard to find. Suspects are young black males between the ages of 12 and 30 who are hanging around corners, driving in cars or can be seen gathered together through a window in an apartment . . . an excuse rather than a legal reason more accurately describes what the members of the RDU (Rapid Deployment Unit) are looking for. For young black males driving in a car the best excuse is some minor infraction: a broken tail light, an ornament hanging from the mirror, a license plate light that is not working." Occasionally, if the RDU officer has a "strong feeling" or a "solid hunch" that a suspect may possess drugs or weapons, the officer may stop the car and "create the broken tail light with a quick slap of his pistol butt." Once an excuse to stop a "suspect" is found, the RDU officer calls in other cruising officers. The police cars quickly surround the suspects' car and the officers emerge with guns drawn. Chambliss notes that all this action evolves from an "officer's 'hunch' often based on the age and skin color of the occupants of the car. . . . The only 'crime' being committed here is that the car being stopped had a broken tail light or some ornament hanging from the mirror. The occupants of the car are instructed at gun point to get out of their car with their hands up. Racial slurs usually accompany the commands: 'Get out of the car motherfucker and don't reach for nothin' or you'll be eating this gun for dinner.' 'We're gonna search your car, OK?' An affirmative answer is assumed by either silence or any bodily gesture such as a shrug or a nod. Failing to get either a shrug or nod, . . . the officers look for some reason to enter the car: a piece of paper in the back seat that could appear to be a marihuana paper in poor light, something white on the floor mat that might be cocaine. While two or three officers search the car the other two or three have instructed the suspects to empty their pockets 'slowly' – all the while at gun point." Not infrequently, the next step is arrest and at least a brief stint in a police lockup, detention center, or jail.[13]

To an adolescent or near-adolescent, bravado notwithstanding, being arrested and jailed is not just another passing experience akin to going to the local "7–Eleven" – at least not the first or second time. To suggest otherwise is the kind of nonsense we would never tolerate were we talking about middle-class white suburban teens. For African-American youths in particular, the experience of arrest and jailing seems to have become something of a puberty rite, a transition to manhood. However, it all comes with deep, historical racially anchored roots and turns into an internal psychological struggle over whether to meekly assume or to aggressively reject the identity the ritual demands – an ambiguous puberty rite of disrespect and symbolic castration – from "assuming the position"; being handcuffed; placed in a police van; moved from place to place; shackled to a line of peers and older African-American males; posed for a mug shot; tagged with an I.D. bracelet attached to a wrist or ankle; confined in crowded "tanks" or holding cells (a common toilet or open hole in the middle) – to appearing before a robed judge; being assigned a lawyer who controls one's destiny but whom one seldom meets; having a price set on one's head as bail; and, finally, joining one's peers or anxious relatives outside.

This criminal justice rite of manhood confers the label of a renegade (or perhaps a "weed") fit to be treated as trash. The "secrets" of the experience are shared with peers and adult males, the majority of whom have been subjected to the same rites. The experience in this sense touches archetypal memories in both races. As West Coast urban affairs writer Mike Davis put it:

The L.A.P.D's "Operation Hammer" and other antigang dragnets that arrested kids at random . . . have tended to criminalize black youth without class distinction. Between 1987 and 1990, the combined sweeps of the L.A.P.D. and the County Sheriff's Office ensnared 50,000 "suspects." Even the children of doctors and lawyers from View Park and Windsor Hills have had to "kiss the pavement" and occasionally endure some of the humiliations that the homeboys in the flats face every day – experiences that reinforce the reputation of the gangs (and their poets laureate, the gangster rappers like Ice Cube and N.W.A.) as the heroes of an outlaw generation.[14]

One may get a sense of how inured we have become to this particular criminal justice ritual from conservative legal scholar and federal judge Richard Posner's comment: "It is curious to reflect," he writes, "that the arrest of Joseph K in the first chapter of [Kafka's] *The Trial* is immensely more *civilized* than any arrest would be likely to be in the land of freedom at the threshold of the twenty-first century" (emphasis in original).[15]

Indeed, the rite is now so universal that some have taken to offering rehearsals so that the postulants may act their roles appropriately. Take, for example, a model "class" being conducted in 1994 in a majority black high school just outside Washington, D.C. Here is how a reporter described it: "With his fingers laced behind his head and the Prince George's County police officer grabbing hard at the pager clipped to his waistband, the smile disappeared from 17-year-old Carl Colston's face. Later, Colston described his thoughts as the officer frisked him. 'You feel uncertain. You don't know what they are going to do.' "[16] The courses were cosponsored by the county police, educators, the local chapter of the NAACP, and the Black Lawyers' Association in an attempt to teach people how to handle themselves if stopped by police. "I have been pulled over by the police numerous times," said Hardi Jones, president of the county NAACP. The classes included personal searches by police, immobilizing techniques and role playing. "Three male students are lined up in front of the stage, with their legs spread apart and their hands on the stage floor. A young officer, Cpl. Diane Salen, is patting them down. Minutes later, Cpl. Salen demonstrates on one of the students how an officer attempting to handcuff a suspect maintains control by holding the suspect's thumbs."[17]

It was an entirely common experience for a black man. In a sense, the classes constituted a bizarre admission by its sponsors. As most black youths and young men could expect to be brought under justice onus of some sort whether or not they had broken the law, it seemed wise to train them for the experience. Significantly, students are not given any information on such crucial issues in police–youth confrontations as their Miranda rights or how they should protect themselves if taken into custody.

Likewise, rather than combating crime in public-housing projects through adequate community policing and alternative programming for children, housing projects have come to resemble prison camps. As this movement progresses, we can expect an escalation of such procedures as random searches, segregation, curfews, and resident counts – all familiar procedures of efficient prison management. As one 61-year-old resident commented when the District of Columbia spent almost $1 million on a fencing system to divide his project into quadrants so residents could be more easily separated and herded for identification-card checks and signing in, "It's as though the children in there are being prepared for incarceration, so when they put them in a real lock-down situation they'll be used to being hemmed in."[18]

Snitching: Feeding Violence

No single tactic of law enforcement has contributed more to violence in the inner city than the practice of seeding the streets with informers and offering deals to "snitches." It is no small matter. It is no coincidence that wanton violence exploded in some cities simultaneously with the massive use of informers in the inner cities. And it has been very massive indeed. An investigation by *The National Law Journal* revealed that the federal government alone paid approximately a half-billion dollars to informers from 1985 through 1993.[19]

Law-enforcement agencies see informers as crucial in breaking criminal organizations. However, arrests have become so pervasive in the inner city that they have affected most families and peer relationships. As a result, relying on informers threatens and eventually cripples much more than criminal enterprise. It erodes whatever social bonds exist in families, in the community, or on the streets – loyalties which, in past years, kept violence within bounds.

The pandemic use of informers comes in conjunction with another short-term solution to street crime that carries profound implications for our system of jurisprudence. It is now a common tactic, particularly at the federal level, initially to overcharge defendants in order to accumulate as many charges as possible, in fantasy or the law, thereby threatening them with draconian mandatory sentences unless they give information on a wide array of friends, associates, acquaintances, childhood chums, and relatives – information that must "satisfy" the prosecution – to say the least, a very loose and ambiguous term. The bargains struck are randomly broken. But, in the process, everyone is fair game, and anyone under enough pressure from the "man," is a potential threat. This practice carries even greater potential for undermining our legal system. As Judge Harold Greene of the United States Court for the District of Columbia wrote: "Because of the mandatory minimum sentences and the rigid sentencing guidelines, effective control of sentencing –

from time immemorial in common law countries a judicial function – has effectively slipped, at least in some cases, not only to the
realm of the prosecution but even further to that of the police. This
development denies due process and is intolerable in our Constitutional system."[20]

The nearly universal dependence on snitches, combined with
the use of drug intelligence armamentaria (surveillance cameras,
eavesdropping and night-vision devices, etc.), and the large percentages of individuals in the inner city who have been given criminal
records, feeds a paranoia that is less delusional than reality-based.
Our inner cities now resonate strongly with the destructive experiences of other societies warped by informers and snitches, the most
obvious recent example being Stasi-ridden East Germany.[21]

A Conspiracy of Silence

An incident that took place in Richmond, Virginia, provides an
excellent example of the degree of alienation between law enforcement and the community. In the cases of the 117 murders committed in that city in 1992, at least 20 of the murderers were known
by the police. However, no one in the community was willing to
identify them. Three days after another homicide in Richmond, a
security guard was gunned down execution-style in a McDonald's
parking lot. The killing occurred in full view of hundreds of
teenagers, yet not a single witness was willing to cooperate with
police at the scene. An angry chief of police called it a "conspiracy
of silence." The city manager then proposed an ordinance that
would allow Richmond police to round up witnesses and hold
them for as long as 60 hours as a way of extracting information.
He admitted that he made the proposal "out of absolute, total
frustration."[22] Having relied upon heavy-handed law enforcement
to deal with everything from trespassing to murder, we are now at
a point in the inner city where it is probably a warped sign of

community health that so many who are themselves disproportionately victimized remain averse to turning in young men engaged in
criminal activities.

Adding to the volatility of the situation is the large percentage of
young men in the cities who are alumni of prisons and jails. The
prison snitch is less than a "man." For the authorities to make a
snitch of a young black male on the street is an even more profound
"dissing" – an assault on his identity and masculinity. The most
vicious and bloody prison riot of this century, at the New Mexico
State Prison in Santa Fe in 1980, provides a concrete example of
how the criminal justice system feeds violence in the cities. As
Roger Morris put it: "When two or more inmates gathered any-
where, Rodriguez would boast during his tenure as warden and
afterward, half of them belonged to him. Snitching and informing
in exchange for power, for revenge, for survival, for fear, occasionally even for justice was a way of life at the New Mexico pen."[23]
When the lid blows in such societies, it looses violence directed as
much at peers as at the authorities. It is not simply a matter of
killing a snitch. The anger is elevated to the level of a ritual demonstration to others that one possesses the requisite hardness of feeling to inflict pain or death in random fashion.

It might be well here to reexamine the words of the great American sociologist Gresham Sykes, whose "participant observation"
research study, *The Society of Captives*, remains a classic in American criminological literature. Written almost forty years ago, it describes the process that now runs the streets, overflowing with the
alumni of this crucial stage of criminal justice handling:

Imprisonment [is] directed against the very foundations of the prisoner's
being. The individual's picture of himself – as a morally acceptable adult
male who can present some claim to merit in his material achievements
and his inner strength – begins to waver and grow dim . . . as one of many,
[he] finds two paths open . . . to bind himself to his fellow captives with
ties of mutual aid, loyalty, affection, and respect, firmly standing in opposition to the officials [or] he can enter into a war of all against all.[24]

The central abiding reality in our inner cities is that most of the young men who live in them can anticipate being ushered through a series of hothouses for sociopathy – prisons, jails, and reform schools. There they will learn to nurture the very deficiencies in human interchange that will subsequently be labeled as pathological. The jargon, attitudes, and values that run many inner-city streets do not so much betray a vacuum of morality arising out of single-parent homes as they proclaim the warped ethics that sustains the institutions upon which the criminal justice system depends.

This is not to ignore other more ominous aspects of a criminal justice system frequently run riot in the inner city. Probably the best explication is found, not in a formal study, but in a film made by Los Angeles documentarian Randy Holland, *The Fire This Time*. After a year and a half of speaking with and filming the residents of South Central Los Angeles following the 1992 riots, Holland points to police activities as being a major source of disorganization in the community. *Los Angeles Times* film critic Kevin Thomas noted that the film "suggest[ed] persuasively that inflammatory infiltration activities on the part of police and the FBI have had an even more profoundly destructive impact on black communities than most of us have ever realized, stirring up gang warfare, destroying the Black Panthers and arresting small boys so that they will have records that stick with them for the rest of their lives."[25]

Fronting

On November 22, 1994, a lone 25-year-old gunman named Bennie Lee Lawson quietly entered the District of Columbia's metropolitan police headquarters and climbed the stairs to the third floor, where he randomly and fatally shot two FBI agents and a D.C. police sergeant. He then turned the gun on himself and committed suicide. At the time, it was thought that Lawson might have been part of a group out to kill the detectives who were investigating three murders a month earlier. Police had questioned Lawson regarding them a month earlier. Lawson was described as having been "quiet and civil" but "not cooperative in any way" during the interrogation. However, someone put word out on the street that he had snitched. Not until the following February did it come to light that Lawson himself had apparently committed the murders in order to allay suspicions among his peers that he was a snitch. To prove his loyalty, Lawson left handwritten notes in his home saying he "wanted" the police dead. He told a close friend that he would "prove" that he was not an informer. The multiple murder-suicide was his proof. One police investigator said that Lawson likely felt "squeezed from both sides."[26] In prison parlance, it is a form of "fronting."

As Commissioner of Children and Youth in Pennsylvania, I headed an effort to remove 400 teenagers from an adult prison. In our debriefing of the young inmates as they emerged from this maximum-security prison to be placed in alternative settings, the term *fronting* came up repeatedly. A 16-year-old described his experience to me in this way: "When I first got there this guy threatened me and told me he was going to make me his 'girl.' I yelled that I would beat his butt if he tried. I didn't know it then, but I'd just 'fronted' on him. I had challenged him in front of the others. The other inmates told me that I had only a few days to 'set up' a confrontation with the guy or I was fair game to be gang raped or taken as someone's 'punk.' "[27]

The young man waited for the appropriate moment when, in front of others, he might accuse the other inmate (falsely) of trying to steal his toothpaste. He then hit the inmate full in the face, breaking his nose. An all-out fight ensued. Both inmates suffered injuries and were sent to solitary confinement for a month. But the new boy had publicly demonstrated his willingness to be violent and had thereby established his reputation before his peers. When he emerged from the isolation unit, he would elicit renewed respect. Though the violence was relatively minor, the point was made. Such confrontations are just as likely to involve stabbings, serious injury, or death.

"Fronting" has become integral to the code of the streets. Confirmed by the majority society in a world of detention centers, jails, prisons, and lockups, the youngest emerge aggressively proud of having taken on as their own an identity which, as they act it out on the street, establishes their loyalty to peers while it ensures their alienation from the larger society. It allows a young man to pretend he is in control of a crazy and violent world that verges on spinning out of control. You see it in the pathetic posturing, menacing swagger, and cold stares that have come to define the persona of so many young males on streets of the inner city. Con-like, they tell us to watch out. The dynamic is there for all to see in the gratuitous violence (for the cameras) of those who beat a white truck driver in L.A. It is the stuff of public arguments that turn into shoot-outs. It betrays the person who has learned never to make an idle threat in front of peers. If you run off at the mouth, you had best proudly deliver within a relatively short time. It is the royal road to "respect," and it is the source of the street code.

Fitting the Criminal Profile

In 1992, there were over 14 million arrests nationally.[28] Virtually all of these resulted in a booking into a local jail or police lockup. As many as five million of them were African-American males, most accused of minor offenses. Because many of these arrestees were jailed more than once in the same year, it is difficult to know how many individuals were involved. However, there are only about 5.5 million African-American men between the ages of 18 and 40 (the age groups that make up the bulk of admissions to state and federal prisons) living in the United States. Suffice it to say that the percentage of black men being jailed each year is substantial. The percentages mount cumulatively year by year, as the pool of yet to be arrested black men shrinks.

Most law-enforcement activity in the inner city, as in the suburbs and rural areas, involves domestic squabbles, drunkenness, shoplifting, traffic violations, fights, small-time property offenses, drug use, and a variety of "nuisance" cases. The most common charges for which African-American men found themselves arrested and jailed in Duval County (Jacksonville), Florida, for example, was "resisting without violence." It usually meant that the individual objected to being stopped or searched for a relatively minor infraction. The largest single group of individuals brought to the jail had been arrested for "driving with a suspended license." This was particularly interesting in view of the fact that it is not a charge which is usually reported – that is, called in by a complainant. Rather, it usually arose in the course of some other event wherein an individual was stopped for some other reason and then found to have an expired or suspended driver's license – usually for nonpayment of traffic fines. (In Florida, driver's licenses were regularly suspended if one moved without informing the Department of Motor Vehicles of the change of address.) The practice of stopping "suspicious" cars driven by black men who fit a "profile" was also reflected in many of these arrests.[29] It renewed a southern tradition of a half-century earlier when black men were regularly arrested and jailed for being "suspicious," fitting an earlier profile, but not accused of any particular illegal action.[30]

It is a now a common law-enforcement technique in the "war on drugs" for police to approach individuals in buses and trains, stations and airline terminals, and request that the "targeted" or "suspicious" person give proof of identification, show his ticket, explain the purpose of his trip, and consent to a luggage search. As the practice spreads, its variations have at times bordered on the bizarre. For example, police in Tucson, Arizona, were selectively stopping motorists in order to apply a piece of adhesive tape under their noses. The purpose was to find out if any traces of cocaine might be found and preserved. According to local public defenders, the decision to stop drivers and attach tape to their noses was race-based. Of 63 individuals subjected to nose-taping, 60 were Hispanic. One of those stopped for the procedure had eaten a sugar donut.[31]

In September 1992, it was revealed that the police department in Oneonta, New York, had compiled what came to be referred to as "the black list," consisting of all the black males attending York College at Oneonta. It had been made available to the local police by school administrators following an attack on an elderly local woman who told police she thought she might have cut the intruder on the arm with a knife and she believed her attacker was black. The list was used to track down black and Hispanic students in dorms, on their jobs, even in the shower, and taking them to the local police department for questioning. The police demanded that each student account for his whereabouts at the time of the attack and bare his arms. As one of the school's instructors commented, "The only probable cause they had was, 'You're black, you're a suspect.' "[32]

Another example of the profiling of young black men came to light in November of 1993, when it was discovered that the Denver police department had compiled a list of 6,500 names of "suspected" gang members. The list was put together on the basis of the following: people who flashed gang signals, dressed in the colors of a gang, had been arrested in the company of gang members, or were known to associate with gang members, as well as other information provided by informants.[33]

Although blacks represented only 5% of Denver's population, they accounted for 57% (3,691) of those on the list. Hispanics made up another third of the list, whereas whites, who comprised 80% of Denver's population, accounted for less than 7%. Significantly, the 3,691 blacks on the list of gang "suspects" meant that *over two-thirds of all the black youths and young men between ages 12 and 24 living in Denver had been profiled as "suspect."*

As the Reverend Oscar Tillman, a senior official of the National
Association for the Advancement of Colored People in Denver
commented, "This is not a crackdown on gangs; it's a crackdown
on blacks." Tillman accused the police department of "peddling a
fear of blacks" to answer the demands of public safety. Said Rev.
Tillman: "My own son, who is now in the Army, was targeted many
times. . . . The police would stop him in front of our house and
want to know, 'Where did you get that expensive watch?' He got it
as a graduation present from us."[34]

What was not noted in the press was that similar lists are kept in
most large cities of the United States. They are not public, but the
police use them to target young men for harsher handling in the
criminal justice system should there be an opportunity for arrest.[35]
These nonpublic lists are disproportionately black and are often as
likely to reflect police-arrest activity as to demonstrate a pattern of
violent behavior on the part of the young person so labeled. In
Duval County, the local police department kept such a list, which
was at least as racially skewed as the one in Denver, with well over
80% of the youngsters listed on it being black.

Having a Criminal History

On December 31, 1993, there were 47.8 million "criminal history" records on file in the United States, 38.4 million of them
computerized.[36] According to the Bureau of Justice Statistics,
eight years earlier the (state) repositories held only 30.3 million
subjects in their criminal-history files. By 1989, the number was
42.2 million – an increase of 56 percent from 1984 to 1992.[37]
More disturbing is that most states required fingerprint and arrest
data for felonies to be submitted to the state criminal history
repository, but half of the states did not require law-enforcement
agencies to notify the repository when an individual was released
without being formally charged. Some state repositories listed

information in all misdemeanor cases, others listed only the
"more serious" misdemeanors.[38]

A 1990 audit of Illinois's criminal history records found that 79%
of all recorded arrests lacked information regarding what charges, if
any, were filed by the state's attorney. Another audit conducted two
years later revealed that this information was also absent in 56% of
the records of prison inmates.[39] Even in the 25 states that did require
law-enforcement officials to notify the state criminal-history repository when an arrestee was not formally charged, researchers found
that the likelihood of such notifications varied widely, from 1% in
Alabama, Arkansas, and Maine, to 100% in Georgia and Vermont.
This should have been a particular cause for alarm in the inner city.
In 1989 alone, as the drug war began to realize its potential for the
grossly disparate arrests of African-American and Hispanic males,
more than 6,000,000 fingerprint cards were submitted to state
criminal-history repositories.[40]

As criminologist Jeffrey Fagan summarized matters in arguing
against the public disclosure of juvenile records: "The social costs
of erroneous information transmitted to police agencies and prospective employers will outweigh any gains to public safety from
broader access to juvenile arrest records. The inaccuracy of arrest
records is widely documented. Once employers deny jobs to young
people based on false arrest information, their exclusion from the
labor market becomes a lifetime sentence to criminality and an
unnecessary burden on society."[41]

Even allowing for some duplication, the implications of having
almost 50 million criminal-history records in state files suggests
that not much is being overlooked by the contemporary criminal
justice system. Considering that approximately 90% of criminal
records are of males, and that there are only about 130 million
males in the nation, the figures hardly suggest a society in which
deviance is regularly overlooked or "defined down" as not meriting
attention, as Daniel Patrick Moynihan has maintained – at least,
not by law enforcement. Rather, it suggests a society in which the

net of criminal justice has been so widely cast that it now lays legitimate claim to a substantial part of the citizenry and the absolute majority of its minority citizens. This comes with payback.

When it comes time for the urban poor and minorities to go to trial, the average criminal court bears little resemblance to those on television where competent lawyers do their homework, argue the details, and use whatever technical legal strategies are available. The lawyers available to the poor use very few technicalities to get a client "off." It is not uncommon for a public defender or court-appointed lawyer to meet his or her client on the way into the courtroom. In the real world of most criminal courts in our large cities, defendants are more likely to plead guilty to charges that have been escalated beyond the facts than they are to get a reduced sentence on an easy plea. Whereas a celebrity murder case on *Court TV* may take months of argument, it has been my experience in testifying in a large number of capital cases that the trial is usually completed (and the death sentence frequently imposed) within three to five days.

Intergenerational Crime: Passing It On

Many criminological researchers of the past two decades have disparaged or ignored the major influence on narrative sociological research and theory of "labeling theory."[42] Both social psychology and sociology traditionally suggested that catching and labeling young offenders could have the unanticipated consequence of producing the very behavior it purported to deter. Labeling theory would hold that legal sanctions can in some circumstances actually exacerbate the likelihood of future offending. The stigma of being labeled an offender further alienates the individual from society and promotes the building of closer relationships with others who have been similarly ostracized, contributing to further acting out and creating a self-fulfilling prophecy.

For example, when David Farrington compared a group of teenagers convicted of delinquency with a demographically matched control group of teenagers who had engaged in similar acts but had not been convicted, he found the convicted youth significantly more likely to engage in delinquency at a later age.[43] In studying the punishment of soldiers in the U.S. Army, psychologist R. J. Hart had found that black soldiers were much more likely to be stigmatized by the experience than white soldiers and, as predicted by labeling theory, were also more likely to engage in subsequent offences after having been punished.[44]

Although other studies have been less supportive of labeling theory,[45] it appears to have more than a little relevance to contemporary crime-control strategies based in deterrence – particularly with reference to the drug war in the inner city. This has stimulated Robert MacCoun to call for "an improved labeling theory" that would demonstrate the precise conditions under which labeling might have either a negative or a positive effect.[46] MacCoun points to the work of John Braithwaite as an example of such research. Braithwaite predicted that "the negative effects of labeling can be avoided when (1) the social disapproval is temporary; (2) it occurs in a context of interdependence and communitarianism; and (3) it is followed by gestures of forgiveness and reacceptance.[47]

As MacCoun summarized: "Under such conditions, social shaming is predicted to increase subsequent compliance. In the absence of such conditions, shaming is disintegrative and can foster the stigmatization effects predicted by labeling theory."[48] It seems almost superfluous to suggest that these conditions are notably absent in the case of most inner-city African-American youths and young men who find themselves absorbed into the justice system.

In an attempt to measure such unanticipated consequences, John Hagan and Alberto Palloni reanalyzed data from the 1960s on working-class boys in London.[49] The original study of 410 boys had involved surveys, interviews, and a search of official records. The boys were interviewed at ages 8, 10, 14, 16, 18, 21, and 24.

Retrospective data were also collected on the parents. The British researchers had drawn the expected conclusion that "a constellation of adverse features of family background (including poverty, too many children, marital disharmony and inappropriate child rearing methods), among which parental criminality is likely to be one element, leads to a constellation of antisocial features when sons reach the age of eighteen, among which criminality is again likely to be one element."[50]

Hagan and Palloni also noted that "this conception of a dangerous, criminal class that is concentrated and reproduced across generations is highly durable." Indeed, "durable" enough to provide the central premise of much of the current discussion on crime, single-parent homes, welfare programs, and genetics. The most extensive longitudinal study on criminal behavior currently in progress, under the auspices of the U.S. Justice Department and the John D. and Catherine T. MacArthur Foundation, appears to take a similar tack. As the program's prospectus summarizes the premise, "an inquiry into the causes of crime is at the same time an inquiry into the causes of general defects in character and behavior." The prospectus ignores the possible effects of the criminal justice ritual itself and the destructive potential of labeling. This is unfortunate.

When Hagan and Palloni reanalyzed the London data, they found factors at work more important than "defects in character or behavior." Delinquent careers among inner-city youths – and indeed, patterns of intergenerational delinquency in families – were as likely to be due to justice intervention in their lives as they were to result from "cultural/characterological" variables. The more reliable predictor of future delinquency was whether a boy or his father had been effectively labeled as criminals by the larger society. As would be expected, cultural and characterological variables like income, broken homes, IQ ratings, and peer ratings correlated significantly with self-reported delinquency. However, Hagan and Palloni found that "past labeling of parents and sons affects future delinquency, above and beyond both the effects of past delinquency and all the other cultural/characterological measures."[51] Criminal roles appeared to be passed on as an unanticipated consequence of repeated criminal justice intrusion into the lives of fathers and sons in socioeconomically disadvantaged communities.

Criminogenic Interventions

In a watershed longitudinal reanalysis of the classic American study of delinquents done by Sheldon and Eleanor Glueck, sociologists John H. Laub and Robert J. Sampson found essentially the same negative effects from criminal and juvenile justice interventions.[52] Laub and Sampson compared the effects of punitive discipline *by parents* on juvenile delinquency and, later, adult crime versus the effects of punitive discipline *by the state.*

The Gluecks had studied a sample of 500 white delinquent boys and 500 nondelinquents ages 10–17 in Boston.[53] The boys were matched case-by-case according to age, ethnicity, general intelligence, and low-income residence. Extensive personal information was gathered between 1940 and 1958, including social, psychological, and biological characteristics, family life, school performance, work experiences, and other life events. In addition to interviewing the individual boys, the researchers interviewed family members, employers, schoolteachers, neighbors, justice, and social welfare personnel. The cases were followed up on at age 25, and again at age 32.

Laub and Samson recoded and reanalyzed the raw data kept in the archives at Dartmouth Medical School and found that, though the type of parental discipline might be an important factor in explaining delinquency, it has less relevance to later adult offending.[54] However, when the punishment was administered by the state through incarceration, two distinct patterns emerged. Though incarcerating a juvenile had neither a *direct* deterrent nor a criminogenic (crime-producing) effect, it had a major *indirect* effect; to look only at the direct effects of official sanctions was misleading. The longer a juvenile had been locked up, the less likely he was to have later job stability – regardless of whether he had a prior criminal history or was an excessive drinker. The greatest negative effects of state punishment (i.e., incarceration) appeared to be "indirect and operative in a developmental, cumulative process that reproduces itself over time."[55] Laub and Samson concluded that this was because "incarceration appears to cut off opportunities and prospects for stable employment later in life . . . job stability in turn has importance in explaining later crime. Therefore, even if the direct effect of incarceration is zero or possibly even negative (i.e., a deterrent), its indirect effect may well be criminogenic (positive) as structural labeling theory would predict."[56] Juvenile incarceration had long-term indirect criminogenic effects on adult crime.[57]

The Laub and Sampson study found two factors (if they occurred between ages 17 and 25) that were most likely to turn a young man away from adult crime: finding a stable job that he cared about and where the employer liked him; and marrying a woman to whom he was attached, supporting her and their children. Only 32% of the teenaged delinquents who found a stable job went on to commit adult crimes, whereas 74% of those who did not find such a job went on to adult offending. Of those who were committed to marriage, 34% went on to adult crime, whereas 74% of those not in such a marriage went on to later offending.

Laub and Sampson were clear as to what these findings meant. "Teen delinquents are more than twice as likely to be still committing crimes in their late 20's if they have low job stability or a weak marriage," said Laub. "From our findings I'm convinced that the current policy of locking up young criminals for long periods is counterproductive." Sampson, a University of Chicago sociologist, concluded that "putting young offenders in prison cuts them off from the very opportunities that might allow them to become productive members of society."[58]

Significantly, both the London and the Massachusetts data came from a virtually all-white delinquent population. There is little reason to believe that the routing of so many African-American youths through the justice system would be any less debilitating than it was for white youths in London or Boston. Indeed, for those with so little going for them in the larger society, strategies that rely primarily upon deterrence are probably more likely to exacerbate their already debilitated situation. Laub and Sampson's analysis challenged neoconservatives who see a combination of incapacitation and deterrence through harsher criminal sanctions as providing the best blueprint for lowering crime among inner-city youth.

With this as background, the remarks made by John Hagan in his 1992 presidential address to the American Society of Criminology carry particular relevance. "There is evidence," he said, "that contacts with the justice system have especially negative effects for underclass males. Even if most underclass males who are arrested do not go to jail, the experience of arrest can have long-term, even intergenerational repercussions ... a criminal arrest record has detrimental consequences for labor market outcomes, with negative effects on employment as much as eight years later."[59]

"Embedding" Unemployment

Hagan later concluded that the relationship between criminal justice intrusion into one's life and later unemployment was more complex (and more ominous) than earlier research had suggested.[60] A record of parental criminality had a better-substantiated causal effect on a son's unemployment than did the father's unemployment. Although some might take this as evidence of some genetic factor, Hagan took a different tack. He proposed that researchers consider inner-city crime from the perspective of "embeddedness," a concept previously applied to labor market research, as having relevance to intergenerational crime and delinquency in the inner city. As Hagan summarized it, "the sweeping impact of macro-economic change requires simultaneous consideration of 'the social relationship in which economic life is embedded.' " He proposed focusing on the social embeddedness of crime and unemployment intra- and intergenerationally, suggesting that high unemployment increases the use of "formal controls" (i.e., reliance upon criminal justice intervention), which, in turn, labels the father and son in the community, further "embedding" the cycle of failure. As he put it, "this chain of causation embeds youth crime within a context that joins parent, peer and court contacts in a process leading to adult unemployment."[61]

Other evidence suggests a strong relationship between unemployment and arrest patterns. In 1954, black and white youth unemployment in the United States was approximately equal, with blacks having a slightly lower rate of unemployment than whites in the age group 16–19. By 1984, the black unemployment rate had nearly quadrupled while the white rate had increased only slightly. Hagan suggests that exposure to justice handling exacerbates the problem considerably, noting that between the ages of 14 and 16 there is an intergenerational effect that "intensifies the involvement in delinquency of officially convicted sons whose parents also have experienced criminal convictions." Hagan concludes that the official convictions "create a trajectory of publicly known as well as privately experienced stigma that is difficult to reverse, disguise or ignore."[62]

Simply being processed through the justice system hurts a person's chances of getting a job, whether or not he/she is found guilty. This has been known for at least a generation. In one interesting 35-year-old experiment, four separate employment files were prepared and personally presented by an employment "agent" to 100 different potential employers looking for seasonal help in a resort area.[63] The files were the same in all respects except for the criminal court record of the applicant. All the files described the applicant as "a thirty-two-year-old single male of unspecified race, with a high school training in mechanical trades, and a record of successive short-term jobs as a kitchen helper, maintenance worker, and handy-man." However, one applicant was described as having been con-victed and sentenced for assault; a second, tried and acquitted; a third, also acquitted, but with a letter from the judge certifying the finding of not guilty and reaffirming the legal presumption of inno-cence. The fourth made no mention of any criminal record.

The employers were asked whether they could use the man described in the file. As far as the prospective employers knew, each showing of the file by the "agent" was a legitimate offer to work. Of the 25 employers shown the "no criminal record" file, 9 were interested in hiring the man. Of the 25 approached with a "convict" folder (in which the applicant had been tried and sen-tenced for assault), only 1 had any interest in the applicant. More significantly, of the 25 employers given the "accused but acquitted" folder, only 3 offered jobs; even when presented with a letter from the judge, only 6 of the 25 were interested. The authors concluded that "legal records are systematically related to job opportunities." This study did not factor in race and was done long before the computerization of criminal records for use in employment screen-ing, the current deterioration in the job market in the inner city, and the societal perception of out-of-control violence among young African-American men.

Iatrogenic Punishment

In their sweeping analysis of "recorded patterns of crimes and violence in 110 nations and 44 international cities, covering the period from 1900 to 1970, Dane Archer and Rosemary Gartner assessed the effects of the ultimate deterrent measure – the death penalty. They found that the deterrence hypothesis had little rele-vance when it came to homicide. In comparing the short-term effects of abolishing the death penalty in 14 countries (one year after abolition), they concluded: "there is no evidence for the deterrence hypothesis. *De jure* abolition appears to have little effect. If anything, there appears to be a slight downturn in homicide rates."[64] Testing "residual deterrence" (five years after abolition), Archer and Gartner found even less support for the deterrence hypothesis. Indeed, when these researchers looked at "specific offense deterrence, they found support for the contention of some researchers that state executions actually produce homicides. Archer and Gartner concluded, "in general, the data run strongly counter to the hypothesis of offense deterrence. While this hypothesis predicts that capital crimes will increase more rapidly after abolition than non-capital offenses, precisely the opposite pattern obtains – rates of homicide were stationary or declined."[65]

In the 1970s, Marvin Wolfgang, Richard Figlio, and Thorsten Sellin found that, though Philadelphia's juvenile justice system was relatively efficient in identifying and punishing delinquent boys, *the greater the punishment, the more likely the youths were to get in further difficulty later.* They concluded that harsh sanctions had no effect on the subsequent behavior of adolescent boys and in fact often had a deleterious effect on future behavior.[66]

A 1978 study of youth crime by criminologists at Ohio State University bolstered the latter interpretation. Using the concept of "velocity" (the amount of time that elapses between a youth's receiving a justice sanction and his first arrest after release), they found that the average youth in their sample was rearrested in about 9.3 months. However, those who had been sent to a state reform school were rearrested within 4.8 months, while those sentenced to an adult county jail cut the "street time" before rearrest to only 1.2 months. The "least intrusive" alternative – informal supervision outside the courts – lengthened the time before rearrest to 12 months. All of this could be chalked up to differences in the selection of youngsters for the various sanctions. However, the researchers took these factors into account, controlling for types of offense, race, and economic status. They concluded:

the most significant finding in this study is that with all else controlled, there is a moderate to high *inverse* relationship between the severity of the sanction for the first in every pair of crimes and the time elapsed until the arrest for the second in the pair. Institutionalization increases the velocity of the second arrest; informal supervision retards it most. . . . Only the mildest intervention, informal supervision, retards the speed of arrest of the next crime.[67]

These findings were replicated by others. A 1982 study of juvenile crime in Wisconsin found "an *increase* in the frequency and seriousness of misbehavior in the periods following those in which [justice] sanctions were administered."[68] A 1992 study by the Institute of Government at the University of North Carolina at Chapel Hill on recidivism among adult criminal offenders in that state found similar patterns. Using a regression model whereby the association of a number of independent variables (e.g., age, race, prior arrests) with a dependent variable (e.g., probability of rearrest) could be estimated, the North Carolina researchers concluded that "increasing imprisonment generally did not have a deterrent effect on imprisoned offenders, and in fact may have increased their chances of rearrest." They noted that contrary to the "specific deterrence" hypothesis of the law, increasing sentences did not lower the chances of rearrest. On the contrary, increased imprisonment increased the likelihood of rearrest for property offenses.[69] Although the authors acknowledged the possibility of sampling bias in their conclusions – "offenders who serve a longer time in prison may be inherently more dangerous than are those who serve a shorter time" – they noted that this explanation was weakened by the fact that their analysis took into account other major factors, like prior criminal activity, which usually predict later recidivism.[70]

In a recent meta-analysis of 443 studies of juvenile correctional programs, M. W. Lipsey found that 64% of the studies reported reductions in favor of the treatment group, with an average reduction in recidivism of 10%. However, dramatic differences emerged between and among the programs being evaluated. For example, programs that focused on employment lowered recidivism by as much as 18%. Those which were run by state or local juvenile justice bureaucracies (as opposed to smaller, privately run alternatives) were generally less effective.[71] Canadian researcher Paul Gendreau broke rehabilitative programs down even further and found that some were able to reduce recidivism "in the range of 25–80% with an average of about 50%."[72] Programs that relied on deterrence and fear, such as "shock incarceration" and so-called scared straight tactics, not only failed to reduce recidivism but actually tended to escalate the amount of delinquent behavior.

In his interesting historical analysis of juvenile justice programs, criminologist Theodore Ferdinand found similar patterns.[73] He asked the intriguing question "Juvenile Delinquency or Juvenile Justice: Which Came First?" Building on a thesis of Stanley Cohen[74] that the models devised over the years to deal with delinquents tended to be bifurcated into two distinct categories, *exclusionary* (punitive) or *inclusionary* (rehabilitative), Ferdinand found that throughout the 19th century the *exclusionary* approach was reserved for those who were handled formally by the justice system and had been labeled as hard-core or antisocial. In general, these programs failed and their alumni were more likely to go on to more serious crime later. In contrast, *inclusionary* programs were seen as rehabilitative rather than punitive and were reserved for a "quasi-normal" population of lesser offenders who tended to be handled informally, if at all, by the justice systems. As these individuals moved on into adulthood, they usually did reasonably well, often associating themselves with other informal but "inclusionary" programs or groups later in life. Ferdinand confirmed Cohen's thesis.

However, as time passed, the rehabilitative *inclusionary* programs were gradually transformed into punitive *exclusionary* models. The shift did not appear to be related to any dramatic changes in patterns or incidence of delinquency. More commonly, the definition of who was a "delinquent" was widened to include relatively normal individuals. This had the effect of qualifying mildly troublesome youths for more severe handling. The least successful and most destructive approach was applied more universally, while the more successful programs were jettisoned to make room for more punishment and retribution. Moreover, Ferdinand found "a sizable, disproportionate increase in juvenile crime" as the punitive juvenile institutions began taking in less serious delinquents and a "shift toward more serious crimes" as the inclusionary programs became more exclusionary.[75]

An Exception to the Rule

The one modern study claiming to demonstrate that harsher handling of juveniles lowers the chances of repeated crime was by Charles Murray and Louis Cox.[76] Their 1979 study of Illinois delinquents, *Beyond Probation*, provided grist for the policymakers at the Reagan administration Justice Department under Attorney General Edwin Meese, who at the time was preaching the scrapping of rehabilitative approaches in favor of just deserts and deterrence for juvenile delinquents. Murray and Cox concluded that incapacitating juveniles in state reform schools was the most effective means of lowering recidivism. Incarceration had a "suppression effect" on later delinquency, cutting repeat crimes and ultimately lowering juvenile crime rates. Based in the intrinsic value of the congregate institution, Murray's policy recommendations anticipated those he would make 15 years later for children of single-parent welfare mothers – that they be removed to state orphanages.

As it turned out, Murray's original study had hardly proved his own thesis. Criminologist Elliott Currie discovered that, in their haste to tout deterrence, threat, and reform schools for young offenders, Murray and Cox had ignored significant facts. Their own data did not show that incarceration was superior to its alternatives – even for serious delinquents. The best results were found among

juveniles who attended out-of-town camps or who were treated in
psychiatric hospitals or group homes. Murray had glossed over the
fact that juvenile delinquents who were simply placed at home
showed suppression effects as large as those produced by incarceration within two years after the youths' discharge.[77]

Because I was mentioned critically by Murray in the first draft of
his *Beyond Probation,* I was called by a *Washington Post* reporter for
my comments shortly after its publication. Halfway through the
interview, she became perturbed, asking me if I had any idea why
she had been assigned by her editors to do a story on what seemed
to be an obscure and not very interesting study. She had apparently
underestimated the ability of the Right to market its material in the
popular press – usually before peers in academia had a look at it.
The publicity surrounding Murray and Cox's study far outpaced
that which usually accompanies such academic studies on delinquency and crime, which are more commonly doomed to obscurity
in professional journals on university library shelves. The strategy
was developed further with Murray's next book, *Losing Ground.* It
reached its apotheosis with *The Bell Curve.*

I had observed the consequences of prematurely dragging young
offenders deeply into the justice system early on in my career. As
head of the Massachusetts youth corrections system, I tried to
discern the benefits and drawbacks to locking up delinquent kids
before trial. Observing youngsters in our Boston detention center,
researchers from Harvard's Center for Criminal Justice had concluded that one of the best predictors of later delinquency was
whether the youth had been kept in juvenile detention early on in
his teens. When I was first told of this finding, I was unimpressed.
It simply meant to me that we locked up certain youths based on
our ability to screen out the more potentially dangerous who would
be more likely go on to commit more crimes later.

This was not the case. When the researchers looked more
closely at those youths who were detained, they found that, with the
exception of a small minority of violent offenders (so few as to have

no effect on the overall findings), the decision to keep a teenager in detention was not based on background information, or even on criminal history. Rather, it was based on two other factors: (1) socioeconomic status and (2) whether there was space available in the detention center on the day the youngster was arrested. In fact, it was our "treatment" – confinement in a juvenile detention center – that carried the virus of later delinquency. It didn't end there. Being detained in a locked juvenile facility in their mid-teens also increased the youths' odds of later being committed to a state correctional facility, while lessening the chances of being allowed to return home.[78]

The idea that governmental intrusion into one's life, home, or history might carry lasting, even intergenerational, consequences is readily accepted when it comes to such matters as government aid, poverty programs, or welfare. Murray had argued that, as virtually all government welfare programs promote dependency, they should be abolished. In fact, this reasoning had to do with "unintended consequences."[79] In a 1992 news conference, then Congressman Newt Gingrich of Georgia commented, "the welfare state, despite the noble intentions of its founders ... has become a wretched life style, passed down from generation to generation."[80] "The city welfare state" must be replaced with a society of conservative values, including strong support of police, prosecutors, and prisons.[81] It should, then, not be so difficult to acknowledge the possibility of similar dynamics resulting from overreliance upon decidedly more traumatic intrusions into one's personal or family life and space.

Shattering Communities

And what had been the effect on the community of the drug war? Had all this "toughness" directed at black youth and young men worked? Noting that law enforcement had, at best, only modest success in raising drug prices and had not reduced middle-class access to drugs, Rand researcher Peter Reuter suggested that the harmful consequences of the punitive approach needed to be examined. Reuter's list included: the imprisonment of large numbers of African-American males for long terms in institutions that do not rehabilitate them; locking up primarily "small fry" of the drug trade; and exacerbating violence in the inner city. As Reuter put it: "Taken singly, it is impossible to estimate the significance of these harms. . . . In the aggregate, however, they add up to this: Politically powerless urban communities not only suffer the most from the drug trade's effects – from crime, violence, AIDS, crack babies, and a host of other ills – they also bear the brunt of harshly punitive policies."[82]

In a similar vein, California researchers Jonathan Marshall and Peter Scott concluded that the prosecution of the war on drugs had done more to shatter the inner cities of America than decades of neglect and ineffective social programs.[83] Meanwhile, as a $30 billion "Crime Bill" wound its way through Congress, the obvious evidence of racism continued to elude most of those who fashioned the nation's policies on crime. As we approach the end of the 20th century, and the criminal law is ever more exclusively concentrated on minorities, the white majority has apparently forgotten that criminal law remains a "hostile procedure," unanticipated consequences of which extend well beyond the narrow purposes of law enforcement.

On March 6, 1990, an 18-year-old African-American man was acquitted of a felony by a black jury in the District of Columbia. "One young juror was crying when the verdict came. The prosecutor gaped as it was read. The crashing sound in the courtroom was the defendant, whose elation propelled him backward over his chair."[84] Three weeks later, a letter arrived at D.C. Superior Court from one of the jurors, who wrote that though most of the jury believed the defendant to be guilty, they had bowed to those who "didn't want to send anymore Young Black Men to Jail." The incident was an unsettling example of one of the unanticipated consequences of the war against crime. It would be repeated in a number of jurisdictions nationally.[85]

The depth of the alienation could be seen in an informal *Wall Street Journal* survey of affluent African-Americans in Los Angeles. Many so-called well-off blacks apparently saw inequalities in the justice system's treatment of the white policemen who were convicted of beating Rodney King and the young African-Americans charged with beating Reginald Denny during the riots which followed. Although most whites saw no comparison between the two cases, blacks, poor and affluent, got a different message. When asked about justice for people who, like him, are black, John W. Patton, an affluent 40-year-old black senior litigator for Litton Industries Inc., told the *Journal* reporter, "The justice system just doesn't work when we're involved, unless it's justice on our heads." He went on to recall that his current success "may forever be colored by an experience he had in Cleveland 28 years ago." In that instance, he and a friend who were driving an older automobile were pulled over by three police cars. The officers emerged with drawn guns and Patton and his friend were made to "assume the position." They were later told they were stopped because one of them was riding in the back seat, and that "made us look like we were about to commit a robbery." Patton told the reporter, "You can't even imagine all the ways a black man can be killed where a white man would not even be at risk."[86]

Six months after the 1992 Los Angeles riots, the residents of economically strapped South Central Los Angeles turned down a $1 million federal anticrime "Weed and Seed" grant, in the process jeopardizing an additional $18 million that the federal prosecutor said was targeted for social services. Local African-American Councilman Mark Ridley-Thomas, representing the district, told the City Council, "My fear is that [the grant] will widen the chasm between police and the community – against a backdrop of what can still be described as a volatile situation. . . . In fact . . . the

Weed portion of this program has been imposed on communities of color with the purpose of incarceration and not rehabilitation." The federal prosecutor was to have overseen the process. A local community leader who had attended the meetings in which the anticrime strategies were outlined said that the plan was really about "seeding" the community with informers and "spies" who would identify young black men for eventual arrest and imprisonment. The contrasting views on "Weed and Seed" were best summarized in the statements of the protagonists. President George Bush characterized it as an effort on the part of federal, state, and local forces to "weed out" violent criminals and drug dealers and, "when we break their deadly grip," seeding the neighborhood with expanded educational programs, social services, and jobs. The Los Angeles Urban Strategies Group saw the "Weed and Seed program as imposing a police state on the public life of low-income communities of color."[87]

The Demise of Probation

And what about rehabilitation? Probation, invented over a hundred years ago by Boston shoemaker John Augustus as a way of advocating alternatives to jail and prison, has deteriorated to the point where the average probation officer is indistinguishable from a policeman. Indeed, the "Mission Statement" of the California Probation Officers Association could be that of a SWAT team. The shift from rehabilitation to enforcement was noted in a study by Harris, Clear, and Baird. They reported that, over the decade of the 1980s, "community supervision officers" had become markedly less concerned with an offender's rehabilitation and more focused on enforcement and authority.[88] A 1994 national survey of police chiefs, sheriffs, prosecutors, judges, and probation/parole directors revealed that the latter were the least likely to want alternatives to incarceration implemented in their jurisdictions.[89]

Other developments bolster the view that the rehabilitation model of probation has been largely abandoned. For instance, in recent years it has grown increasingly common for probation officers to carry guns, and even in those states which forbade such practices, the majority of probation/parole officers supported their being able to be armed. In 1987, the federal probation division developed a firearms training program for its officers, who were then armed with a .38 revolver. A 1990 survey of the Southern District of Texas revealed that 70% of the federal probation officers there carried firearms.[90]

As William Dickey, a University of Wisconsin law professor and formerly that state's Director of Corrections, summarized the problem: "Parole board members, parole agents, and prison social workers read the newspapers. They do not see anything but 'get tough' proclaimed there and see the same thing in the policy statements and actions of political leaders. They have no desire to be 'on front street' when the system misfires, as it inevitably must in the complex world of corrections. The messages from leaders and the public are clear: When in doubt, do not grant parole; when in doubt, revoke parole; when in doubt, do not approve a person's furlough or other off-grounds leave." Dickey notes that these messages feed a preoccupation with avoiding blame should the system misfire, creating "a bureaucratic culture that reinforces in the world of unwritten rules the same culture that is reflected in the press, in politics, and in academic writing."[91]

As a result of such trends, probation is now as likely as not to *increase* the risk of rearrest and imprisonment. For example, making restitution a condition of probation enhances the chances of a probationer being rearrested. Although researchers allowed for the possibility that probationers required to pay restitution to victims were "different in some important (unmeasured) way," it seemed more likely that the additional financial pressure placed on probationers who were already having difficulty earning a living made it harder for some to remain law-abiding.

This sad state of affairs apparently presents little problem to the contemporary American probation officer. The chief probation officer of Los Angeles County offered his own explanation as to why, for example, "intensive probation" did not lower recidivism. "Reduced recidivism was not listed as the highest priority," he wrote. "The goal of community protection is not always compatible with rehabilitation, a low recidivism rate was not an adequate criterion to determine whether [intensive supervision] works." Turning the traditional view of probation on its head, he asks: "Why is revocation and sentencing of a probation violator not considered a 'success'? I believe it should be, and that is why the goals of [intensive probation] here in Los Angeles placed recidivism as a lower priority."[92] In this upside-down world, "intensive probation" is equated with increasing the odds of uncovering a "technical violation" of probation or a minor misdemeanor, which can then be used to justify revocation of probation and recommitment to prison.[93] The more of this adversarially based "help" the client receives, the more likely it is he or she will end up in prison or be tagged with the "career criminal" label.[94]

A perusal of the official publication of the American Probation and Parole Association clearly demonstrates to what point this particular group of former "helpers" have come. We see advertisements for: Brinks "full service offender monitoring"; Syva "emit" immunoassays in drug testing; Ontrak, "Drug Abuse? *Yes* or *No* in 3 Minutes with Ontrak" – "Ontrak allows no time for excuses and gives you complete control of the testing situation"; "The Mitsubishi Electronic Monitoring System provides positive visual identification of a client's curfew, and his alcohol status," and Digital Products, "Guard Mobile Monitoring System"; "A radio frequency link allows interrogation of the home receiver unit without alerting the offender. What's more, a set of lights on the compact handset offers at-a-glance status reports on everything from curfew compliance to tamper condition to outbound message requests." Articles on proper "practice" are of the same genre. In one, for example, a professional social worker explains how to use urine tests with juveniles to justify violation of probation and return to reform school, or to bring about prosecution in previously "adjusted" cases. An article contributed by Psychemedics Corporation in Santa Monica, California, describes "a new and fascinating technique of drug testing based on hair analysis." As the editors comment approvingly, "Their article identifies some important advantages hair analysis provides over the more conventional body fluid testing."[95]

The fact that we are now at a point where "intensive probation" increases the odds of rearrest is a commentary on the deterioration of probation over the past two decades. Caught up in an ersatz cop role (called "attack" probation by the British criminologist Andrew Rutherford),[96] most contemporary probation officers are not interested in offering the kind of assistance that might keep a probationer out of prison. Increasingly, American probation officers, in concert with the prosecution, see their role as one in which to search out any means possible to get the probationer into prison. The motto for this practice was mounted on the office wall of one of California's chief probation officers: "Trail 'em, Surveil 'em, Nail 'em, and Jail 'em."[97]

The effects have been only too obvious. In 1993, more than one-third of the 120,000 inmates in California's state prisons had been put there by their probation officers (supervised and managed by professional social workers and counselors). These inmates were imprisoned for "technically violating" the conditions of their probation or parole – such things as missing appointments, not attending Alcoholics Anonymous meetings, being unemployed, moving or marrying without permission, having "dirty" urine, and a host of other reasons. They had not engaged in behavior sufficient to warrant an arrest or criminal charge; rather, they had aggravated their helpers.[98] Between 1977 and 1991, those being returned to prison as "technical" violators of conditions of probation or parole more than doubled from 14.5% to 30.5% of *all* prison admissions nationally.

Perverting Help

Social commentators from Michel Foucault to Ivan Illich have observed that the disciplined ethic of the punitive state eventually infects all segments of the society. Nowhere has this been more obvious than among the so-called helping professions. Northwestern University's urban affairs expert John McKnight has pointed out the grossly negative effects on the community of the "professionalization" of the war on poverty. "Certified experts" in everything from social work to grief counseling now come from outside the community to replace the indigenous individuals who, in the past, worked locally to combat the problems plaguing their own communities. The destructive potential of these developments was exacerbated as professional "helpers" took on the mantel of criminal justice authority.

A blatant example of this surfaced in early 1994, when it was discovered that a university hospital in South Carolina had been testing pregnant women (virtually all African-American) for drugs without their consent. After the fact, when the women were told that they had been tested for drugs, they received a letter, which stated in part, "During your recent examination you tested positive for drugs. . . . If you fail to complete substance abuse counseling, fail to cooperate with the Department of Social Services in the placement of your child and services to protect that child, or if you fail to maintain clean urine specimens during substance abuse rehabilitation, you will be arrested by the police and prosecuted." At least 40 of the women were reported to the police and subsequently prosecuted.[99]

Indeed, professional "help" for a substantial proportion of African-American citizens now comes tied to the criminal justice system. So-called helping professionals lend a gloss of clinical validity to what in fact are criminal justice spectacles. As these unlikely sectors of the population have succumbed to a philosophy of life rooted in the justice system, social workers, psychiatrists, psychologists, school counselors, and teachers have increasingly come to see themselves as covert agents of law enforcement – in effect, willing to allow the justice system to define the symptoms, provide the diagnostic labels, and prescribe the preferred treatment, particularly where African-American and Hispanic clientele are concerned. The very idea of lifting ever so slightly the heavy hand of law enforcement and the threat of incarceration from a broad array of complex human affairs has come to be seen as "unprofessional," if not subversive.

In a Faustian bargain, a large segment of helping professionals now view themselves as agents of a benign criminal justice endeavor. The criminal justice system has spawned a new generation of "helpers" grown comfortable with culling the elect from the wicked while offering little more than threat and intimidation to those who fall short of the mark. Trashing such traditional ethical principles as confidentiality and individualization, they resemble those functionaries H. G. Wells referred to in his most dystopian fantasies as "psychojusters." For the urban African-American male in need of help, there are ever fewer helpers whose first allegiance is not to law enforcement, the courts, or corrections. As the blurb for one counseling/drug treatment group proudly proclaims: *"Right-Turn Inc.* understands that CORRECTIONS is our client – not the INMATE" (emphasis in original).[100]

These "unanticipated consequences" of tying help to the authority of the justice system make eminently sensible the advice civil libertarian Ira Glasser, who has recommended that clients treat their helpers – psychologists, counselors, or social workers – as they would a policeman: with respect and civility, saying nothing.[101] In the world of criminal justice, professional diagnosticians and therapists are expected to deliver one basic commodity, what the late British social anthropologist Sir Edmund Leach called "treatment" when applied to delinquents: "the imposition of discipline by force – the maintenance of the existing order against threats which might arise from its own internal contradictions."[102]

In this milieu, even child care workers are often indistinguishable from police investigators. After hearing an allegation of
child abuse, those who in past years would have attempted to
understand and treat the family while protecting the child now
rush to gather evidence for the prosecution – often destroying
the victim and family in the process. Wedded to law enforcement, "child protective services" might more properly be characterized as "family dismemberment services" – particularly where
African-American families are concerned. With ever-shrinking
budgets for family support programs, children are removed from
birth parent(s) and sent into the labyrinth of state-given foster
care and institutionalization, with little evidence it does anyone
much good.

Predictably, as black children and teens have become the primary focus of social-policy discussions, the ground has shifted
mightily. We hear less about the need for adequate family-support
services and alternatives to long-term institutionalization, and more
about the halcyon days of the congregate orphanage. The rationale
is that in-home services and family preservation services have failed
to meet the needs of children, particularly many of those on welfare
and living in single-parent homes. Of that, there can be little question. However, it is an apples-and-oranges comparison. Were $150
to $250 per day (the cost of most contemporary children's institu-
tions) spent on temporary foster care or support services for the
natural or extended family, things would probably "work" fairly
well. But that might smack of welfarism; spending these amounts to
exile children somehow seems safer. At the end of this road one
will find, once again, a mimicking of the criminal justice system.
Family members are more likely to be prosecuted for abuse and
neglect and children "placed" with little regard to the ultimate
consequences, either for the children or their parents. The search
will be for a "perpetrator" – someone who can be labeled, punished, and exiled.

Controlling the Marginalized

What will be the long-term consequences for a society that uses its justice system so readily and so heavy-handedly with its black population? Will the measures the white majority has prescribed for the inner city ever come back to haunt them? Alexander Nehamas put it well:

the mechanisms used to understand and to control marginalized and ostracized groups [are] also essential to the understanding and control – indeed, to the constitution – of "normal" individuals. Thus, the constant surveillance of prisoners that replaced physical torture as a result of penal reform came to be applied also to schoolchildren, to factory workers, to whole populations (and, we might add, to average citizens, whose police records, medical reports and credit ratings are even today becoming more available and more detailed).[103]

Occasionally, matters move in the opposite direction as in the so-called Abscam "sting" operation in 1981 whereby law enforcement aggressively sought out potential offenders among congressmen by offering them bribes. The FBI operation netted a large number of congressmen – proving that some could easily be set up to take bribes. At the time, this new approach to law enforcement was seen by legal experts as something of a one-time anomaly. As George Washington Professor of Law Gerald M. Caplan wrote at the time in the *Washington Post*: "As to the future, it would be surprising if the bureau were to do it again. Abscam appears to be a one-time thing that punished a few thieves without providing the country – or the FBI – with a better map of the scope of official corruption or ways of coping with it."[104] Caplan was a bit off target. Sting operations became a staple of American law enforcement at both the federal and local level, with particular relevance to the drug wars being conducted in the inner cities.

If there were an aggressive police presence in the white suburban communities similar to that which defines the relationship between police and citizens in the inner city, how many white citizens might be netted by the criminal justice system?[105] The dismal prospects are not as farfetched as some might imagine. Halfway into my tenure as the jail monitor, I was taken aback to discover that, in Duval County, Florida, with its 700,000 inhabitants (75% white, 25% black), the local police maintained 330,000 individual criminal records. On any given day, there were 75,000 outstanding (unserved) arrest warrants for persons charged with misdemeanors and 10,000 warrants for those charged with felonies.[106] On one of my visits, while sitting in my hotel room writing reports, I turned on the local TV evening news to find the sheriff announcing "Operation Safe Streets" – a massive effort by police to arrest and jail an additional 82,000 citizens thought to be driving with suspended licenses in the county.[107] As the sheriff put it: "If you are bent on a life of crime, we will deal with you severely. We have your pictures." The implications of defining one in every six adult inhabitants of the county as "bent on a life of crime" went unaddressed.

However, when it comes to dealing with the vital social issues of the urban poor, national policy has devolved into a simple axiom: "If you can't understand it, threaten it. If you can't make it go away, jail it." Formal criminal justice procedure offers an easy solution to problems too daunting to consider seriously; even those who know better are seduced by its coercive potential. Social-policy planners, helping professionals, teachers, social workers, and school counselors will find out too late that they have placed their trust in a system distinguished mostly by its failure to make communities safer and its alienation of large segments of our population.

4

The Politics of Crime

At a 1948 Paris conference three years after the fall of Nazism, with the debris of a regime built upon what he called "fictitious entities" strewn over half the world, Graham Greene observed that "the totalitarian state contrives, by educating its citizens, to suppress all sense of guilt, all indecision of mind."[1] It is an apt description of the current state of the politics of crime in the United States. Spurred on by the alienating procedures of a criminal justice system spun out of control, a media bereft of a minimal sense of responsibility, a dehumanized research establishment, and a management-obsessed justice industry, as citizens we have been effectively relieved of whatever vestigial "sense of guilt" we might once have felt for our present condition.

Punitive Punditry

A metaphor for the politics of crime that overtook the United States during the 1980s and 1990s can be found in the transformation of former Harvard management professor James Q. Wilson into a pundit on crime. British criminologist Jock Young describes

Wilson's approach to crime as one that "evolves a series of measures which would step beyond the bounds of justice in order to defend the existing order . . . if one does not wish fundamentally to restrict the economic and judicial system, then coercion and discipline are the only alternatives to maintain order." The practical problem with this approach is that, as Young put it, "coercive policies tend to increase disrespect for law rather than the reverse."[2]

Wilson's "commonsense" musings, published under the title *Thinking About Crime* (1975), moved the parameters of the debate to the right and eventually came to shape the nation's policy on crime for most of the 1980s, culminating in the misinformed and destructive legislation of the 1990s. Initially reveling in the fact that he was not expert in these matters, Wilson cast a critical eye on traditional sociological and psychological theories about crime and the "root-cause" anticrime stratagems of academic criminologists, some of whom had been advisers to the Johnson Crime Commission.[3] Wilson viewed their analyses and policy recommendations not only as ineffective but as having contributed to the conditions for more crime, although in fact the recommendations of the commission had not been implemented in any significant way.

Alternately representing himself as a reformed liberal or a committed conservative, Wilson became a highly effective behind-the-scenes advocate, acting as consultant to politicians of both the Left and the Right. His Harvard association provided academic cover for his politically driven solutions. Charging that the justice system had "encouraged the calculators" and "trifled with the wicked," he disparaged rehabilitation and called for greater reliance on punishment and deterrence. Wilson had little time for addressing "root causes" when it came to combating crime. "[When I hear the phrase] 'Crime and drug addiction can only be dealt with by attacking their root causes,' I am sometimes inclined, when in a testy mood, to rejoin: 'Stupidity can only be dealt with by attacking its root causes.' I have yet to see a 'root cause' or to encounter a government program that has successfully attacked it, at least with respect to those social problems that arise out of human volition rather than technological malfunction."

Wilson's rejection of governmental intervention into the lives of citizens was not unconditional, however. Although he spurned rehabilitative and preventive programs, he strongly supported the wide expansion of aggressive law enforcement, stricter laws, harsher sentences, and building more prisons. Wilson used the work of sociologist Robert Martinson to bolster the view that "nothing works" in rehabilitating offenders (a position which Martinson later disavowed) and moved from there to propose more reliance on deterrence and "incapacitation." However, in his argument against rehabilitating offenders, Wilson failed to mention that Martinson had been an abolitionist regarding prisons, having written a series for *The New Republic* two years earlier in which he held that we should consider doing away with most prisons because they make matters worse for most of those sent to them. A year after Wilson's *Thinking About Crime* appeared, and while he was touting the failure of rehabilitation and using Martinson as his expert source, Martinson wrote the following:

A particular pox should be visited upon those who support mandatory incarceration on the basis of questionable assumptions about how many crimes are "saved" by incarceration, when they do not make similar estimates of the numbers of crimes contributed as a result of damage done to the offender by imprisonment.

And a pox on those who do not realize the massive overkill involved in using prison to restrain criminal behavior. Penal restraint is a very inefficient method. . . . And yet, we over-restrain offenders when we incarcerate them. Furthermore, it should be recognized that this overkill restrains good and neutral behavior as well as criminal behavior. If there is any thought that penal restraint might lead the offender to "unlearn" criminal behavior, we must also think about the possibility of his "unlearning" good and neutral behavior as a result of restraint.[4]

Marketing as Research

For the most part, Wilson eschewed the peer-review process of standard academic and scientific publications in criminology, preferring to write for conservative magazines – Norman Podhoretz's *Commentary*, Irving Kristol's *The Public Interest* (where Wilson serves on the publication committee), the Heritage Foundation's *Policy Review* – or for popular magazines like *Fortune, Forbes, The New Republic, The National Review*, and *Atlantic*. Thus Wilson was afforded both a large audience for his views and wide dissemination to policymakers through the highly effective publicity machinery that has come to characterize conservative "think tanks," by now a staple of the Washington political scene.

This was a process entirely foreign to the academic criminological researchers Wilson had left in the dust, in much the same fashion as social-welfare experts would later be undone by Charles Murray's well-financed and well-marketed jeremiads against welfare.[5] It was to become a common strategy of neoconservative "think tanks" on social-policy matters. The tactics all but guaranteed that by the time the bona fide experts got around to replying in the professional journals, they had already lost the day in the media and in the minds of policymakers. William Hammett, president of the conservative think tank The Manhattan Institute, best summarized how social policy on crime and welfare in the 1980s and 1990s was formulated, "Marketing is fun . . . and we're marketing ideas."[6]

Wilson brought his own version of "supply-side" economics to justice policy. Initially, he portrayed the average offender as viewing the world through the eyes of a Harvard Business School graduate who weighed the "risks" of apprehension against the "benefits" to be gained, and proceeded accordingly. Wilson would cut crime by simply increasing the risk. It made eminent sense to white middle-class policymakers of both parties who, having a stake in society and a fair amount to lose, could relate to the deterrent value of perceived risk. Although there was virtually no credible research to suggest that this approach had much application to street crime, it was an immediate hit with politicians.[7]

As E. J. Dionne noted in his study of American politics, "Among the major figures of neoconservatism, James Q. Wilson may have been closest to the feelings of angry whites in the cities." Wilson argued that white anger toward the black poor is less a matter of racism than the perception that blacks refuse to live by the standards that whites see as appropriate. As he put it, "Much of what passes as 'race prejudice' may be little more than class prejudice, with race used as a rough indicator of social class."[8] But, while acknowledging that Wilson's analysis "was truer to the real sentiments of most rebellious urban whites than the contention of some liberals that such whites are racists, pure and simple," Dionne added, "using race as a 'rough indicator of social class' sounds suspiciously like racism."[9] In fact, Wilson's proposals laid the groundwork for the disastrous racial twists and turns that would come to define the criminal justice system in the late 1980s and 1990s.

Ronald Reagan's 1981 anticrime address to the International Association of Chiefs of Police on the wickedness of human nature outlined the concepts Wilson had set forth. In supporting the construction of prisons over schools, then New York Mayor Ed Koch acknowledged his debt to Wilson. Senator Edward Kennedy's support for the federal "Omnibus Crime Bill" and its call for harsh mandatory sentences and the trying of juveniles in adult courts came out of private seminars on crime conducted by Wilson for Kennedy and his staff.[10] Wilson's ability to balance his credibility with liberal politicians while guarding his status as a darling of the Right was probably less a reflection of his political skills than of the emptiness of liberal thought on crime. Wilson got a free ride in the establishment press and among policymakers of both parties.

Whether Wilson's more recent fascination with the putative genetic (i.e., racial) influences on IQ and crime will be as enticing to

liberal politicians as his punitive approach to crime remains to be
seen. (This is discussed in more detail in Chapter 5.) If properly
packaged and marketed, however, his frankly racially loaded proposals will probably ultimately be welcomed by white politicians, conservative and liberal alike. As neoconservative theorist David Frum
put it, "You no longer get far in public life by preaching that the
poor are poor because someone else is not poor, or that criminals
can be rehabilitated. . . ."[11]

When asked about the "underclass," Wilson has been uncharac-
teristically blunt. "The reason why it is called an underclass and
why we worry about it," he writes, "is that its members have a bad
character: They mug, do drugs, desert children, and scorn education."[12] His views are reminiscent of those of the 19th-century
English writer Charles Booth who, in looking out upon the streets
of London, observed that "The inhabitants are mostly of lowest
class and seem to lack all ideas of cleanliness and decency . . . the
children are rarely brought up to any kind of work, but loaf about,
and no doubt form the nucleus for future generations of thieves
and other bad characters."[13] Wilson gave little reason to hope that
we could do much through rehabilitation or socialization. "Individual differences," he noted, "are to a large extent immutable."

Designer Research

Early in the Reagan administration I was invited to lunch by a politically appointed official in the Office of Juvenile Justice and Delinquency Prevention, the Justice Department agency that funds research and demonstration projects in delinquency. He wanted to
discuss some of my views on the "tougher" stance his agency would
be taking relative to delinquents (the head of the agency ultimately
came to support the death penalty for juveniles). As we relaxed over
drinks, he proffered as an example of the new administration's progress the fact that an eminent "liberal" criminologist had recently
"come around" to their views on juvenile crime and was being more

careful about what she was writing. He fairly crowed his belief that researchers had finally gotten the message. If they were to receive government funding, their conclusions had best be in line with the philosophy of the Justice Department. My host's comments presaged what was about to happen in criminology nationally.

The social critic James Kincaid has commented that the subtleties of a complex world too often give way to the metaphors of the powerful and end up expressed in "enforced dualisms."[14] As he characterizes the process, "We seem to return always to the security of binaries, no matter how vicious they may be . . . unable to recognize the price we pay for the joy of affixing distinct names and assigning classes."[15] That is an apt description of the state of American criminological research in the 1980s and 1990s. The ready availability of research monies from an ideologically driven U.S. Justice Department led to the ascendancy of a new stable of researchers who all but jettisoned any critical sense. Narrative all but vanished from the scene, receding in proportion to the infusion of governmental funding. Critical theory was replaced by an obsession with techniques directed toward finding better ways to identify and catch the criminal, widen police authority, improve prosecutorial efficiency, develop more intrusive and lethal anticrime armamentaria, justify harsher sanctions, and build and manage more jails, prisons, and camps. The research agenda followed the money, and the conclusions followed the power. In this sense, the observation of sociologist Paul Starr that "in a generally conservative time, sociology may seem expendable" is too narrowly conceived.[16] Though traditional sociologists might be expendable, an eminently durable new type of sociologist-criminologist has emerged on the scene. Often lacking hands-on experience in the criminal justice system, they nevertheless provide academic and scientific cover for politically driven anticrime policies. These developments profoundly affected the study of racial bias in the criminal justice system.

This marriage of criminological research to politics helped governmental policymakers to avoid the uneasiness that potentially

"value-loaded" conclusions might bring. Criminologists set themselves the task of carefully sifting, twisting, and pounding ambiguous
realities into forced dualities to fit the political metaphors that fed a
"melodrama of monsters and innocents" while assuring policymakers that "there are no complex issues and none that threaten."[17] As
Kincaid further specified the process: "It allows us to overlook both
contradictions and cruelties in our logic, in our family structure, and
in our social system at large. It allows us unlimited and gratuitous
talk on the subject."[18] And what more characterized the legislative
process on crime in the late 1980s and early 1990s than "gratuitous
talk"?

As the social sciences grew increasingly vulnerable to shifts in
the political winds, some researchers began grinding out studies
that were generally supportive of the anticrime agenda of the
Reagan-Bush Justice Departments. It was not simply a matter of
political partisanship. Rather, one came away with the impression
that, should we enter a more progressive political era, these positiv-
ists would just as eagerly provide the prerequisite statistical validation for whomever their new funders might be.

Predictably, as what possibly looked to be a more liberal new
national administration appeared on the horizon, the same conservative "think tanks" that had designed models for selecting offenders for long-term "incapacitation," began suggesting that imprisonment itself was among the least desirable strategies for decreasing
crime and might, in fact, be "criminogenic."[19] This kind of analysis
slowed as it became clear in the second year of the Clinton administration that its anticrime policies would not differ that much from
those of the Reagan and Bush administrations.

Abandoning the Narrative

Criminological research of the past had produced empiricists and
theorists like Clifford Shaw, William Thrasher, W. I. Thomas,

George Mead, Robert E. Park, Ernest W. Burgess, Erving Goffman, and Howard Becker, civilized men who gave evidence of
having read books outside their field, who wrote as well as they
conceptualized, and, while pondering theory, managed to keep in
touch with the stuff of their studies – people and the worlds they
populated. One was seldom allowed to lose sight of the complex
human tragedies that weave their way through the mundane labeling and processing we call criminal justice.

Although narrative criminological research from the 1930s
through the 1960s concerned itself primarily with young white
males,[20] the hands-on methodology held promise of eventually
yielding the kinds of rich data on African-Americans that we had
seen from writers like Shaw, whose autobiographies taken from
the sons of white immigrants provided classic insight into criminal
careers. But it was not to be. With the exception of the gang
studies of Walter Miller and a few others, African-American
youths were excluded from this rich narrative tradition. Although
studies like Richard Cloward and Lloyd Ohlin's *Delinquency and
Opportunity* developed important theories upon which social policy
might be based, with particular reference to race, class, and
crime, if one wanted to know about the lives of African-American
youths, one had to turn to a small cadre of African-American
writers and poets relatively unknown to white researchers.[21]

The narrative quality of most earlier criminological research had
inhibited writing off predominantly white delinquents as "other"
from the rest of us. Sociological researchers like W. I. Thomas and
Florian Znaniecki, whose study *The Polish Peasant in Europe and
America* remains a classic of American sociological literature, saw the
personal "life-history" as providing the *only* grounding from which
to draw conclusions. As they commented, "whether we draw our
materials from sociological analysis, from detailed life-records of
concrete individuals or from the observation of mass-phenomena,
the problems of sociological analysis are the same." They held that
even in the search for abstract laws the "life-records" of individuals

were superior to any other kind of data. Indeed, they held "that personal life-records, as complete as possible, constitute the perfect type of sociological material, and that if social science has to use other materials at all it is only because of the practical difficulty of obtaining . . . a sufficient number of records . . . and of the enormous amount of work demanded for an adequate analysis of all the personal materials necessary. . . ." In a comment that must seem odd to sociologists of today, Thomas and Znaniecki concluded that, if the researcher is "forced" to use mass-phenomena "without regard to the life-histories of the individuals who participate in them, it is a defect, not an advantage." They believed that social institutions (families, communities, religions) could not be understood simply by studying their formal organization. Rather, it was crucial that the researcher be able to analyze "the ways in which they appear in the personal experience of various members of the group and follow the influence which it has upon their lives. . . ."[22] It was research geared to plumb such matters as the psychosocial interplay of such factors as family and community ties; the effects of labeling; the personal and social dynamics that go into forming a delinquent career, and a myriad of other issues. To paraphrase the psychologist Jerome Bruner, it was research that was less concerned with *processing information* than with the *construction of meaning*.[23] The paradox is that, with the invention of computers, the "practical difficulties" which confounded Thomas and Znaniecki in the 1920s are no longer so overwhelming. There is no longer a valid excuse for not grounding criminological research in such matters as "detailed life-records."

Indeed, the ground for the ascendancy of right-wing ideology in American criminology was laid in the 1980s when its research models were ceded to the paradigms of modern economics, described by one observer as manifesting a behaviorist faith that "there were no ideological issues left to solve; the country faced only . . . 'technical problems [and] administrative problems.' "[24] American criminological research came to resemble that generated for the Pentagon during the Vietnam War – focused on narrow issues for technical purposes in the service of ideology. It was the kind of research that had led a besieged president to see "light at the end of the tunnel" by looking at charts of "body counts," even as the country was torn apart and his presidency was being destroyed. Indeed, as the Vietnam conflict wound down, many of those individuals and research organizations that had worked mostly for the Defense Department migrated to criminal justice and began receiving substantial Justice Department contracts and grants.[25] It was not an atmosphere conducive to studying a politically loaded issue like racial bias. Indeed, as the prisons, jails, and reform schools began to overflow with disproportionate numbers of people of color, race was aggressively ignored.

Prisons as Savings Banks

This kind of research reached an apotheosis of sorts with the appearance in spring 1989 of an article by Assistant Attorney General Richard B. Abell in the Heritage Foundation's *Policy Review*. Using data from a 1983 Justice Department–funded study conducted by the Rand Corporation, Abell concluded that every 100 offenders put in jail generate a *savings* of approximately $40.5 million. He based this on the assumption that the average offender commits 187 to 287 crimes per year at an average cost of $2,300 per crime. This led him to estimate the average annual damage in crime costs of $430,000 per offender. Subtracting the average cost of a year's incarceration ($25,000), Abell concluded that "a year in prison costs $405,000 less than a year of criminal activity. For 100 such offenders, the savings would be $40.5 million."[26] Using Abell's formula, for example, leads one to conclude that the 1.5 million offenders in the nation's jails and prisons generate approximately $675 billion in annual savings. The inflated crime profile of the average bumbling offender would be laughable to anyone who had spent more than a few days with accused defendants in courts across the nation. Abell's figures were ultimately cited by former President Bush in an anticrime speech to law-enforcement and correctional officers, and were still being quoted by Texas Republican Senator Phil Gramm in 1993.[27]

A variation on Abell's theme was taken up by then Attorney General William Barr, who argued the cost-effectiveness of prison by contrasting per capita imprisonment rates of $15,513 annually (in 1990) with the savings generated by incarcerating one inmate for a year – benefits that Barr placed at between $172,000 and $2,364,000 per inmate. As University of Minnesota criminologist Michael Tonry commented, Barr's conclusions contained "improbable estimates of the costs of crime to victims . . . [and] exaggerated estimates of the number of offenses committed by an average prisoner."[28]

At a 1992 Attorney General's Summit on Corrections, Barr used opinion surveys which showed that the public would be willing to spend up to $2.6 million to avert one death through funding better highway safety or asbestos removal to float the proposition that, as about 6,500 homicides are committed each year by persons on bail, probation, or parole, the public would be willing to spend $17 billion (6,500 × $2.6 million) to imprison more people. He did not address the issue of how one picks the 6,500 for incarceration – .001% from among the roughly 6 million individuals on probation, parole, or out on bail or being sought on arrest warrants on any given day nationally.[29]

Barr's later claims for the deterrent effects of prison were so grandiose as to impel criminologist Tonry to note that, if Barr was correct, crime should have disappeared sometime in the mid-1980s: "The 237,000 prisoners added between 1977 and 1986 would have been 'incapacitated' from committing as many crimes as were reported [nationally] in 1977."[30] Nevertheless, Barr's conceptualization provided the theoretical basis for much of the anticrime legislation that surfaced during the early days of the Clinton administration. The fact that it had little basis in reality was of no

importance. Again, race was not mentioned in any of these formula-
tions, even though prison populations were growing increasingly
black and Hispanic.

In its neglect of history and scandalous ignorance of the worka-
day realities of the justice system, the new criminology built its
paradigms on sand. Despite its positivistic pretensions, it was obsessed with means – but to what end? Cambridge University political scientist Quentin Skinner posed the dilemma well: "One of the
first victims of this development [positivism] proved to be the 'end-
of-ideology' argument . . . the thesis itself amounted to little more
than an ideological reading of consensus politics, one in which
silence was (recklessly, as it turned out) taken for agreement."[31]

The Rhetorical Wink

Replete with images of dark-skinned predators, crime has become
a metaphor for race, hammered home nightly on TV news and
exploitative crime shows. Traditionally in this country, welfare and
crime have never been far from the reach of any politician who
wishes to posture on race without ever having actually to mention
it. These issues provide the backdrop for the "rhetorical wink,"
whereby code phrases communicate a well-understood but implicit
meaning while allowing the speaker to deny any such meaning.[32]
Although there may be occasional ambivalence among politicians
when it comes to welfare (particularly where young children are
involved), the "wink" is all but blinding when the rhetoric turns to
matters of crime and punishment. It carries minimal political risk
when presented in terms of getting "tough," while promising massive returns for the politician on the make.

Race-baiting on welfare and crime has a long tradition. In his
1992 try for the U.S. Senate, David Duke, despite his history as a
leader in the Ku Klux Klan and American Nazi party, garnered a
two-thirds majority of white votes in Louisiana by focusing on

welfare and crime – avoiding all but the slightest direct mention of race. The demagoguery had its roots in the post-Reconstruction period. As the sociologist Shirley Vining-Brown noted, "After the [Civil] War, the crime problem in the South became equated with the 'Negro Problem' as Black prisoners began to outnumber White prisoners in all Southern prisons. . . . the terms 'slave,' 'Negro,' and 'convict' were interchangeable."[33]

By the 1990s, what began in the South had overtaken much of the nation. The caricature of the big-time (i.e., African-American) drug dealer riding around in a BMW had replaced the Reagan-era "welfare queen" as an urban myth characteristically reserved for minorities – in this instance, that of the young African-American male as "criminal." As television critic Walter Goodman put it, "the suspects seen on television being arrested in muggings and shootings are almost always black men in their teens and 20's, and they figure hugely in the prevailing anxiety, among blacks as well as whites, over personal safety. . . . No positive stories can compete with the recurrent images of shackled black youths."[34]

Defining Social Problems

As I noted earlier, the American "symbolic interactionist" sociologist Herbert Blumer concluded that we decide what are to be our "social problems" in vague and wispy ways. "Problems" are not problems until we decide they are, and this process does not depend upon either their seriousness or frequency of incidence. As Blumer put it, "[t]he societal definition, and not the objective makeup of a given social condition, determines whether the condition exists as a social problem."[35] Blumer concluded that, if his thesis were correct, it "would call for a drastic reorientation of sociological theory and research in the case of social problems."[36] Expressing frustration with his professional peers for ignoring this phenomenon, he wrote, "I would think that students of social problems would almost automatically see the need to study this process by which given social conditions or arrangements come to be recognized as social problems . . . the role of political figures in fomenting concern with certain problems and putting the damper on concern with other conditions . . . the role of powerful organizations and corporations doing the same thing."[37]

Blumer contrasted this to the impotency of powerless groups to gain attention for what they believe to be problems and the role of the mass media in selecting social problems, along with "the influence of adventitious happenings that shock public sensitivities." As he wrote, "We have here a vast field which beckons study and which needs to be studied if we are to understand the simple but basic matter of how social problems emerge. And I repeat that if they don't emerge, they don't even begin a life."[38]

The experience of the 1980s and 1990s suggests that the pollsters and pundits of the Right learned very well how to define social problems, generate crises, and set the parameters of the debate – with little obeisance to academic niceties. It has to do with creating "moral panics."

Public Policy and Moral Panics

In 1994, Professor Barry O'Neill took the time to uncover what he termed "the history of a hoax." O'Neill was referring to the results of a "survey" attached to a Yale University bulletin board comparing the top problems of public schools in the 1940s to those in the 1980s. According to the survey, in the 1940s the main problems (in order of seriousness) were: talking, chewing gum, making noise in the halls, getting out of turn in line, wearing improper clothing, and not putting wastepaper in the wastebasket. In the 1980s, the survey listed the problems in schools as: drug abuse, alcohol abuse, pregnancy, suicide, rape, robbery, and assault.

The survey results were quoted by a wide range of writers and social commentators of both the Left and the Right, from the Heritage Foundation to the Brookings Institution. Its validity was accepted by mayors, senators, state education officials, university professors, and deans. William Bennett, the former secretary of education and "drug tsar" in the Reagan and Bush administrations, used them in speeches, editorials, and TV appearances to promote his book on moral decay in America, *The Index of Leading Cultural Indicators.* The survey also showed up in the commentaries of Anna Quindlen, Carl Rowan, Rush Limbaugh, George Will, and Bernard Goldberg on *CBS News.* Former Harvard president Derek Bok quoted the survey in an appearance before the Harvard Club of Chicago. Publishing magnate Morton Zuckerman attributed the frightening findings to television violence. As O'Neill commented, the survey became the "most quoted results of educational research, and possibly the most influential."[39] However, he grew suspicious in November 1992, when the *Wall Street Journal* reprinted the list from the *Congressional Quarterly Researcher*: the date of the survey had mysteriously jumped from 1980 to 1990.

It turned out the survey had been invented by T. Cullen Davis, a born-again Christian in Fort Worth, Texas, who devised the lists as an attack on the public schools. He and his brother Ken had built a billion-dollar conglomerate of the family business in oil equipment. In 1976, Davis had been charged with the double murder of his stepdaughter and the lover of his estranged wife. The trials were filled with lurid stories of his wife's drug and sex parties at the Davis mansion. According to O'Neill, after Davis's acquittal, he "turned from the fast life to Christianity . . . and plunged into a reading program on public schools, fought plans for sex education and lobbied for the teaching of creationism."[40] The wide acceptability of this bogus school survey on the state of American public education comes as close as any to describing the moral panic over "exploding crime rates" in the early 1990s and the destructive policy proposals that resulted therefrom.

"Moral Panics" and Race

Moral panics in the United States traditionally have been associated with welfare, immigration, and crime. Outlining the recent history of how crime was hyped into a major political issue in the United States, William Chambliss began with the 1964 presidential candidacy of Barry Goldwater. Goldwater described his platform this way: "Tonight there is violence in our streets, corruption in our highest offices, aimlessness among our youth, anxiety among our elderly. . . . Security from domestic violence no less than from foreign aggression, is the most elementary and fundamental purpose of any government."[41] Goldwater then placed matters in a distinctly racial context – one clearly geared to the white majority:

Our wives, all women, feel unsafe on our streets. And in encouragement of even more abuse of the law, we have the appalling spectacle of this country's Ambassador to the United Nations [Adlai Stevenson] actually telling an audience – this year, at Colby College – that, "in the great struggle to advance human civil rights, even a jail sentence is no longer a dishonor but a proud achievement." Perhaps we are destined to see in this law-loving land people running for office not on their stainless records but on their prison record.[42]

The 1966 Republican congressional campaign built on the themes introduced by Goldwater in 1964, linking crime with the antiwar and civil rights movements.[43] By 1968, the Nixon presidential campaign was traveling a similar path – tying the 1968 riots and disorder in the cities following the assassinations of Martin Luther King and Robert Kennedy to "lawlessness" and crime – with a distinctly black face to it. Nixon's campaign manager, John Mitchell, attacked the Johnson administration's Justice Department with its putative "permissiveness" on crime – and criticized the U.S. Supreme Court. In polls, "crime, lawlessness, looting and rioting" headed the list of the most important problems facing the country.[44]

History repeated itself a quarter-century later. On January 23,

1994, the Sunday preceding President Clinton's State of the Union speech, which was to deal with crime as a major national issue, a *New York Times/CBS* poll revealed that 19% of its respondents cited "crime and violence" as the single greatest problem facing the nation. The *Times* noted, however, that there were contradictions: "Despite studies showing that crime had generally held steady in the past year, 73% said crime had increased in the country, and 58% said crime had risen in their own communities. . . . Yet surprisingly, there has been no appreciable increase in the past 20 years in the degree to which people say they fear walking at night within a mile of their homes."[45] In the weeks following the president's speech, crime moved even higher in the polls as the defining issue of American politics. It had been molded into a major issue, not on the merits of rising crime rates, but through manipulation of the issue by politicians, think-tank commentators, special interests, and a media that fed on the sensational.

More than a decade earlier, Mark Fishman produced an interesting study of the workings of the media in creating nonexistent "crime waves" with racial overtones. Fishman, a sociologist at Brooklyn College, found that during a period in which there was literally no documentable evidence of an increase in incidents of violence directed at the elderly in New York City, the three largest daily newspapers and five local television stations reported a surge of such violence. The muggers, murderers, and rapists of the elderly were usually reported to be black or Hispanic youths with long juvenile records. They tended to come from ghetto neighborhoods, near enclaves of elderly whites who, usually for reasons of poverty, had not fled the inner city. In the wake of the media-reported "crime wave," bills were introduced into the legislature to deal harshly with juveniles, mandate longer prison sentences, and make juvenile records available.[46]

Fishman concluded that "Newsworkers make crime waves by seeing 'themes' in the news. Crime waves are little more than the continued and heavy coverage of numerous occurrences which journalists report under a single theme (e.g., 'crimes against the elderly')."[47] Fishman labeled this a "crime wave dynamic," whereby, "once journalists notice each other reporting the same crime theme, that theme becomes entrenched in a community of media organizations." He found that, as the theme persisted, news organizations already using it did not hesitate to report new instances of it, as they served to confirm their previous judgment that "this thing really is a type of crime happening now." Each use of the theme confirmed and justified its prior uses and helped to spread it even more.[48]

By late January of 1994, Richard Morin, the director of polling for the *Washington Post*, could proclaim, "Crime's Hot." Whereas in July 1993 only 5% of those interviewed saw crime as their primary concern, six months later 21% rated it as the nation's biggest problem. By mid-January of 1994, that percentage had risen to 31%, with fully half of those interviewed listing crime as one of the country's top two problems. Relying on an analysis remarkably similar to that posed by Blumer a quarter-century earlier – "adventitious happenings that shock public sensitivities" – Morin saw it as mostly an artificially created crisis with a political purpose:

Helped along by the news media and a conjunction of tragic incidents, public concern about crime has risen in the polls from one of many American worries to the No. 1 concern. And suddenly in the White House and on Capitol Hill, the cry of "three strikes and you're out" is echoing down the corridors of power – and the politicians aren't talking baseball. Yet there's plenty of cause for pause when listening to all this tough talk about crime. Inconveniently for those poised to demagogue, the available evidence suggests that concerns about crime are soaring at precisely the same time that nearly every major type of crime is going down.[49]

Morin called it a "disconnect" between image and reality. Citing University of Texas communications professor Maxwell E. McCombs, Morin compared the current hyping of crime to "a similar journalistic feeding frenzy over the drug problem in the late 1980s." McCombs had made note of the fact that, once the *New York Times* discovered drugs, other news organizations took up the theme. "The reality was that nothing had changed regarding the incidence or use of drugs. The high spike of public concern was very much driven by media concern."⁵⁰ Noting that "the media direct, shape and inflate public concern," McCombs concluded that the staying power of the crime issue would probably depend upon how long the media remained interested in crime stories.⁵¹

One saw similar patterns in the hyping of drug abuse as the greatest national problem. The public perception changes, often with little regard to statistical evidence. The Bureau of Justice Statistics noted, in its *1993 Sourcebook of Criminal Justice Statistics*, that the percentage of Gallup Poll respondents describing drug abuse as the single most important problem facing our country has shown dramatic shifts over the past decade (Table 7).

A study released in March 1994 by the Center for Media and Public Affairs suggested that the moral panic over crime was being nurtured and sustained by the media. While both government crime reports and victimization surveys showed that the overall national crime rate remained virtually unchanged in 1993, the three major TV network evening newscasts had more than doubled their coverage of crime (Figure 7). In 1993, network newscasts aired 1,642 domestic crime stories, with NBC accounting for 636, CBS for 557, and ABC for 449. In contrast, during 1992, the three network newscasts together had aired a total of 830 crime stories. From January through July, violent crime averaged 66 stories per month. During the rest of the year, coverage jumped 68%, to a monthly average of 111 stories. In addition, the networks developed new crime-oriented features, such as NBC's "Society under Siege," which focused on urban violence and street crime.

As Robert Lichter, codirector of the center that conducted the study, told the *Washington Post*: "I'm not arguing there is no crime problem, but when the media make more of it than they have, the

Table 7. *Public Opinion about Drugs,*
1985–1994

Date of poll	Drug abuse most serious problem (%)
January 1985	2
July 1986	8
April 1987	11
September 1988	11
May 1989	27
November 1989	38
April 1990	30
July 1990	18
March 1991	11
March 1992	8
January 1993	6
January 1994	9

Source: U.S. Justice Department, Bureau of Justice Statistics, *Drugs and Crime Facts: 1994*, NCJ 154043, June 1995, p. 32.

media coverage can really ratchet up public concern. . . . People's fear of crime doesn't come from looking over their shoulders. It comes from looking at their television screens."[52] The Lichter study did not include local news coverage, which in many markets based ratings races on the sensational coverage of local crime stories; nor did the study include the popular national tabloid shows like "Hard Copy," "Inside Edition," and "A Current Affair," which tend to revolve around particularly bizarre crimes, and "Cops," which gives the inaccurate impression that most police work has to do with chasing down and catching young men of color.

James Q. Wilson, when asked why there was such public outcry

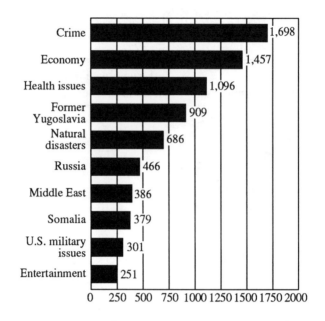

Figure 7. Top ten television news topics of 1993. *Source*: Center for Media and Public Affairs, Washington, D.C., March 1994.

about crime during a time in which crime was actually decreasing, responded in a most unscientific way: "People are not responding to statistics, but what they hear reported. . . . It's rational to be scared."[53] Wilson was correct. The actual incidence of violent crime meant relatively little when placed next to the presentation of crime by the media. An assignment editor or TV producer can now create "crime waves" whether or not they existed.

Crime as Kitsch

The focus of the drug war on mostly poor neighborhoods was a particular boon to "infotainment" news broadcasters, publicity-conscious sheriffs, drug-enforcement agencies, and politicians on the make. It provided a treasure trove of crime kitsch for public consumption. The political draw was so great that the publicity-conscious sheriff of Broward County, Florida, began manufacturing and selling his own crack cocaine for deputies to use as bait for drug users.[54] It played well to a media obsessed with photo-ops and sound bites, all the while feeding white middle-class citizens with a vicarious "walk on the wild side." In most of these gut-satisfying forays, the villains turned out to have black or brown faces. The concentration of law-enforcement armamentaria – listening devices, night-vision scopes, battering rams, SWAT teams, "jump out" narcotics squads, and paid informers – on African-Americans was so massive that it could only be characterized as a full-scale assault.

None of this is to say that crime should not be a concern or that it has not been at unacceptable levels for at least a quarter-century. However, the ways in which the problem is being defined and hyped call for political "solutions" that played to the worst impulses of all concerned and had increasingly racially skewed outcomes. The political "solutions" that followed on the heels of moral panics over crime came with an institutional afterlife not easily undone when the press moves on to other matters. The prison systems we are building and staffing in the United States will not be easily dismantled. On the contrary, inmates will be found to fill them, regardless of actual rises or falls in crime rates. A self-fulfilling, self-feeding industry has been created – one aimed primarily at the underclass and minorities.

Most of the public musings on criminal justice policy now flow to, from, and through an increasingly irresponsible electronic media that allow no room for shades of gray. Transforming the mundane into hyperreality, television has nurtured a new kind of national moral indignation, best described by the Italian filmmaker Vittorio De Sica as "2% moral, 48% indignation and 50% envy."[55] Poseurs and victim stand-ins find ratings, votes, and no-risk heroism by immersing themselves in a peculiar kind of third-party ire, transforming human tragedy into soap opera. Ever on the lookout for these trends, politicians have fallen in line, mouthing the familiar self-righteous inanities while avoiding complex issues that might dampen the public fervor for retribution or cause an individual citizen to take pause.

Contemporary prosecutors seldom resemble the media image portrayed in its most idealized form in the early 1990s by Michael Moriarty on the National Broadcasting Company's series *Law and Order*. In my experience in courts in a number of states and in the federal court system, they are mostly indistinguishable from other run-of-the-mill local "pols," with the possible exception that they have been afforded greater resources and staff than most to go about their business of getting a "win" or a shot at higher office.

Police and prosecutors have grown skillful in engaging the media in this task, not so much to serve effective enforcement as to reinforce what has become a largely racially defined, socially destructive ritual. Major actors in the justice system – police, prosecutors, judges – can now be regularly counted upon to perform their roles using the unctuous hyperbole of the Victorian stage actor summoning up a vision of the criminal as "monster." Perhaps the best example of the modern prosecutorial ideal can be found in Jeanine Ferri Pirro, District Attorney for Westchester County, New York. A *New York Times* profile of Ms. Pirro, headlined "Leading the Charge and Loving the Lights: Westchester Prosecutor Courts a TV Jury," is bordered with ten photos of Ms. Pirro during television appearances. Using the language of the theater, the *Times* reporter noted, "already the stage seems too small to contain her."[56] Ms. Pirro pays an assistant district attorney to do press relations full-time. The day of her interview with the *Times* reporter, she was on Geraldo Rivera's cable television show arguing that the jury should be permitted to hear evidence of spousal abuse in the O. J. Simpson case. Earlier in the day, she was on a local TV "Live at Five" newscast. As a prominent local defense attorney remarked, "I think Jeanine is probably a D.A. for the 1990's."

By the early 1990s, the country had virtually immersed itself in a world of crime kitsch – one peopled by coifed TV hosts and news readers shedding crocodile tears over the current state of the country while turning human complexity into melodrama.[57] This highly successful exercise shielded the citizenry from the uncomfortable realities that cause and nurture crime, while encouraging them to join in maudlin spectacles that further dull the capacity for civic responsibility. According to TV critic Janet Maslin, America is obsessed with "escapist trivia as a means of avoiding real discourse."[58] Garrison Keillor put it more bluntly: "Every murder turns into 50 episodes. It's as bloody as Shakespeare but without the intelligence and the poetry. If you watch television news you know less about the world than if you drank gin out of a bottle."[59]

As citizens have grown increasingly dependent upon portrayed scenarios rather than authentic experience, the seeds for the culture of kitsch have taken root from New York to California. People are now more liable to shed what the Czech novelist Milan Kundera has named the "second tear." "Kitsch causes two tears to flow in quick succession. The first tear says: How nice to see children running on the grass! The second tear says: How nice to be moved, together with all mankind, by children running on the grass. It is the second tear which makes kitsch kitsch."[60] This "wallowing in emotion" leads nowhere. It is, in William James's words, "the weeping of a Russian lady over the fictitious personages in the play while her coachman is freezing to death on his seat outside."[61]

There is an even darker side to all this – particularly when it becomes a national characteristic. The need to detach oneself from unpleasant realities and to see matters in kitsch-like ways runs deep. Woe betide whoever might question these perceptions by dragging before a kitsch-obsessed public those unpleasant reminders that would tie personal concern to civic responsibility. This is what the criminal represents in such a society – a reminder that all is not right. He must therefore be quickly invalidated and driven from view lest we become aware that we all have a share in the deviance. Behind it all stands a bureaucracy unparalleled in American history, having as its central task the apprehension, labeling, sorting, and managing of the absolute majority of young African-American males.

The Nelson Eddy Effect

The increasingly florid trappings of the criminal justice system are a tacit admission that less and less is happening on the crime front. During my years in the United States Air Force medical service corps, a close friend, a military orthopedic surgeon, observed that his 18 years in service had convinced him that whenever conflicts with other nations flagged, the uniforms of military officers seemed to become more extravagant. Simply joining up made one eligible for an array of epaulets, medals, stripes, and braid, whether or not one had done anything personally to deserve them. "Were we to enter a long stretch of peace," he said, "our generals would start to look like Nelson Eddy in *The Chocolate Soldier.*"

As serious criminal activity in the country goes unaddressed, the formal trappings, ritual, and language of criminal justice assume greater importance – from the robocop attire of SWAT teams to the Speer-like edifices springing up across the country labeled as "justice centers" or "New Generation" jails. The "thin blue line" of police officers holding back the tide of criminals ready to engulf the citizenry, the prison guard working under conditions of stress and danger while he watches over depraved criminals; the ethically driven, conscience-ridden prosecutor of the TV crime show – all these images bear little resemblance to reality.[62]

New York City's commissioner of police expressed concern that most recruits "come in expecting to chase people and do shoot-ups," whereas "the average police officer in America is never going to draw his gun in his entire career."[63] A policeman is at half the risk of death or injury while on the job as is a farmer, fisherman, trucker, or logger, and considerably less at risk than a heavy-construction worker, roofer, or coal miner (the most dangerous job). Likewise, being a prison guard brings about as much risk of injury or death as being a teacher or a nurse. Despite the occasional tragedy, a police officer is no more at risk of a fatal injury while on the job than is an electrician or a construction supervisor. A construction worker is two and a half times, and a taxi driver four times, more likely to be killed while on the job than a police officer.[64]

Notwithstanding the concern about violent crime in the 1980s and 1990s and the putative danger to law-enforcement officers, policing got progressively *less* risky over those two decades. In 1990, there were 66 felonious deaths among the 600,000+ federal, state, and local "sworn" law-enforcement officers. This represented a 40% drop from the number of such deaths in 1980 (104). The number of police in the country had grown by at least 20% in the intervening years. The risk associated with police work had, in fact, declined precipitously from an average annual number of 124 line-of-duty deaths in 1974–1976 to 66 such deaths in 1990–1992.[65] Criminologists Mark Blumberg, Victor Kappeler, and Garry Potter attribute the cultivation of the myth that policing is one of the most dangerous occupations to the fact that it is likely to increase public support for police actions:

Citizens who have an exaggerated sense of the danger that law enforcement personnel routinely confront are more likely to give the police the benefit of the doubt when it comes to various controversies involving the propriety of certain actions ... the public perception that the police are armed and ready to deal with danger 24 hours a day can be beneficial when it is time to engage in contract negotiations (Fyfe, 1982) ... the belief that being a law enforcement officer is akin to the work of a soldier on the frontlines ... this pervasive sense that their mission is a dangerous one cannot help but affect the way that police officers deal with the public.[66]

Despite the fact that there is virtually no relation between the number of police on the streets and crime rates, there is a demand from both political parties for more police equipped with more sophisticated technology. Even were the current federal crime bill to result in 100,000 new police on the streets (in addition to the already existing 600,000), it may not be enough to satisfy the national mood. Adam Walinsky, whose efforts were crucial to obtaining the funding for 100,000 police in the original Clinton anticrime legislation, has called for a minimum of *five million* police nationally.[67] This recalls the old joke about Franco's Spain: with a uniformed policeman or uniformed government guard around every corner, it was a country occupied by itself.

Expedient Politicians

After the burning and looting subsided in Los Angeles in the spring of 1992, politicians of both parties were crawling over one another to assign "root causes." Any hope that the serious problems in urban America would either go away or remain latent until the election had been dashed in a few hours, with ominous portents for other cities around the nation. Los Angeles Police Chief Daryl Gates blamed "criminal gangs." Then President Bush's press secretary, Marlin Fitzwater, attributed the riots to wrong-headed social-welfare programs from a quarter-century back. The vice president suggested that the urban poor had lost their moral fiber because of the social permissiveness of the 1960s, using the acceptance of a single mother on a TV sitcom as an example. Having adopted a strategy to court alienated middle-class white voters, then Democratic presidential candidate Bill Clinton called for a tough-sounding federal crime bill.

Two weeks after the riots, President Bush showcased his "weed and seed" initiative, sandwiching in a visit to the poor, black "Hill" neighborhood of Pittsburgh between a speech to law-enforcement officials at the Washington Monument's Sylvan Theater and a $1,000-a-plate dinner meeting with Pennsylvania Republicans. At the Washington affair, he had said, "We must show less compassion for the criminal and more for the victims of crime." But that note didn't play so well in urban Pittsburgh. "We need your help beyond the weeding part," said Bunny Carter, head of the Three Rivers Employment Agency. "We need more support in the seeding part." A local barber named Napoleon Buice spoke up in a halting voice to tell Bush: "There's people out in the Hill. There's drug addicts out in the Hill that need help. And there are intelligent boys out there who don't have any hope." The president responded by committing $1.1 million in federal funds for law enforcement in Pittsburgh. There were no specific commitments for social programs.

As the 1992 presidential race swung into gear, the successful African-American lawyer, lobbyist, and chairman of the Democratic National Committee, Ron Brown, wrote: "Let's get it all out on the table. Race and crime. Kerosene and a match. Bush and Horton. Republicans since Richard Nixon have 'used' crime as an issue 'better' than we Democrats have. They've 'tied' it well to racial fears and stereotypes, and that has won them many votes."[68] In a variation on a Broadway show tune, "Anything you can do, I can do tougher," Brown noted that Democratic leaders in Congress had proposed 15,000 more federal prison cells than the Bush administration had requested.

Striking that same rich political vein, liberal Massachusetts Democratic Congressman Barney Frank wrote an op-ed piece for the New York Times. "Race and crime together," he wrote, "show the 'notsaposta' syndrome at its worst. Liberals are notsaposta take note publicly of the fact that young black males commit street crimes in a significantly higher proportion than any other major demographic group." Frank concluded, "we liberals have allowed ourselves to be restrained from saying what the public at large wants – and has every right – to hear: that people who assault, rape, rob, or otherwise terrorize others are bad people from whom the innocent majority must be protected."[69]

The political attractiveness of being tough on black men was amply demonstrated by all the major candidates in the 1992 election. Bill Clinton had already proven his willingness to be "tough" by taking a break from his New Hampshire primary campaign to sign the warrant for the execution of a severely brain-damaged black man in Arkansas. Third-party presidential candidate H. Ross Perot hinted at similar draconian measures with reference to defendants accused of drug offenses. Using the war analogy in a "Today Show" appearance, Perot proposed that drug offenders be treated like "prisoners of war" with no bail and no release, apparently until the "war" is over. Describing the soft-authoritarian government of Singapore as a vision of the future, Perot mused that if his proposals for dealing with the drug problem were put in place, the result "won't be pretty." He would have to see if citizens "had the stomach" for his unspecified solutions.

The Culture of Neglect

Shortly after his inauguration in 1968, President Nixon brought Harvard professor Daniel Patrick Moynihan into the White House as his special assistant for domestic affairs. As an assistant secretary of state in the Johnson administration, Moynihan had produced an internal report entitled *The Negro Family*, which called attention to what he saw as the disintegration of the black nuclear family into a "tangle of pathology."

Although heavily criticized by African-American leaders, Moynihan's controversial thesis conditioned the national debate on welfare for the next two decades. A Democrat, and occasionally uneasy in the role in which he had been cast, Moynihan became something of a hero to the newly burgeoning neoconservative movement. At the time, as urban geographer Susan Roberts noted, the idea of a "city life cycle" infused most of the debate on urban policy, and Moynihan's views were consonant with that view.[70] The idea was that cities as presently constituted had probably outlived their usefulness. Roberts traced that concept to the conservative politics of welfare:

During the 1970s and early 1980s, the city life cycle idea is found peppered throughout debates on urban policy and in policy documents themselves. In particular, the city life cycle idea found favor among modern conservatives. The New Right, represented in journals such as *Commentary* and *The Public Interest*, used the city life cycle idea and the related but more vague urban death thesis.[71]

The geographer P. E. Peterson summarized the policy implications of the city life cycle thesis: "For many analysts," he wrote, "especially those with a training in economics, the incapacity of cities to redistribute goods and services is not a cause for alarm. . . . For these scholars industrial societies are plagued by the negative impact on societal productivity of an inefficient public sector. The issues simply require 'benign neglect.' "[72] The economic and social deterioration occurring in the cities was seen as inevitable and, in the long view, even desirable.

A variation on this theme was proposed by what the journalist Roger Starr termed "planned shrinkage." Starr who, along with Moynihan, Murray, Krauthammer, and Wilson, served on the publications committee of the conservative journal *The Public Interest*, proposed that the country simply recognize the fact that cities were going to shrink in population and that we begin cutting back on services to help the process along, thereby realizing the savings.[73] Another influential journalist, urban commentator Marvin Stone, proposed that the big cities be left to die.[74] The British magazine the *Economist*, considering the deterioration occurring in the South Bronx, was more direct: "The bleak truth is that this is the natural and inevitable consequence of a shrinking city. The destruction, poverty and hopelessness that cluster around the burnt-out wrecks is abhorrent. That something should be done to stop it is the immediate reaction. That something should be done to speed it up is nearer the mark."[75]

Indeed, by 1995, there were indications that a strategy of "planned shrinkage" was being put into place in New York City by the Giuliani administration. In an article aptly headlined "Honey, I Shrunk N.Y.: Does Mayor Giuliani Have a Secret Plan to Drive the Poor Out of the City?" the *Washington Post's* New York City bureau chief, Malcolm Gladwell, wrote that something had happened in New York that was "so strange that people here still don't know quite what to make of it." Republican governor George Pataki and New York City mayor Rudoph Giuliani had both asked for deeper cuts in welfare and Medicaid. For every dollar the governor cut, New York City saved 25 cents. However, it seemed illogical to give up 75 cents of someone else's money in order to save 25 cents of your own. Gladwell proposed "a much more sinister explanation, one that says as much about so-called 'welfare experiments' now going on around the country as it does about New York City politics." Giuliani and Pataki had set out to solve New York's poverty problem simply by slashing the state's welfare system and driving the poor from the state. It was a strategy that had first been proposed in the 1960s by conservative columnist William F. Buckley, Jr., in his run for mayor. "The half million plus people in New York City who are unemployed and/or on relief do not contribute anything tangible to the city's welfare," he said. "What is the point in encouraging them to stay, when they might go elsewhere?"[76]

The Myth of the "Era of Rehabilitation"

The great myth of the 1990s debate on crime and corrections – a myth that justified the country's investment in policies of deterrence and incapacitation – was that we had tried rehabilitation in the 1960s and 1970s and it hadn't worked. Having served at the cabinet level for three governors and having run two of the ten largest states' youth correctional agencies (Massachusetts and Pennsylvania) and another's child welfare agency (Illinois), I learned long ago that the only way to judge commitment to a policy is to follow the budget. When that exercise is completed, one can only conclude that, even in the heyday of putative permissiveness, the bulk of criminal justice budgets went to arrest, prosecute, and imprison offenders. Alternative diversionary and rehabilitative programs were, at best, small appendages to the massive state institutional budgets geared to incapacitate and deter.

The truth is that there never was a shining hour of even minimal retreat from basic reliance on jails, prisons, and detention centers. President Johnson's Crime Commission had called for the nation to take a different direction, stressing the need for preventive programs, alternatives to incarceration, and diverting of the young from the justice system whenever possible within the constraints of public safety. James Vorenberg, the executive director of the Johnson Commission, summarized its goals in this way: "to show how police, courts, and correctional agencies could *both reduce crime and treat people more decently [by lowering] the level of hostility between the police and young people, particularly blacks*" (emphasis added).

Although planners like Vorenberg and the criminologists who acted as consultants to the Johnson Commission conceived these new approaches to crime, their proposals never got off the ground. The legislation that resulted from the commission's recommendations was passed, but it fell to the Nixon administration to implement it. Attorney General John Mitchell, who had led the strident 1968 "law and order" campaign for Nixon, told a House subcommittee, "No problem is of higher priority than the ever increasing crime in our nation." Crime increased 30% in the first three years of the Nixon administration. The Nixon-appointed administrators of the newly established Law Enforcement Assistance Administration (LEAA) set about funding the very approaches the Johnson Commission had sought to undo. As an article published in *The Nation* in late 1970 put it, "The Cops Hit the Jackpot."[77]

By the second year of the Nixon administration, a concerned Vorenberg wrote: "It would be a tragic mistake to assume that we can look to the law-enforcement system to control crime. . . . The view that the level of crime is determined less by law enforcement than by the extent to which we make life worthwhile for those at the bottom of the economic and social ladder is not a partisan one."[78] Noting that the Johnson Commission had among its members such staunch conservatives as former Secretary of State William Rogers and Nixon's subsequent Supreme Court nominee Lewis Powell, Vorenberg pointed out that these men "[had] no doubt whatever that the most significant action that can be taken against crime is action designed to eliminate slums and ghettos, to improve education, to provide jobs, to make sure that every American is given the opportunities and freedoms that will enable him to assume his responsibilities." Vorenberg then accurately predicted where things would head: "The country seems to be proceeding on the contrary assumption. Against the background of the tremendous increase in crime committed by blacks, whatever notions of fiscal soundness or social justice are thought to underlie the Administration's apparent acceptance of Daniel P. Moynihan's proposal for 'benign neglect' of blacks, that policy seems almost certain to have disastrous effects on crime."

In a style that was to become de rigueur in an increasingly politicized Justice Department, after Vorenberg's comments appeared in the *Atlantic,* the Center for Criminal Justice he then headed at Harvard Law School was threatened with loss of its Justice Department grants.[79] Annual funding for the Department of Justice, FBI, and LEAA reached more than $3.4 billion before disillusionment with the LEAA set in during the late 1970s and its allocations were cut. However, by 1980 annual funding was still at $2.6 billion.

Two decades after his original call for benign neglect of urban areas, Daniel Patrick Moynihan (by now a senator) looked out again upon the urban terrain and, in a highly publicized article in *The American Scholar,* suggested that America's troubles were the result of our society having become too tolerant of uncivil and criminal behavior.[80] We were "defining down" deviance. James Q. Wilson was saying much the same thing – giving the subject an ever so slightly genetic (and, by implication, racial) twist.[81] Moynihan's thesis, this time drawn from the work of the 19th-century French sociologist Emile Durkheim and of the contemporary American anthropologist Kai Erickson, was that a society can stand only so much social deviance. When overloaded with unacceptable behavior on all sides, it redefines matters, making "acceptable" what was formerly "unacceptable" so as to keep social deviance within bounds and at a relatively fixed level. In a related speech entitled "Toward a New Intolerance," delivered before the Association for a Better New York and published in *The Public Interest,* Moynihan amplified his views:

[When] I settled down to work on the *American Scholar* article . . . I remembered the St. Valentine's Day Massacre. I have a World Book Encyclopedia, a wonderful thing. I looked it up. The St. Valentine's Day Massacre in 1929 in Chicago has two entries in the World Book Encyclopedia. Two. Along with the Battle of Thermopylae and things like that. The country was outraged. Al Capone had sent four of his men dressed as police. They rubbed out seven of Bugs Moran's men. All adults; they knew what they were up to and in for. But it shocked the country. We changed the Constitution. We said this was not acceptable behavior.[82]

Moynihan then went on to decry a contemporary society that had lost its sense of outrage. Citing Wilson, he noted that "Los Angeles has the equivalent of a St. Valentine's Day Massacre every weekend." In some ways, Moynihan was correct. For example, the overall national homicide rate (the crime most likely to be reported and the best barometer of violence in a society) was as high in 1929 as it

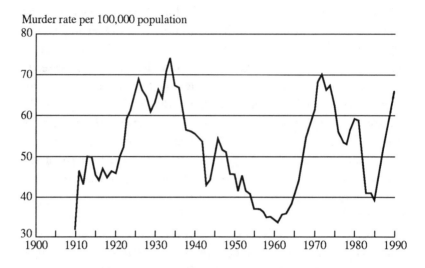

Figure 8. Homicide rates for nonwhite males, 1910–1990. *Source*: Adapted from Paul Holinger, *Violent Deaths in the United States: An Epidemiologic Study of Suicide, Homicide, and Accidents* (New York and London: Guilford Press, 1987), pp. 209–210; and Albert J. Reiss, Jr., and Jeffrey A. Roth, *Understanding and Preventing Violence* (Washington, D.C.: National Academy Press), p. 50.

was in the late 1980s.[83] But of particular relevance to the racial issues implicit in Moynihan's discussion was the fact that homicide rates among African-American males (as measured by victimization rates) were higher in the putative halcyon days of the early 1930s than they were throughout most of the 1980s and early 1990s. Homicide rates for nonwhite males spanning the half-century from 1930 to 1990 reached their all-time high in this country *in 1934*, after having soared earlier in the century at a pace equaling or outstripping recent growth in violent crime.[84] Homicide victimization for nonwhite males was as high in 1934 as it was throughout most of the 1980s.[85]

It is likely that a significantly higher percentage of black males were killed in the 1920s and 1930s by white men than was probably the case in the late 1980s and early 1990s, when it appeared that black victims of homicide were more likely to have been killed by other blacks. This puts Moynihan's thesis in a somewhat different light, however. Although he acknowledges that in the wake of the St. Valentine's Day Massacre the country changed the Constitution, he implied that the nation responded by sending a strong message that it would not allow the violence to continue. As he would have it, the citizenry stood up and said, "No more!" In reality, the government had further "defined down" deviance by abolishing Prohibition, thereby legalizing behaviors that for the previous fourteen years had been illegal.

Although Moynihan had drawn his thesis from Durkheim's theory, he downplayed Durkheim's more important point: that should actual criminal behavior recede, new crimes would be legislated to ensure that the populace could easily identify the enemy.[86] This is not to suggest that American society had at any point freed itself of crime. However, there is ample evidence that during the years in which crime rates were falling, the criminal justice system had a life of its own – growing exponentially in a manner virtually unrelated to patterns of rising criminal behavior. Over the past three decades, the tendency has been toward extending the net of justice control ever more widely into the community where traditionally other agents of social control defined matters (e.g., family, church, school, etc.). Criminal justice saturation of minority urban areas came to be most strongly supported by the majority white population, few of whom lived in the inner cities.

Indeed, in light of the victimization surveys, which for 20 years had found a stable or falling crime rate in the nation, one could argue that the swath cut by the justice system had little to do with stemming violent or serious crime. Rather, while it chipped away at the edges, millions of African-American and Hispanic young men accused of lesser offenses were formally dragged into the justice system – individuals who earlier would more likely have been dealt with informally – by friends, families, churches, schools, and other traditional groups and agencies of socialization. This had little to do with "defining down" or ignoring deviance. The arrest statistics among African-Americans and the poor suggested that very little was being overlooked by the police.

Investing in the Industry

It remained for the Reagan and Bush administrations and a cowed Democratic Congress to deliver the final coup de grâce to any brief flirtations with alternative approaches to controlling crime. Federal, state, and local funding for justice (police, judicial, prosecutors, public defenders, and corrections) rose from about $11.7 billion in 1972 to $62 billion by 1988. In 1981, there were 54,422 employees in the U.S. Justice Department; by 1992, there were almost 100,000. In 1988, $3.1 billion was going to the federal "war on drugs" alone. By 1989, it was $4.7 billion, and by 1992 the federal government was spending $11 billion annually. And in the hysteria surrounding crime in 1993, the Democrat-controlled United States Senate passed a $22.5 billion Crime Bill – the bulk of which went to new prisons and police. Even this was not sufficient to fit the tenor of the times. As of this writing, the new Republican majority House of Representatives had revised it to take out the so-called prevention monies and transfer an additional $3 billion to building prisons. A kind of "criminal justice–industrial complex" was being set in place. Nationally, criminal justice expenditures were soaring into the hundreds of billions. This in itself would come to be a major driving force for anticrime legislation – unrelated either to law and order or crime rates.

Meanwhile, as cities continued their downward spiral and social-welfare programs fell more deeply into national disfavor, the country turned to the justice system to pick up the pieces. The centerpiece of law enforcement was its preoccupation with highly visible groups who could be relatively easily and *publicly* arrested. The crown jewel was the handcuffed black youth or young man paraded before TV cameras so all might behold this symbol of lawlessness and disorder.

Genuine rehabilitation flows from relationships and a predisposition to care on the part of those who dispense it. That is now impossible when it comes to young offenders. Indeed, we have reached a point where rare or occasional concern must be camouflaged by pseudo-macho rhetoric. Boot camps confirm the metaphor of the black man in need of taming – one whose "reform" rests in his keepers' ability to make him run, jump about "double time," and, on command, to spout back "Yes, sir!" and "No, sir!" as ersatz "drill instructors" heap abuse on their charges.[87]

The Great Divide

The Wall Street Journal suggested that the Los Angeles riots placed in "stark relief" the divisions between black and white, rich and poor, suburban and urban:

growing up in the 1960s and 1970s, liberal children of conservative parents vowed they would be different. In fact, many of them have become so detached that the cognoscenti have a phrase for them: "People Like Us," or "PLUs". . . . It means "People Like Us" as opposed to "People Like Them" – who we find threatening. It's a term of distinction, exclusion, and lately, it stresses defensiveness and escapism.[88]

Noting the great gap between the public's perception of crime and the realities of crime, the *Journal* headlined a front-page article on the subject, "People with the Least to Fear from Crime Drive the Crime Issue." The *Journal* cited a 1992 survey conducted by the Joint Center for Political and Economic Studies, which found that suburban upper-income blacks were more likely to see crime as a critical issue than were low-income blacks in urban areas.[89] As if to reinforce this view, in the New York mayoral election of 1993, those boroughs with the highest crime rates and in which citizens were more likely to be victimized by violent crime voted for the incumbent David Dinkins, rejecting the harsh "law-and-order" rhetoric of Rudolph Giuliani, whereas the whiter and the more removed voters were from high-crime areas, the more likely they were to vote for Giuliani.

Similarly, hundreds of suburban whites bought guns in the wake of the Los Angeles riots, even though the disturbances never came close to their neighborhoods – all this despite the fact that, in a detailed survey of the 75 largest urban counties, over 80% of both white and black murder defendants had a victim of the same racial background and 8 out of every 10 were killed by relatives or acquaintances.[90] As Northeastern University criminologist James Fox commented to a reporter, "One of the worst things affecting our feeling of safety was probably the development of the video camera."[91] University of Pennsylvania communications researcher George Gerbner, who had collected data on 20 years of television and movie violence, told the reporter that "violence on television is vastly exaggerated compared to real life and has a totally different demography." Noting that there were an average of six to eight acts of violence per hour in prime time, with two murders per night, Gerbner was less concerned that this might stimulate real-life violence than he was alarmed over how it exaggerated "feelings of insecurity, dependence and fear" – mostly among middle-class whites.

The policy implications of this are immense. Whereas black ghetto residents identify jobs or the economy as their first concern, suburbanites identify theirs as violent crime.[92] As the *New York Times* noted, urban residents who were the most likely to have to contend with real-life crime seemed to be more able to separate fact from fantasy.[93] When it came to developing policy and legislation to combat crime, those who were least likely to be victims of serious crime ended up defining the debate, while those most likely to be personally victimized by crime were for the most part excluded. Had they been included, it is more likely that the discussion would have centered more on "root causes," particularly unemployment. In effect, crime control came to mean finding the best way to deal with "people like them."

In 1969, Attorney General John Mitchell advised observers to "watch what we *do*, not what we say." It proved to be good advice. The effect on crime of all this Sturm und Drang has been minimal. However, the social detritus left behind has been considerable. As a result, arrest and jailing is now routinely proposed as the optimum means of dealing with a growing range of personal, economic, and social problems, from family breakdown to alcoholism, welfare, homelessness, mental illness, child abuse, and school failure – all problems often exacerbated by criminal justice handling. Beneath the cacophony of threat and demagoguery, the politics of crime has finally proved to be the politics of race.

5

Race, "Applied Science," and Public Policy

The Case of the Criminaloid

Coauthored by the late Harvard psychologist Richard Herrnstein and neoconservative Charles Murray, *The Bell Curve: Intelligence and Class Structure in American Life*[1] was published in November of 1994, setting forth the controversial view that blacks as a group are seriously disadvantaged, if not cursed, in modern industrial society because of their low IQs – mostly a result of fixed genetic endowment. *The Bell Curve* contained no original research but was a guided tour through the selected work of others, often of greatly differing expertise and ideology.[2] The book was a bestseller virtually upon release; within 60 days, there were 400,000 copies in print.[3]

Virtually none of the assertions on the genetics of race and IQ in *The Bell Curve* emanated from molecular geneticists. The cited studies for the most part were associated with "behavioral genetics" based in statistical methods of regression analysis tying the artificial construct of IQ to various life outcomes. As University of California sociologist Troy Duster wryly observed:

Arthur Jensen, who vaulted to national fame with a claim on the relationship between genetics and intelligence, is an educational psychologist. . . .

David Rowe and Sarnoff Mednick, who argue the genetic basis for crime, and [H. J.] Eysenck, who argues the genetic basis of psychopathology and intelligence, are all psychologists. Richard Herrnstein (a psychologist) has not only argued the genetics of intelligence, but has even speculated that "the tendency to be unemployed may run in the genes." Herrnstein . . . teamed with James Q. Wilson, a political scientist . . . ask for a more sympathetic reading of the possible "biological roots of an individual's predisposition to crime." . . . Each of these men lays considerable claim, and achieved considerable attention in the popular media postulating the importance of heredity in the explication of human behavior.[4]

A vastly more important study based in genetic data culled from blood samples worldwide was published by Princeton University Press at about the same time *The Bell Curve* appeared. However, the landmark 16-year study by Stanford University population geneticist Luca Cavalli-Sforza and his coresearchers Paolo Menozzi and Alberto Piazza, entitled *The History and Geography of Human Genes*, went unnoticed at the time.[5] These geneticists concluded that once the genes for coloration and stature are dealt with, the differences between and among individuals are so great as to render the concept of "race" virtually meaningless. In his presentation to the American Association for the Advancement of Science in February 1995, Cavalli-Sforza commented on the notion that genetics has made one race more intelligent than another: "The truth is," he said, "that there is no documented biological superiority of any race however defined. There are some superficial traits like skin color and body build. They are striking and we notice them. That is what misleads us. It makes us think races are very different. They are not, when we look under the skin." Cavalli-Sforza noted that he had found the biggest genetic differences between African and Australian aborigines, despite the fact that many aborigines have skin as black as many Africans.[6]

Noting that *The Bell Curve* contained no new arguments and presented no compelling data, Harvard paleontologist Stephen Jay Gould concluded that the book's success "must reflect the depressing temper of our times – a historical moment of unprecedented ungenerosity, when a mood for slashing social programs can be powerfully abetted by an argument that beneficiaries cannot be helped, owing to inborn cognitive limits expressed as low IQ scores."[7] The popularity of *The Bell Curve* was not to be found in the scientific rigor of the studies, nor in the equivocal assertions regarding race and IQ by the surviving author in his talk-show book tour, but in the feasibility of the implicit policy imperatives. The process was particularly familiar to Murray. In the mid-1980s, a tract on welfare he produced for The Heritage Foundation was turned into another best-selling book, *Losing Ground.* The marketing strategy, as described by journalist Sydney Blumenthal, was put in place by Murray's conservative funders to create a "classic" before the research was done. As Sydney Blumenthal noted, with some irony, "Conservatives, after all, do not blindly invest their hopes in the marketplace of ideas; they prefer marketing to natural selection."[8] The effort was highly successful. *Losing Ground* redefined the political debate on welfare policy.

Whether *The Bell Curve* will have equal influence is still open. Its frankly racial premises (also at the heart of *Losing Ground,* though better disguised) present a somewhat greater challenge to the opinion makers of the Right. However, the fact that Murray was invited as a principal speaker to the December 1994 orientation meeting for the incoming "freshman" class of newly elected Republican congressmen suggests that it is not likely to be as much of a political chore as some might have thought. Murray clearly had things other than scientific enlightenment in mind for *The Bell Curve.* Lewis Lapham notes that, in the original manuscript submitted to two separate publishers, "Murray didn't mince words about the bigotry that he meant to confirm and sustain." "[There are] a huge number of well-meaning whites who fear that they are closet racists," wrote Murray, "and this book tells them they are not. It's going to make them feel better about things they already think but do not know how to say."[9]

An End to Ideology?

The average observer presumes that we formulate enlightened public policy by researching the issue and drawing conclusions accordingly. It seldom happens that way. When it comes to criminal justice policy, matters work in precisely the reverse order with the ideological tail wagging the probabilities dog.

As Cambridge University political scientist Quentin Skinner has observed, one of the first victims of social-science positivism was the "end-of-ideology" argument. "[T]o claim that politics is a purely technological affair, and thus that ideology must have come to an end," writes Skinner, "has the effect of grounding the stability and even the legitimacy of the state on its capacity to maintain a high level of technological success."[10] It amounted, he said, "to little more than an ideological reading of consensus politics, one in which silence was (recklessly, as it turned out) taken for agreement."[11] The process lent support to the late British psychiatrist Ronald Laing's thesis that the theories we devise to label those who threaten us are, in fact, "social prescriptions."[12] In effect, we take stock of what we are already disposed to do, assess the political landscape, and create our scientific rationales accordingly.

Citing the social theorist Jürgen Habermas, who stressed the need for social researchers openly to acknowledge the political and ideological worlds within which they operate and from which they come (and, one might add, which fund them), Skinner notes that researchers who acknowledge their ideological bent can at least be confronted at that level and can defend their arguments accordingly.[13] However, Herrnstein and Murray insisted that they were not making an ideological statement. Our contemporary situation is, in many ways, analogous to that which prevailed earlier in the century, during the heyday of the American eugenics movement. As historian Stefan Kuhl has noted, at the time "pure" research scientists were indistinguishable from "applied science" ideologues. He attributes this to the "complex interaction between science and politics within the various branches of the American eugenics movement" of the time.[14] The proliferation over the past two decades of ideologically inspired "think tanks" has fueled a similar process. Despite their positivistic pretensions, they have spawned a generation of politically inspired researchers and commentators who are obsessed with the means to predetermined ends. Distinguishing the scientist with an ideological agenda from the politician in search of validation grows more difficult day by day. It has blurred our understanding of a wide range of social issues. In the case of loaded issues like IQ, race, and crime, the distinctions between science and ideology all but disappear.

Gould characterized *The Bell Curve* as a latter-day version of the previously discredited "social Darwinism" that followed the publication in 1859 of Darwin's seminal work popularly referred to as *The Origin of Species*.[15] Its full title gives some presaging of the directions in which matters might turn: "On the Origin of Species by Means of Natural Selection, or the Preservation of Favoured Races in the Struggle for Life." The American critic and philosopher Jacques Barzun characterized its publication as being "greater as an event than as a book . . . as much because of what it brought seething out of the European mind, as because of what it put into it."[16] Among the theories it bred was the view that the "Mongol" and the "Negro" were but human saurians who had long ago reached their full development and were now "moral fossils," and that the missing link between the chimpanzee and the Negro was the idiot.[17]

The Case of the "Born Criminal"

Given the policy implications of *The Bell Curve*, it might be useful to look briefly at one strand of its genetic presuppositions – namely, that the *criminal* is innately predisposed to crime – as that view wound its way from "applied" research into public policy earlier in the century and as it appears once again to have become an unuttered premise of contemporary criminal justice policy in America. In this arena, society's predispositions are decidedly more critical than any putative innate criminal tendency in an offender. It all gives an odd sense to the recurring "Aha!" in societies under stress that the criminal is, after all, a different breed, if not a subhuman species (as one well-known forensic psychiatrist has recently suggested).[18] Those who would lead us down this path characteristically start by suggesting biology and end in shouting race. As Duster had predicted, with our prisons getting darker and darker it would only be a matter of time before there would be "a convergence of the halo of the new genetics and the appropriation of that halo by other researchers."[19]

In their 1985 book, *Crime and Human Nature*, James Q. Wilson joined with Harvard School of Education psychologist Richard Herrnstein to raise the old idea that genes, IQ (and race) seriously influence criminal behavior.[20] The book tested what the public market might bear when it came to genetic and implicitly racial explanations for socially unacceptable behavior. As it turned out, opinion makers and the press were unusually receptive to such theories. Like *The Bell Curve*, *Crime and Human Nature* was a best-seller (a rare occurrence for a criminological text). Its positive reception in the popular media also breathed new life into the old canard that the way a society perceives the convicted criminal is as good a barometer as any of what that society is all about and where it is headed.[21]

The great crusades against crime and drugs of the late 1980s and early 1990s rather quickly produced sufficient numbers of demons, savages, and psychopaths against whom to rally the national will. Though there were some political glitches as it appeared that the country's new enemies tended to have dark skin, the refurbished biological theories of criminal behavior gave us leave to ignore this. We were invited to dismiss whatever out-of-date liberal guilt we might still entertain over the societal conditions that accompany crime and deviance and lie back. It wasn't long before the

same genetic imps which had been confined to their cages since the
late 1930s were once again set loose to roam the terrain.

The Wilson/Herrnstein thesis, with its emphasis upon such contentions as the insensitivity of criminals to pain and the supposed
low IQs of criminals, though couched in the civil language of management and careful politics, was in fact very close to the traditions
of earlier 20th-century theory on crime, genes, and race.[22] Before
the invention of the IQ test, British sex researcher Havelock Ellis,
for example, had tied innate criminality to mental retardation and
consequent insensibility. "[T]he instinctive criminal resembles the
idiot," he wrote, "to whom pain is 'a welcome surprise.' " Leaping
quickly to matters of race, he concluded that the criminal "may be
compared with the many lower races, such as those Maoris who did
not hesitate to chop off a toe or two, in order to be able to wear
European boots."[23]

The 19th-century criminologist Cesare Lombroso was equally
forthright. "The characteristics found in savages and among the
colored races," he wrote, "are also to be found in habitual delinquents." The putative insensibility to pain of criminals, for example, recalled "that of savage peoples who can bear in rites of
puberty, tortures that a white man could never endure. . . . All
travelers know the indifference of Negroes and American savages
to pain," he commented. "[T]he former cut their hands and laugh
in order to avoid work; the latter, tied to the torture post, gaily
sing the praises of their tribe while they are slowly burnt."[24] The
research questions being posed were in the tradition of earlier
organic and genetic theories of social deviance like those of the
American physician Samuel Cartwright who sought to prove that
"Negroes consume less oxygen than white people" and that slaves
suffered from "drapetomania" – that is, "an insane desire to run
away."[25]

The consequent diagnoses came with their own set of political
premises and social policy imperatives. Lombroso put this view
succinctly. "[T]he white races," he wrote, "represented the tri-

umph of the human species, its hitherto most perfect advancement." As historian Daniel Pick noted, the theories provided a rationale for a political response to social instability – in Lombroso's case, the threat to southern Europe from the "Dark Continent" of Africa and the need to control a "riotous peasantry" within Italy itself. Lombroso's schema allowed political authorities to comprehend the rabble scientifically while excluding them politically.[26]

Similar views had great currency in American penal practice. As A. J. McKelway, Secretary for the Southern States of the National Child Labor Committee, asserted in his 1910 report to the International Prison Congress: "One subject for discussion is . . . whether or not the Negro race can be fitly governed under Anglo-Saxon law. . . . Whether this ignoring of racial differences is the best thing for the Negro in America is a question which I am sure must finally occupy the thoughtful consideration of humane and patriotic men."[27] But it wasn't simply a matter of innate inadequacies: it also had to do with innate evil.

This conception stalked the fictional netherworld as well. As Pick observed, Oscar Wilde's *The Picture of Dorian Gray*, Robert Louis Stevenson's *The Strange Case of Dr. Jekyll and Mr. Hyde*, and Bram Stoker's *Dracula* were "all based in the ideas and prejudices of the time regarding the physiognomy of 'degeneration.' "[28] As Pick further notes, to upper- and middle-class whites of the late 19th century, the term "degenerate" applied to *all* those of color. However, there were other physical signs as well. As Lombroso had put it in "The White Man and the Coloured Man" (1871), "Only we White people [*Noi soli Bianchi*] have reached the most perfect symmetry of bodily form."[29]

Consider Wilde's vision of Dorian Gray moving about "this grey monstrous London, flitting between 'polite' society and a grotesque East End underworld peopled by 'hideous' Jews, 'half-castes,' opium addicts, prostitutes and alcoholics – a vast gallery of 'monstrous marionettes' and 'squat, misshapen figure[s].' "[30] Stoker said it another way, describing Count Dracula as "a criminal . . .

predestinate to crime." He wrote: "This criminal has not full man-brain. He is clever and cunning and resourceful; but he be not of man-stature as to brain. He be of child-brain in much . . . Lombroso would classify him, and *qua* criminal he is of imperfectly formed mind."[31]

Indeed, Herrnstein immersed himself in the foggy Victorian world. As he told a *Baltimore Sun* reporter in 1986, it was no accident that the potion which changed the law-abiding Dr. Jekyll into the criminal Mr. Hyde "also made him pale and dwarfish . . . stooped . . . with a ferret, animal-like face."[32] Of course, there has never been a dearth of those willing to describe criminals as animal-like, devilish-appearing, or simian. Take this 1940s description of a young Jewish offender by a New York City prosecutor: "[H]e had a round face, thick lips, a flat nose and small ears, stuck close to his kinky hair. His arms had not waited for the rest of him. They dangled to his knees, completing a generally gorilla-like figure. He was, investigators concluded, 'an animal in human guise.' "[33]

Proper Breeding

In the late 1800s, a committee of biologists associated with the American Breeders' Association was formed to promote "the value of superior blood" and warn of "the menace to society of inferior blood."[34] It formed the nucleus for what would become the eugenics movement in America. In 1896, as part of a state-sponsored breeding strategy, Connecticut began regulating marriage, making it a crime punishable by three years in prison for a feeble-minded woman to marry or have extramarital relationships if she was under age 45. Kansas, New Jersey, Ohio, Michigan, and Indiana followed suit, forbidding marriage to a wider range of persons: the insane, syphilitic, alcoholic, epileptic, and criminal.[35] However, these marriage laws came under fire from some quarters for reasons of practicability. Martin W. Barr, chief physician at the Pennsylvania School for Feeble-Minded Children at Elwyn, complained in 1904 that the laws were not sufficient to the task of gathering up "the waifs and strays, the vicious and lawless, and above all the unrecognized, unsuspected defectives in all ranks of society."[36] Protection of society demanded that the laws be further extended to allow authorities to "desex" the unfit if we were to avoid tainting future generations. Asexualization was seen as both a cure and a deterrent.

The medical profession occasionally proceeded with the eugenic agenda without benefit of enabling legislation. Dr. F. Hoyt Pilcher, superintendent of the Kansas State Home for the Feeble-Minded, claimed great success in castrating 44 boys and removing the ovaries of 14 girls at his facility.[37] In a 1905 report on the good effects his method had had on 88 boys and youths ages 14 to 22, he noted that, "In every case, there was a marked mental and physical improvement, the children growing stout, and acquiring large frames. There was no hair on the pubes or face, and the cheeks became round and prominent; indeed, they resemble large women."[38] Among those who were castrated was one boy who had "solicit[ed] women on the road, and was extremely vulgar." According to Pilcher, after the operation, the youth improved "in temper and habits" and became "languid in movements," developing "a most excellent soprano singing voice."[39]

Involuntary sterilization through vasectomy eventually replaced surgical castration. In 1899, Dr. Harry Sharp the physician superintendent of the Indiana Reformatory in Jeffersonville, first performed a vasectomy on a boy to break him of his habit of masturbating four to ten times a day. Sharp went on to sterilize 300 more delinquent boys. Like his counterparts in Kansas, he recommended the practice as "both a punishment and a way of helping individuals to control their criminal proclivities."[40]

In 1907, Indiana passed a bill making mandatory the sterilization of confirmed criminals, idiots, imbeciles, and rapists in state institutions when recommended by a board of experts.[41] The doctor and board of managers of the institution decided each case and proceeded accordingly. As the populace grew concerned about the so-called dangerous classes, eugenic measures were seen as applying to an ever-widening range of individuals and classes – including criminals, Negroes, idiots, tramps, poor farmers, slum dwellers, unskilled laborers, and immigrants, all of whom were seen as engulfing "the intelligent elite." Eugenic procedures were also prescribed for victimless crime as a deterrent to "accentuat[e] the social dangers of 'vice' and 'debauchery.' "[42]

Unsexing African-Americans

It was recommended that these procedures be applied in massive fashion when it came to African-Americans. Many influential southern whites had long favored castration and sterilization as a protection for white women from rape by black men. Rape was the "New Negro Crime" attributable to black frustration at not gaining social equality during Reconstruction. In 1906, southern newspapers waged a campaign calling for the castration of all black men who had been involved in incidents with white women. Although there was no record of any such trend, blacks were portrayed as "avid rapists of white women." Some newspapers proposed that, as a preventive measure, all black women be "unsexed" early in life to forestall the rise of another generation of rapists.[43]

When it came to stemming criminal behavior among blacks, the eugenic procedures were fashioned in such a manner as to be as excruciatingly painful as possible. As Dr. Jesse Ewell wrote in a Virginia medical journal, "castrate the criminal, cut off both ears close to his head and turn him loose to go where he will."[44] In addition to emasculation for black males and ovariotomies for black females, physicians recommended genital and other maiming.[45] Another physician concluded that "the violator loses not only the desire, but the capacity for a repetition of his crime, if the operation [castration] be supplemented by penile mutilation according to the Oriental method." He noted that "[t]he fierce criminal would become mild" as a result of this treatment, and might even "become a useful member of society as a clergyman, choir singer, or dry nurse."[46]

In 1909, California enacted its version of what would come in the 1990s to be called "three strikes and you're out" legislation. The law mandated the "asexualization" of prisoners who had been committed twice for sexual offenses, three times for any other crime, or were serving a life sentence if the inmate demonstrated while in prison "that he is a moral or sexual pervert."[47]

"The Howls of the Demos"

In their 1928 book, *The New Criminology: A Consideration of the Chemical Causation of Abnormal Behavior*,[48] Max Schlapp, a professor of neuropathology at the New York Graduate Medical School, and Edward Smith, a mystery writer, posited the theory that crime is caused by glandular disturbances resulting in chemical imbalances in the blood and lymph of the criminal's mother during pregnancy. As Friedman points out, when it came to criminals, there seemed to be "a burning faith in glandular tinkering" of all kinds. The chief surgeon in San Quentin prison in California performed more than 10,000 "testicular implantations" in that one prison alone between 1918 and 1940.[49]

The political philosophy underlying Schlapp and Smith's approach to crime was based in the same meritocratic paradigms that underlay the theories of Wilson and Herrnstein. Unlike their modern counterparts, however, Schlapp and Smith unashamedly laid out the social prescriptions their theories demanded. "In spite of the howls of the demos," they wrote, "mankind probably must go back to some sort of caste system founded on productiveness, upon ability, upon service to the state."[50] As an individual's ability to produce was central to such a political philosophy, virtually any physical malady would suffice for eugenic intervention if it were combined with criminal behavior. Schlapp and Smith's policy recommendations for the criminal victims of maternal blood imbalance were relatively straightforward: euthanasia, compulsory treatment for defectives, registration, sterilization, and forced labor.

The British satirist G. K. Chesterton put these matters in context, "At root," he noted, "the eugenist [sic] is the employer." Chesterton saw eugenics as the logical outgrowth of unfettered capitalism, the question posed by his biographer: "what to do with the masses of wretched, half-starved, stunted 'unemployables' in the slums of the great cities?" As Chesterton put it:

In short, people decided that it was impossible to achieve any of the good of Socialism, but they comforted themselves by achieving all the bad. All that official discipline, about which the Socialists themselves were in doubt or at least on the defensive, was taken over bodily by the Capitalists. They have now added all the bureaucratic tyrannies of a social state to the old plutocratic tyrannies of a Capitalist state. For the vital point is that it did not in the smallest degree diminish the inequalities of a Capitalist State. It simply destroyed such individual liberties as remained among its victims. [51]

Indeed, the nostrums do not seem to change very much over the years. In the wake of the controversy surrounding the publication of *The Bell Curve,* the editor of the newsletter of the Los Angeles chapter of the high-IQ society, Mensa, suggested more direct routes to controlling the underclass, proposing that the homeless "should be humanely done away with, like abandoned kittens." Another Mensa writer widened the population at risk to include "those people who are so mentally defective that they cannot live in society," who "should," so he wrote, "as soon as they are identified as defective, be humanely dispatched."[52]

Quod licet Jovi non licet bovi

The idea of desexing criminals emerged again in the 1970s. Ernest Rodin, a neurologist in charge of Detroit's well-known Lafayette Clinic Project, recommended castrating "dumb young males who riot."[53] Again, race was not mentioned. Psychosurgery alone, however, was not enough for this group. It only ensured, said Rodin, that "the now hopefully more placid dullard can inseminate other equally dull young females to produce further dull and aggressive offsprings."[54] Rodin put his proposals for urban peace in rural terms. "Farmers have known for ages immemorial that you can't do a blasted thing with a bull except fight or kill and eat him," he said. "[T]he castrated ox will pull his plow; . . . It is also well known that human eunuchs, although at times quite scheming entrepreneurs, are not given to physical violence."[55]

Touting what he called an "authoritarian life style," Rodin declared that "[t]olerance and encouragement of free thought is probably excellent for the high IQ Bracket, but not advisable for the lower one." He argued that children of limited intelligence tend to become violent when treated as equals. "Quod licet Jovi non licet bovi [what is allowed for Jupiter is not allowed for the ox]," he wrote. "The problem is that the ox may not recognize himself as an ox and demand Jupiter's prerogatives."[56] Rodin's comments resonated with Wilson's mockery of "egalitarian impulses"[57] and Schlapp and Smith's contempt for the "howls of the demos."

In the wake of the urban unrest of the late 1960s, a number of respected psychiatrists and psychosurgeons had advocated neuroleptic drugs and, in selected cases, brain surgery for violent rioters. Drs. Vernon Mark, W. H. Sweet, and Frank Ervin published their proposal in the *Journal of the American Medical Association*, headlined "The Role of Brain Disease in Riots and Urban Violence."[58] They concluded that many of those who engaged in rioting probably suffered from brain diseases and needed to be diagnosed and treated "before they contribute to more tragedies." Although race was not mentioned, "brain diseased" clearly referred to inner-city black males. The policy implications surfaced three years later when, in their book *Violence and the Brain,* Mark and Ervin called for the establishment of a federal hospital for the "sociobiological study of violent persons." Genetic tests, surgical implantation of electrodes deeply in the brain, and removal of parts of the amygdala were among the recommended procedures.[59] The federal prison then being planned for Butner, North Carolina, was slated for this purpose. However, the plan was abandoned in the wake of the controversy surrounding the proposed surgical procedures.·

Searching Out the Criminaloid

In the same year that Wilson and Herrnstein's *Crime and Human Nature* appeared, it was revealed that a University of Florida professor had been collecting portions of the amygdala from the remains of prisoners recently executed in Florida's electric chair. As the head of the department of psychiatry remarked to a university sociology professor, the brains were "in a bucket upstairs." The sociologist mentioned it to his class later that day, and as it happened a reporter from Jacksonville's *Florida Times Union* was auditing the course. The secret was out. The professor had made private arrangements with the state's medical examiner to have the brains delivered to her. As neither she nor the medical examiner had sought permission from the families of the deceased, the matter had been kept quiet. The idea of examining brains in order to understand criminal behavior is not new. Following Washington State's 1993 execution by hanging of Westley Allan Dodd – convicted of sexually molesting and murdering three children – the medical director of the local state mental hospital requested Dodd's brain so that he might conduct brain scans and extract vials of the dead man's blood for possible gene oddities.[60] In the late 19th century, Moriz Benedikt, a Viennese neuropathologist, collected the brains of 19 beheaded criminals and claimed to find specific abnormalities in their fissures and gyres.[61] Likewise, in 1910, a Chicago physician did an autopsy on a "colored murderer," claiming to find "incontrovertible evidence" that he was a "born criminal."[62]

When the incident of the purloined brains in Florida was made public, corrections authorities stopped the practice. Florida State University criminologist C. R. Jeffery, who had long held that the future of criminology lay in discovering the "genetic codes and brain codes" of the criminal, responded sarcastically: "I assume this means that the causes of crimes are social and not biological. Even the conservative James Q. Wilson now recognizes this role of biology in criminal behavior." Although Wilson's neoconservative views on social issues were well known, he had given few hints that he thought offenders might be predisposed toward criminal behavior by their genes. Assuming the theologian-as-economist role, Wilson had until then preferred to portray lawbreakers as "wicked" persons who commit crimes after weighing the odds and estimating the risk of punishment.

The Politics of the Search

Conversely, psychologist Herrnstein donned the robes of the political scientist. "The privileged classes of the past," he wrote, "were probably not much superior biologically to the downtrodden, which is why revolution had a fair chance of success." In modern America, "[b]y removing artificial barriers between classes, society has encouraged the creation of biological barriers." He continued, "When people can take their natural level in society, the upper classes will, by definition, have greater capacity than the lower."[63] As Richard Lerner commented, it was the kind of politics that saw contemporary American society as "totally 'just and fair' . . . the poor, weak, homeless, and unemployed were in their proper biological place."[64] It was a classic description of the contemporary "meritocracy" in the United States – characterized by Christopher Lasch as "a parody of democracy," with a progressively widening social gap between those at the bottom and those at the top – a hodgepodge elite he enumerates as "brokers, bankers, real-estate promoters and developers, engineers, consultants of all kinds, systems analysts, scientists, doctors, publicists, publishers, editors, advertising executives, art directors, moviemakers, entertainers, journalists, television producers and directors, artists, writers, [and] university professors."[65]

In his review of *Crime and Human Nature* for the *Scientific American*, then Princeton University psychologist Leon Kamin characterized the Wilson/Herrnstein research in much the same way that Harvard paleontologist Stephen Jay Gould was to describe *The Bell Curve* a decade later.[66] As Kamin put it:

Tiny snippets of data are plucked from a stew of conflicting and often nonsensical experimental results. Those snippets are then strung together in an effort to tell a convincing story, rather in the manner of a clever lawyer building a case. The data do not determine the conclusions reached by the lawyer. Instead the conclusions toward which the lawyer wants to steer the jury determine which bits of data he presents.[67]

Noting that he had read a few hundred of the studies cited, Kamin found that, among other things, Wilson and Herrnstein had described a control group that did not exist, reported statistically nonsignificant results as though they were significant, and cited a preliminary study as though it were definitive without mentioning "later, larger and better-controlled studies from the same laboratory, which produced contradictory outcomes." In frustration, Kamin concluded, "[I]t is hard for me to believe Wilson and Herrnstein have actually read those papers . . . very few of [their] citations are accurate . . . still fewer are adequate."[68]

However, Kamin's judgments were not shared by others. *Crime and Human Nature* struck a responsive chord in the popular media, eliciting positive reviews in most of the major news and opinion magazines, including *Time, Newsweek, The New Republic,* and the *New York Times,* and culminating in an unusual two-part interview with Wilson on National Public Radio's "All Things Considered" by NPR correspondent Nina Totenberg, who hailed the Wilson/ Herrnstein opus in near-Olympian terms. Similarly, entitling his glowing review of the book "The Mugger and His Genes," New York Mayor Ed Koch summarized its thesis in this way: "certain individual biological – indeed genetic – traits can barely be changed if at all. The authors find only marginal roles for schools, neighborhoods, peer group values, television violence, and job market conditions as causes of crime."[69] Koch correctly saw the Wilson/ Herrnstein book as a ringing rejection of traditional social "root cause" approaches to understanding and dealing with crime.

Born Criminals

Early in the Nixon administration, Arnold Hutschnecker, a former personal physician and adviser to the president, had proposed that the nation begin chromosomal screening of every six-year-old male in the country as a preventive anticrime measure. Screeners would look for XYY chromosomes, and a program for sending these "hard-core six-year-olds" to camps where they could be taught to be "good social animals" would be implemented.[70] The program was in fact begun in Massachusetts with karo-typing of all new births in some local hospitals. It was stopped only after it came to the attention of civil liberties groups.

At about the same time, Georgetown University psychologist Juan Cortes was proposing that the Justice Department fund a delinquency prevention project based on the now discredited theories of William Sheldon regarding the relationship between "body-type" (e.g., endomorph, ectomorph, mesomorph, etc.) and delinquency. Cortes wanted to set the program up in Washington's "wickedest" precinct in order to identify families who had children under the age of seven who might fit the physical profile of being potential delinquents. Both "cooperative" and "uncooperative" families would be pressured to get "help."[71]

Graeme Newman, associate dean of the Department of Justice at the University of New York at Albany, had put forth his thesis that "some people may be born with a physiology that is likely to predispose them (or even in some rare cases determine them) to become killers."[72] Similarly, as president of the American Society of Criminologists, C. Ray Jeffrey had posited a connection between criminal behavior and genetically determined low IQ. He saw a new era of "biosocial criminology" based in "cybernetics" and "psycho-pharmacology." Like Wilson, Jeffrey dismissed traditional sociological theories of crime such as differential association, anomie, opportunity structure, social learning, conflict, and labeling theory. He also rejected the idea that genes have any relevance whatsoever to white-collar offenders or offenders from the upper classes. "They," he said, "should be regarded not as a problem in criminology but as a problem of politics and economics."[73]

Until *Crime and Human Nature* appeared, however, those who held to the belief in a strong link between crime and genetic endowment had loitered on the fringes of the modern criminological scene. With its publication and the hype surrounding it, they soon took center stage.

All in the Family

Which modern-day studies pointed to genes as playing a significant part in criminal behavior? The ideal research model would be one that examined commonalities in criminal behavior between and among identical or fraternal twins, particularly those raised separately. Identical (monozygotic) twins share the same genes, whereas fraternal (dizygotic) twins share about half their genes. Though some early research showed a slight concordance in criminal behavior between both kinds of twins, there were problems regarding how criminality was defined and whether the twins were raised in similar ways. Twins separated at birth who had criminal histories and were raised in different home environments were so rare that no credible research studies were available. A logical extension of this model was to look at (non-twin) brothers separated at birth and raised in different family environments – for example, foster homes or adoptive homes as opposed to the home of the natural family.

The most widely cited studies of this type were those of University of Southern California psychologist Sarnoff Mednick, who compared the criminal records of 14,000 adopted Danish males with those of their biological and adoptive fathers. Mednick found that boys placed for adoption whose natural fathers had a criminal history were slightly more likely to break the law than those whose natural fathers did not have a criminal history. This was particularly true if, in addition to breaking the law, the natural father was an alcoholic. Mednick concluded that there was a possible genetic association with property crimes; he could find none with violent crimes. Although some suggested that a significant number of the adoptees who later became delinquent had actually been placed in adoptive homes wherein the adoptive father also had a criminal record (probably a result of social-class matching by child-adoption caseworkers), Mednick challenged this.[74]

A panel convened by the National Academy of Science in 1993 to assess the adoptive studies concluded that they "suggest at most a weak role for genetic processes in influencing potential for violent behavior: the correlations and concordances of behavior in two of the three studies are consistent with a positive genetic effect, but are statistically insignificant."[75]

Other data seemed at first glance to be suggestive of genetic influences on criminal behavior. For example, a 1991 study of incarcerated juveniles and imprisoned adults found that 52% of the juveniles and 35% of adults had close relatives who had also been locked up. Twenty-four percent of the teenagers had fathers who had served time in jail or prison and 9% said their mother had been incarcerated. Another 25% had a brother or sister who had been incarcerated.[76]

The stampede to genetic explanations was unstoppable. A Fordham University associate professor of law, Deborah W. Denno, immediately concluded that the high rates of incarceration among family members were probably related to hyperactivity transmitted genetically across generations, thereby creating a "biological predisposition to criminal behavior." "These results are stunning statistics," said the redoubtable Herrnstein. The data provided fresh proof to him that "the more chronic the criminal, the more likely it is to find criminality in his or her relatives . . . [criminality] is transmitted both genetically and environmentally. So kids brought up in criminal families get a double exposure. That accounts for this enormously dramatic statistic."

It fell to Marvin Wolfgang, professor of criminology and law at the University of Pennsylvania, to put matters in perspective. "You should remember," he said, "that most of these people come from low socioeconomic backgrounds, disadvantaged neighborhoods, where a high proportion of people will be sent to jail whether they are related or not." Indeed, other studies showed that in the 1980s and 1990s (as distinct from the 1940s, 1950s, and 1960s), African-Americans were being arrested in our inner cities in such large numbers that a person who *did not* have a friend or close relative who had been jailed or imprisoned would have been an odd exception.[77]

Princeton researcher Anne Case and Harvard sociologist Lawrence Katz found that juveniles who had family members in jail were much more likely to become involved in criminal activities. However, they saw not a genetic but an environmental effect, the behavior of both older family members and nonfamily peers affecting levels of criminal activity, drug and alcohol use, child-bearing out of wedlock, schooling, and church attendance "in a manner suggestive of contagion models of neighborhood effects . . . 'like begets like.' "[78]

"Analogical" Brothers

In one of the more interesting twists on the statistical methods of so-called behavioral geneticists, Temple University's Joan McCord devised an experiment that compared the criminal histories of 34 pairs of biological brothers born between 1926 and 1933 with each other and with the histories of artificially constructed "analogical" brothers.[79] Between 1935 and 1939, each biological brother was matched to a child of similar age, intelligence, personality, physique, and family environment – creating the "analogical brothers." Both sets of "brothers" were from deprived, disorganized neighborhoods. The biological brothers shared exposure to family interaction as well as genetic loading, while the analogical brothers resembled the biological brothers in age, physique, and family environment, but not in genetic endowment or in living in the same home.

McCord then looked for any evidence of criminal behavior among the grown men 40 years later. A man was considered to be criminal if he had been convicted for a serious (index) crime. The follow-up revealed that 24 of the biological brothers and 24 of the analogical brothers had been convicted of such crimes. McCord then took matters a step further by comparing the "concordance" of the biological brothers with that of the analogical brothers. Brothers were considered "concordant" if both, or neither, had been convicted for an index crime. Again, the rate of concordance was similar for the two groups: 22 pairs of biological brothers and 18 of the analogical brothers were concordant for crime.

Finally, McCord compared each brother separately to determine whether the differences in the number of convictions for serious street crimes were greater for the biological brothers or for a biological brother and his analogue. She found that although genetic brothers were more similar than analogical brothers among 16 pairs, they were less similar among 18 pairs (with differences equal among 34 pairs). The mean difference in convictions among biological brothers was 1.4; among analogical brothers, the mean difference was 1.5. McCord concluded that "whatever impact genetic factors have on crime is mediated through criminologically relevant social factors."

At Last, the Gene

In 1993, a rare study done by a group of Dutch and American researchers focused on actual genetic structures in a single Dutch family with a history of erratic and hostile behavior.[80] Hans Brunner, the lead author and a geneticist at University Hospital in Nigmegen, the Netherlands, noted that although other studies had "implicated" biological and inherited factors in aggression, "[t]his is the first that actually pinpoints a specific gene and a specific mutation within that gene."[81] The researchers claimed to have identified a tiny genetic defect that appeared to predispose some of the men toward aggression, impulsiveness, and violence.[82] Comparing genes in five "afflicted" and twelve "nonafflicted" males in the family, the scientists found a difference in a single "point mutation" in one building block among the thousands that made up the gene of those who appeared to manifest "aggressive or impulsive behavior." The researchers hypothesized that, lacking a metabolic enzyme, the brains of the afflicted men contained excess deposits of serotonin, dopamine, and noradrenaline. They concluded that a surplus of these neurotransmitters had stimulated erratic and hostile behavior.[83]

Commenting on the study, Dr. Xandra O. Breakefield, an associate neurogeneticist at Massachusetts General Hospital in Boston, cautioned that even in a seemingly straightforward case like an enzyme disorder, the spectrum of the behaviors in the five "afflicted" men could not be explained by a single genetic defect alone. She noted that different members of the family had behaved differently; some were doing quite well, and one married, had children, and held steady employment. As she put it, "Obviously, how this syndrome is manifested as a behavior depends on many factors."[84] Dr. Jonathan Beckwith, professor of microbiology and molecular genetics at Harvard Medical School, noted that the study, like others before it, had not adequately defined what was meant by "aggressive behavior." "It's been a long-term problem in this area, an insufficient characterization of the behaviors you're looking at . . . that's one reason why there have been so many announcements of genes that have later been retracted. There's often a lot less here than meets the eye."[85]

These molecular genetic researchers – unlike their "behavioral genetic" counterparts from the fields of psychology, sociology, political science, and business management – were somewhat more modest in assessing the implications of their study. They estimated that the gene they saw as putatively associated with aggressiveness in the Dutch family would probably afflict no more than one in 100,000 people. Again, not all of those afflicted would actually become pathologically aggressive. Were this finding to be replicated and the same gene defect to be found in the general population, it would affect about 1,300 of the 130 million males in the United States. Moreover, only a very small percentage of them would be likely to be involved in the justice system. As Dr. Emil F. Coccaro, clinical director of neuroscience at the Medical College of Pennsylvania in Philadelphia, commented: "It ain't a gene for all those people who are committing murder left and right."[86]

The "Violence-Prone"

Harvard psychologist Jerome Kagan has proposed that some individuals who engage in impulsive crimes of violence may have a "special biology" characterized by lower-than-average heart rates and blood pressure.[87] In assessing the impact of biological and genetic factors upon violent crime, Kagan suggested that a range of biological tests might be available within 25 years which would allow us to pick out 15 children who may be prone to violence out of every thousand. Noting that no more than one of the 15 would actually become violent, he asked, "Do we tell the mothers of all 15 that their kids might be violent? How are the mothers then going to react to their children if we do that?" The question of what a society obsessed with violence might to do with a test that claimed to identify 15 potentially violent juveniles out of every 1,000 – falsely predicting violence for 14 of the 15 – presents vexing problems for social policymakers.[88]

To give some idea of the minimal effect Kagan's biological markers would have on everyday crime (were they to prove valid), about 2,300 of the 2.3 million juveniles arrested in 1993 would have been correctly identified as biologically predisposed to violence and would subsequently have engaged in some sort of aggressive behavior (which may or may not have resulted in involvement in their juvenile justice system). But in the process of identifying these 2,300 violence-prone juveniles, 32,000 others would have been labeled as violence-prone who in fact would never have become violent.

It is true that a small number of offenders commit a disproportionate amount of violent crime. This was the conclusion of Marvin Wolfgang and David Farrington, who followed a "birth cohort" of African-American males from 1945, and another from 1958 to the present. "Cohort" studies by Ohio State University researchers Simon Dinitz, Donna Hamparian, and others yielded similar results. However, the implication of Mednick, and even of Kagan,[89] that high-rate street offenders will be the same persons whom biological or genetic tests might identify, seems unwarranted. Wolfgang estimated, for example, that were the Scandinavian adoptive studies regarding heritability to prove predictive of later violent behavior (which they have not), they would probably have relevance to no more than 3% of the violent offenders identified in his Philadelphia cohort. Simon Dinitz estimated approximately the same percentage in his Ohio cohort study of chronic and violent delinquents.[90]

Punishing the Genetically Flawed

Genetic conceptions of crime have inevitably ended in vicious social policies.[91] The phenomenon is striking and, at first glance, illogical. One might normally conclude that if a person were born with a predisposition to crime, his personal culpability might be somewhat mitigated. Just the opposite happens: demands for pain and punishment pile up, one upon another. For example, though maintaining that certain criminals were probably born that way, Newman proposed in 1983 that we devise an electric-shock punishment machine to which each offender could be strapped and from which he or she might receive jolts calibrated both to the seriousness of the offense and to the individual's personal threshold for pain – in order to ensure that the punishment might reach its optimal excruciating level. Although Newman proposed his bizarre contrivance as an alternative to imprisonment, his musings carried him ominously near the concentration camp. "It is time that we . . . realized that these few criminals, these bad people, have been sent [to prison] for punishment and that is what they should get." Newman then spelled out what he meant. "[O]n the simplest level, it seems morally required that incarcerated murderers . . . should see it as quite deserving that they should risk their lives for others. Their use for risky medical research might well be justified on this basis."[92] Newman's argument was similar to those made earlier in the century by British eugenicists who proposed that criminals be subjected to vivisection.[93]

Wilson and Herrnstein recognized the contradiction in punishing the genetically predisposed criminal and then dismissed it out of hand. "Scientific explanations of criminal behavior do, in fact, undermine a view of criminal responsibility based on freedom of action," they wrote, "[a]nd it is also correct that this book has taken pains to show that much, if not all, criminal behavior can be traced to antecedent conditions. Yet, we view legal punishment as essential, a virtual corollary of the theory of criminal behavior upon which this book is built."[94] They went on to rationalize the contradiction with a reference to British legal philosopher H. L. A. Hart (who) "has formulated

> . . . an account of criminal behavior that seems to us to resolve the apparent paradox of holding people responsible for actions that they could not help committing, and to do so in a way that fits naturally with the theory of criminal behavior proposed in this book. An act deserves punishment . . . if it was committed without certain explicit excusing conditions. In Hart's scheme, free will is a negative, rather than a positive, attribute of behavior . . . for purposes of the law, behavior is considered "free" if not subject to these *excusing conditions*. One such condition is insanity, but there are others, such as duress, provocation, entrapment, mistake and accident.[95]

A closer reading of Hart reveals that he advanced his argument in response to social theorists like Lady Barbara Wooton, who held that we might not be able to hold *anyone* responsible for *any* criminal act, all behavior having been preconditioned.[96] There is nothing in Hart to suggest that, were the genetic predeterminants posed by behavioral geneticists to be proven, they would not be mitigative or even exculpatory of individual responsibility for some criminal acts.

In the years since the publication of *Crime and Human Nature*, both Wilson's and Herrnstein's' views on the contribution of genes to social deviance apparently hardened. In a glowing review ("Uncommon Sense about the IQ Debate") of *Forbes* magazine columnist Daniel Seligman's book, *A Question of Intelligence: The I.Q. Debate in America*, Wilson wrote, "[i]ndisputable facts . . . worry many decent people who feel that it is impolite or impolitic to acknowledge group differences in a society committed to the proposition that 'all men are created equal.' " Wilson attributed the problem to an "egalitarian impulse," which "makes . . . people willing victims of academic charlatans and political demagogues who argue that differences in IQ are chiefly or entirely a matter of environment." Accepting Seligman's "dysgenic" thesis regarding overbreeding among the lower classes, Wilson held out the hope that "group differences, . . . depending on marriage patterns and birthrates . . . may well change."

Wilson's use of the term *group differences* seemed particularly disingenuous in light of the fact that Seligman's book was entirely focused on presumed *racial* differences in IQ scores. Seligman vigorously argued that IQ is racially determined, and he praised the eugenic principles set forth by Singapore's prime minister, Lee Kuan Yew, in condemning the relative infertility of the highly educated classes. (Similar remedies were being proposed by Johns Hopkins University sociology professor Robert A. Gordon. Describing himself as "a man unfettered by the liberal guilt of many academics," Gordon suggested that remedial educational and social programs be scrapped and that it be national social policy to persuade less intelligent people to have fewer children.)[97] Among the "dysgenic" social policies Seligman targeted were federal welfare programs, affirmative action, and federal restrictions on abortions for the "poor and ignorant." He looked to a future in which the political failures of past eugenics movements in the United States would be followed "by a kind of invisible, unorganized triumph of private sector [eugenics]."[98]

Herrnstein was less circumspect. In his review of the same Seligman book, he boldly plunged in. "Looking to a more distant horizon," he wrote, "Seligman considers the possibility of declining [IQ] scores from generation to generation, if people with high scores continue to reproduce at low rates." Admitting that "talking about differential fertility harks back to eugenics," Herrnstein went on, "before eugenics was perverted by the Nazis, it was seen by such respectable and upright people as Oliver Wendell Holmes Jr.

as a matter of designing public policies to improve human hereditary endowment in humane and voluntary ways."[99]

Indeed, Herrnstein's comments notwithstanding, eugenics did
not need to be "perverted by the Nazis." Its worst qualities were
becoming evident long before National Socialism appeared on the
horizon. For example, Karl Pearson, professor of eugenics at London University (and a disciple of Galton), declared in 1912, "The
death rate is selective, and if we check Nature's effective but
roughshod methods of race betterment, we must take her task into
our own hands and see to it that the mentally and physically inferior
have not a dominant fertility."[100] Pearson went on to propose a
series of "remedies," which, as Canovan notes, "amounted to leaving paupers, tramps, and the insane to starve; for 'if we leave the
fertile, but unfit, one-sixth to reproduce half the next generation,
our nation will soon cease to be a world power.' "[101]

Similarly, Charles Wickstead Armstrong's 1931 book, *The Survival of the Unfittest*, which attacked unemployment relief on eugenic grounds, was well received in Great Britain.[102] Armstrong
wrote that "the nation which first begins to breed for efficiency –
denying the right of the scum to beget millions of their kind . . . is
the nation destined to rule the earth." Observing that there were
three methods of diminishing "the dangerous fertility of the unfit –
the lethal chamber, segregation, and sterilization," he laid out a
program of eugenic classification of the population. The "A-1s"
would be given tax privileges to have more children, while the "C-
3s" would be sterilized or segregated.[103]

Herrnstein's reference to Justice Holmes was part of a long
tradition of making the argument for eugenics from authority. The
American eugenics movement earlier in the century had counted
not only Holmes among its members but also such luminaries as
Benjamin Rush, Margaret Sanger, Justice Louis Brandeis, Harvard
University president Charles W. Eliot, and psychologist Edward
Thorndike (who pioneered much of the work in IQ testing).[104]
Herrnstein omitted mention of the somewhat less felicitous policy

effects of *Buck v. Bell*, the Supreme Court decision written by Holmes in 1927. The case revolved around the constitutionality of a 1924 Virginia law permitting the involuntary sterilization of persons in state institutions who were thought to be feebleminded.

Holmes's views carried considerably more mischief than Herrnstein suggested. As the historian Carl Degler has noted, to Holmes the subject was not all that complicated. "If a state may compel a young man to serve in the army in time of war, thereby putting his life in jeopardy . . . it certainly ought to be able to call upon those who already sap the strength of the state for . . . lesser sacrifices . . . in order to prevent our being swamped with incompetence. . . . [t]he principle that sustains compulsory vaccination is broad enough to cover cutting the fallopian tubes." "It is better for all the world," wrote Holmes, "if instead of waiting to execute degenerate offspring for crime, or let them starve for their imbecility, society can prevent those who are manifestly unfit from continuing their kind." [105]

In the wake of *Buck v. Bell*, involuntary sterilization of selected populations spread across the United States and eugenics laws were enacted in over half the states. Oklahoma had its Habitual Criminal Sterilization Act, and California embarked on a massive program that resulted in the sterilization of 11,000 inmates. It is estimated that 58,000 Americans had been sterilized by 1956. [106] The procedures were primarily confined to institutionalized populations. Indeed, Kuhl concludes that the early Nazi eugenicists took many of their cues from American scientists and populizers of eugenics. [107] Virginia's eugenics legislation (out of which the *Buck v. Bell* decision emerged) provided the legal framework for the early Nazi legislation that sanctioned the sterilization of retarded children, the physically or mentally handicapped, and selected offenders. [108] Just as enthusiastic as their American counterparts, the Nazis were not constrained by the legislative process, eventually involuntarily "desexing" 350,000 of the physically disabled, mentally retarded, mentally ill, and criminals in order to stem "degeneration." According to estimates of the German government, approximately 5% (17,500) of those upon whom the surgical procedure was performed died in the process.[109] We do not have an estimate of what the mortality rates were among Americans who were sterilized during those same times.

When it came to the criminal, a kind of a priori culpability first advanced by Carl Schmitt, the leading constitutional lawyer for the Third Reich, was the guiding force of state preventive programs. The character of the offender was as integral to the policy as the illegal act itself.[110] Indeed, a similar logic was outlined by Supreme Court Justice Oliver Wendell Holmes in an address to the Boston University School of Law in 1897: "If the typical criminal is a degenerate, bound to swindle or to murder by as deep seated and organic necessity as that which makes the rattlesnake bite," he said, "it is idle to talk of deterring him. . . . He must be got rid of; he cannot be improved, or frightened out of his structural reaction."[111]

The Truth Will Out?

Clearly, there should not be anything inherently wrong with studying the relationship of genes to such factors as race, intelligence, human behavior, or crime. As Harvard sociologist Christopher Winship recently noted, in a society that has become increasingly socially and economically stratified by level of cognitive ability, "it is critical that we understand the relationship, if any, between intelligence and entrenched social problems."[112] Nor is there anything wrong with looking at racial concomitants associated with low IQ and crime.

As Duster told the *Scientific American*, avoiding race in studying violence and crime plays into the hands of the right wing. If we properly account for racism and related factors, the idea that blacks are innately crime-prone "will fade away into nothing."[113] Maybe. However, such debates have never been notable for valuing facts over ideology. Adding crime to the mix complicates the process considerably. As the "criminal" enters the arena, civility exits from the proceedings and whatever "science" remains is up for grabs. That is why reopening the issue of genes, race, and crime at this time carries decidedly more risk than Duster acknowledges. Even were the assertions of Herrnstein, Wilson, and Murray on genes, IQ, and crime to be found valid – and there is precious little evidence they are – there still remains the question of how, in a democratic society, we choose to define the relationship of scientific positivism to the formulation of social policies. As Kagan asked, "Where are the *a priori* assumptions necessary for ethical decisions to come from? . . . Although science can help . . . by supplying factual evidence which disconfirms the invalid foundations of ethical premises, it cannot supply the basis for a moral proposition. Facts prune the tree of morality; they cannot be the seedbed."[114]

The issue is one of how we set research priorities. The question that conservative political scientist Nathan Glazer asked in reviewing *The Bell Curve* – "whether the untruth is not better for American society than the truth?" – was not as naive as some critics assumed.[115] Although one might take exception to Glazer's implicit acceptance of the validity of the Herrnstein/Murray thesis, his reservations echoed the sentiments of Max Weber who, earlier in the century, though personally receptive to then current theories on inheritance and behavior, saw their potential for mischief as outweighing whatever minimal scientific value they might have had at that time. As Weber wrote in 1921:

I do not see how, in spite of the valuable contributions of anthropological [i.e. genetic] research, it would be possible for the time being to decide with an exactness its share in the evolution here investigated, either quantitatively or above all as regards the manner of its influence and the points where it is exerted. I do not see a basis for guesses about it. Sociological and historical research should therefore first concentrate on the task, as exactly as possible to establish the influences and causal connections which may be explained satisfactorily as reactions to external events and to the environment.[116]

Weber's advice, as we now know, was ignored.

A similar dilemma bothered Weber's contemporary, the German anthropologist Werner Sombart. Sombart, who held that Jews had a genetic tendency to trade and innate abnormally strong sexual impulses, was dismayed that his theories were used politically. In 1911, he wrote: "Of late, everything that is in any way connected with the study of national and racial characters has become a toy for dilettantic whims, and more especially has the study of Jewish character been undertaken as a political sport by rude minds with blunt instincts – to the disgust and surfeit of all who are still possessed of some taste and impartiality in this unpolished age."[117]

All of this suggests that it may be irresponsible to carelessly and publicly toy with the putative genetics of social deviance while at the same time bypassing the more pressing, obvious, and remediable environmental and social factors involved. If there *is* a criminal gene, or a combination thereof, let's *see* it or them – not in factor analysis or artificial constructs like "*g*," but in a microscope.[118] Until then, it might be well for political scientists, mathematicians, and "behavioral geneticists" to hold their tongues, and their pens.

For example, the writer Christopher Jencks has clearly recognized the ominous potential of a genetic schema of crime for leading to brutal treatment of criminals (e.g., "The notion that criminals are 'different' has been used to rationalize horrifying abuses in the past"). He even suggests that "the same thing could happen again." After looking over the controversial Danish "twin studies," Jencks admits that, if genes matter at all, they probably relate only to minor offenses. There is "currently no solid evidence," he notes, "that men's genes affect their chances of committing violent crimes." However, he then gratuitously tosses in the observation, "although such evidence may well emerge," and proceeds from there.[119] "The danger," he writes, "is not that a realistic understanding of genetic influences will lead us to think of criminals as subhuman, but that the mythology surrounding genetic explanations will do so. The most serious risk is that we will come to think of criminals as incorrigible."[120] Jencks muses that criminals just might use their genes as an excuse: "It's not my fault I keep breaking the rules. I'm just one of those people who can't follow the rules no matter how hard I try. Some people are just born to be criminals." Jencks makes no comment about how such an imagined scenario might play out in social policy – particularly in times such as our own.

The neoliberal political commentator Mickey Kaus engages in similar flights of fancy, pointing at Herrnstein's disturbing syllogism that "social standing (which reflects earnings and prestige) will be based to some extent on inherited differences among people." Despite his concerns over what he dubs "The Herrnstein Nightmare," he gives undeserved and relatively unquestioning credibility to Herrnstein's hypothesis that we are headed toward a "Hereditary State."[121] Wilson pounced on the inconsistency, calling Kaus "the first neoliberal to take seriously [Herrnstein's argument] "that . . . immutable human differences limit dramatically the extent to which the distribution of status or power in society can be changed."[122]

Chesterton noted in the 1920s that status and power are what genetic arguments are usually about. He observed that no one seemed to be suggesting that the marriages of the rich should be controlled and concluded that this potentially rich field of inquiry remained "unexplored not merely through snobbery and cowardice, but because the Eugenist . . . half-consciously knows it is no part of his job; what he is really wanted for is to get the grip of the governing classes on to the unmanageable output of poor people."[123]

Trusting the Experts

Part of the problem may lie in a contemporary tendency to place something approaching invincible faith in what appear to be scientific paradigms and credentialed professionals. Historically, however, when social deviance has been tied to such constructs as the genetics of class and race, neither professionalism nor scientific sanction has afforded much protection from inhumane practices and policies. On the contrary, it has spurred on the worst that humankind can conjure. Ironically, as a result, otherwise irrelevant ad hominem factors such as the power, motivations, biases, and marketing skills of the scientist/policymakers end up being crucial to understanding the "scientific" debate.

As the infamous Tuskegee study on syphilis and a number of other human experiments over the last 50 years demonstrate, even a scientifically verifiable diagnosis made by well-trained medical professionals does not guarantee either ethical decisions or humane treatment when the patient is black or poor.[124] As medical ethicist David Rothman recently summarized the dilemma, "[a]nybody who expects physicians to save us . . . from the worst imaginable abuses of twenty-first-century medical interventions, whether they involve genetic engineering, pharmacological interventions or surgical procedures, had better start searching for alternatives."[125]

Of Jungle Life and Mating Strategies

As we enter the mid-1990s genetic conceptions of crime and welfare are once again in full bloom. They were stated in unadorned form in early 1992 by Dr. Frederick K. Goodwin, then administrator of the Alcohol, Drug Abuse, and Mental Health Administration. "If you look, for example, at male monkeys, especially in the wild, roughly half of them survive to adulthood," he said. "The other half die by violence." He continued, "[t]hat is the natural way of it for males, to knock each other off and, in fact, there are some interesting evolutionary implications. . . . The same hyper aggressive monkeys who kill each other are also hyper sexual, so they copulate more and therefore they reproduce more to offset the fact that half of them are dying." Dr. Goodwin then drew an analogy with the "high impact [of] inner city areas with the loss of some of the civilizing evolutionary things that we have built up. . . . Maybe it isn't just the careless use of the word when people call certain areas of certain cities, jungles."

More disturbing than the racist content of his remarks was the fact that an eminent health official at the highest level of government felt no uneasiness in making such statements in a public forum of his peers. It suggested that although he may have committed a public relations faux pas, he probably had not misjudged his audience. Predictably, Goodwin pretty much dismissed the idea of dealing with the social and economic causes and concomitants of crime and violence. "If you are going to leverage that at all," he said, "you are going to leverage it through individuals, not through large social engineering of society. . . . [Y]ou look at genetic factors and violence and aggression which are very strong, and from the few adoption studies that we have. . . . If you are going to say, we have 10 million potential recipients of this intervention, forget it . . . we might be able to hone down to something under 100,000 and then talk about interventions." After his remarks appeared in the *Washington Post*, Dr. Goodwin was "demoted" to head of the National Institutes of Mental Health, where, among other responsibilities, he would oversee governmentally funded research on violence and delinquency.

Although admitting that Goodwin had made "a few seemingly racist" remarks and "injected what some took to be Hitlerian overtones," *New Republic* editor Robert Wright later portrayed Goodwin as a naive, well-meaning individual who made his comments "after a wholly sleepless night." Wright suggested that "modern Darwinian thought" as advanced by the discipline of "evolutionary psychology" held the most promise for future social policy on inner-city crime. Stressing "species-typical mental adaptations" (i.e., that the human mind adjusts itself to social circumstances and this is perpetuated in the genes), Wright hypothesized: "If, for example, early social rejection makes people enduringly insecure, then we should ask whether this pattern of development might have had a genetic payoff during evolution." Nowhere did Wright cite any genetic studies per se. Admitting that this theory was "meagerly tested and is no doubt oversimplified," Wright went on to simplify it further. Seeding his article with phrases like "the biochemistry of low status," and commenting on "groups that find themselves shunted toward the bottom of the socioeconomic hierarchy," Wright noted that it "may be nature's way of preparing them . . . to evade the rules of the powers that be." As he put it, "inner-city thugs may be functioning as 'designed.' "[126]

Wright even held out the prospect of a new kind of medical diagnosis for social problems: "if serotonin is one chemical that converts poverty and disrespect into impulsiveness or aggression or low self-esteem," he wrote, "then it, along with other chemicals, may be a handy index of all these things – something whose level can be monitored more precisely than the things themselves." How Wright would provide a biological or genetic explanation for the dramatic increase in imprisonment rates among young black men in the last decade is unclear. Normally, such adaptations in humans take generations to occur, and there is no evidence that criminality offers an exception to that rule.

In a chilling reprise of Goodwin and Wright, psychologist and behavioral geneticist David Rowe recently introduced his own Darwinian "evolved genetic theory" of delinquency, basing it on what he called the "mating strategies" of baboons, monkeys, and cuckoos. Applying this theoretical model to inner-city crime and welfare, Rowe proposed that we concentrate on identifying (presumably through a statistical correlational process) those, as yet unspecified, genes which maximize "mating" and minimize "parenting" among "certain groups and individuals." In assessing the public-policy options necessary to remedy these defective mating strategies, Rowe said that he was "pessimistic that interventions aimed at altering family conditions . . . would greatly reduce the mating effort traits of children who are at the trait extreme." Using the same bland term as Goodwin – "intervention" – Rowe suggested that "a biologically-based trait . . . raises the possibility of using biological as opposed to social interventions."

Rowe acknowledged, however, that the "interventions" that occurred to him would probably contravene "our most fundamental democratic values favoring freedom of association." Then, in the "what if" tradition of his compatriots, he listed them anyway. They included "eugenic interventions," to control human reproduction, and "therapeutic interventions," which involved "administering drugs to alter nervous system functioning." These interventions could be supplemented with what he termed "ecological intensifiers." "For example," Rowe wrote, "if threshold effects are associated with population composition, one could plan communities to keep the population at risk below the threshold level."[127] Race was not mentioned.

Prisons, Orphanages, and Camps

Given our history, we cannot assume that the diagnoses proposed by Wright and the "interventions" suggested by Rowe will lie indefinitely outside the ethical repertoire of the majority, particularly when it comes to African-American males. The country is already at a point where three out of every four black males will be arrested, jailed, and acquire a criminal record by age 35. As we entered the second half of 1995, Wilson was suggesting that in order to save the Renaissance, we will have to consider writing off a generation of inner-city youth through incarceration.[128] As an adjunct, he proposed that single teenage mothers on welfare be removed along with their children to state-funded reeducation facilities. Should they resist such measures, the children would be placed in "boarding schools" or other congregate facilities.[129]

Not all of these proposals are, in and of themselves, necessarily destructive. There is a legitimate place for congregate child-care facilities such as group homes and alternative family settings in selected cases. However, in light of Wilson's well-known views on the "immutability" of certain traits and his previous writings on preventive and rehabilitative programs for the poor and delinquent, one must wonder why he would advocate state-funded institutions for welfare mothers and children. In this light, the "resocialization" of black children seems more likely to work out in practice as a way of retraining those selected to accept their supposedly innate limitations and consequent place on the bottom rungs of the labor market or – if one wished to give these matters a more ruminative cast – perhaps to advance the meritocracy so treasured by both Murray and Wilson. In his dystopian novel, *The Rise of the Meritocracy, 1870–2033*, Michael Young reminds his readers that the best way to defeat opposition is by appropriating and educating the best children of the underclass while they are still young, thus draining talents away from the lower classes and thereby depriving them of leadership.

6
The Future
From Managerial Efficiency to Biological Necessity

Despite its pretensions, modern criminal justice is no more about crime control than it is about rehabilitation. Nor is it about deterrence. None of that matters. Rather, it is increasingly about "identifying and managing unruly groups,"[1] and its work is fast being distilled down to those two elements which have traditionally characterized racially based social policy – what the British scholar Ivan Hannaford calls matters of "managerial efficiency" and "biological necessity."[2]

The current national mood on crime is hardly distinguishable from that observed by the Danish sociologist Svend Ranulf when he looked across the border into Germany of the early 1930s to see how that country proposed to deal with criminals and crime. Everywhere he saw a "disinterested disposition to punish." He called it "disinterested" because "no direct personal advantage seemed to be achieved by calling for the harsh punishment of another person who had injured a third party." Noting that this punitive inclination was not equally strong in all human societies, and was entirely lacking in some, Ranulf concluded that it did not arise out of concern for deterrence. Rather, it was a kind of "disguised envy" –

less a response to increased crime rates than tied to the economic insecurities of the middle class.[3]

The anticrime program undertaken in accordance with the principles of National Socialism and proposed by the Prussian minister of justice in 1933 seems oddly resonant today: Aggravated penalties added to criminal acts already subject to punishment; mitigation allowed only in the rarest and most exceptional cases; attempts at crime dealt with as severely as accomplished crimes; drunkenness considered an aggravating rather than extenuating circumstance; more liberal recourse to capital punishment; and prisons harsher, with dark cells and hard couches applied as disciplinary measures at the discretion of prison wardens. Criticizing the alleged permissiveness of the Weimar Republic toward criminals, the minister ended his white paper with a familiar slogan. "It seemed," he wrote, "that the welfare of the criminal, and not the welfare of the people, was the main purpose of the law."[4]

As rhetoric, these anticrime proposals seem less strident than what we are hearing from political figures in the United States today. At the beginning of the 1994 fall session of Congress, Representative Jay Dickey (R-AR) drew up a list of anticrime measures – including public flogging (which, as the *Washington Post* noted, would "leave it up to the states whether they beat their prisoners in jail or do it in front of City Hall"), "*two* strikes and you're out" legislation, and televising executions. Dickey also proposed a "three-tiered" system in which inmates who refuse to work get bed and board and nothing else. Dickey also wanted 13-year-old offenders tried as adults, and their victims allowed to sue these juvenile offenders' families.[5]

Although many of these proposals can be scoffed at, they betray a troubling undercurrent. In 1995, the chain gang was returned in Alabama, there were calls for the introduction of castration in Texas, demands for flogging in Mississippi, widening the application of the death penalty nationally, and sending more juveniles to adult prisons.[6] At times, the rhetoric seemed more suited to a pulp-fiction novel. In surveying the disposition of politicians to "mak[e] hard time harder," the *New York Times* cited motions from Louisiana, California, Wisconsin, Florida, New York, North Carolina, Ohio, and South Carolina, noting in particular the "visceral debate" in Mississippi over the passage of a law taking away prisoners' amenities: "there was talk of restoring fear to prisons, of caning, of making prisoners 'smell like a prisoner,' of burning and frying, of returning executions to the county seat and of making Mississippi 'the capital of capital punishment.' "[7]

The U.S. House of Representatives crime bill passed in February 1995 included provisions to ensure that inmates in the Federal Bureau of Prisons not be allowed to "engage in any physical activities designed to increase their fighting ability; and that all equipment designed for increasing strength or fighting ability of prisoners promptly be removed from Federal correctional facilities . . . [i.e., weight-lifting and body-building equipment]." The legislation also calls upon the attorney general to "establish standards regarding conditions in the Federal prison system that provide prisoners the least amount of amenities and personal comforts consistent with Constitutional requirements and good order and discipline" – adding, "Nothing in this section shall be construed to establish or recognize any minimum rights or standards for prisoners."[8] The fact that the recipients of this renewed viciousness would be primarily black and brown males was not mentioned.

Occasionally, the not-so-latent maliciousness surfaces in undisguised form, as in a *Wall Street Journal* Op-Ed article by neoconservative political scientist John DiIulio. The editors chose to entitle the piece "Let 'em Rot." Though DiIulio objected to the title in a subsequent letter to the *Journal* editors, they had clearly received his message that incapacitating ever larger numbers of persons in prisons is the only course for the country, and titled it accordingly.[9] At about the same time, the liberal Republican governor of Massachusetts, William F. Weld, was pushing his own brand of penology. At a law-enforcement "summit" in Washington, Weld shared his wish with the assembled guests "to introduce inmates to the joys of rock-breaking." Detailing his vision, he confided that he was "of the belief that prison should be like a tour through the circles of hell." He added, however, that "in making it so, our task is a formidable one, since we have to undo many years in which we treated crime as a social service matter rather than a public safety problem."

Weld was apparently unaware of proposals already developed among criminal justice academics on the same subject. For example, Graeme Newman, former dean of the criminal justice department at the State University of New York at Albany, though granting that prisoners probably could not "be subjected to the same terrible tortures in prison as Dante dreamed up for Hell or Purgatory," recommended as an alternative that they be used for "risky medical research."[10] Newman's views were strikingly similar to those advanced by Dr. Jack Kevorkian, the controversial Michigan proponent of physician-assisted suicides, who had proposed that condemned convicts submit to medical experiments that would be fashioned in such a way as to begin while the inmate was alive and end in his death. He also wanted to extract reusable organs from inmates before execution damaged them and had tried, without success, to obtain the kidneys of a condemned inmate in Texas in 1992.[11]

Medical doctors in the industrialized Far East had already begun extracting organs from death row. In 1991, 37 organs of 14 condemned Taiwanese criminals were removed and donated for transplants. The condemned inmates were shot dead while hooked up to respirators so their blood circulation and breathing would not stop suddenly. Dr. Masami Kizaki, a Japanese transplant specialist and chairman of the Japan Society for Transplantation, noted that Jun-Jan-Lee, a professor at National Taiwan University, had assured inquirers that the condemned men had agreed to give their hearts, kidneys, and livers in order "to be redeemed from sin."[12]

By mid-1995, reports from mainland China referred to a large and burgeoning business in organ transplants – the organs being obtained from condemned inmates. Chinese refugees testified before the U.S. Senate Committee on Foreign Relations that the Chinese government was removing organs from condemned prisoners and selling them for use in medical transplants in state-owned hospitals. The recipients were usually top officials or foreigners from Hong Kong, Japan, Great Britain, and the United States in need of kidney or cornea transplants and who could afford to pay for the operations in foreign currency. As Gao Pei Qi, a former member of China's Public Security Bureau who now lives in exile in London, put it, "They would take the prisoner's skin, if necessary." He reported that death-row prisoners were made to kneel before being shot in the head or heart, whereupon their corpses were rushed into waiting vans where surgeons removed their organs while the bodies were in transit to local crematories. Prisoners whose corneas were to be used were usually shot through the heart. It was estimated that between 2,000 and 10,000 organs were being taken annually from condemned inmates. The timing of the executions was set according to the immediate market for organs.[13]

Managerial Efficiency

The headline read: "California Prisons Turn On Electricity: Lethal Perimeter to Save Money on Tower Guards." The story was accompanied by a photo of Warden K. W. Prunty standing alongside his new electric fence.[14] The signs surrounding the fence read "Danger! Peligro! High Voltage! Keep Out!" and showed the image of a man being hit by a bolt of electricity, falling backward. The newly installed fence at Calipatria State Prison was designed to spell instant death for any inmate trying to escape. It carries 4,000 volts and 650 milliamperes, though only 70 milliamperes are necessary to kill an average person. Exhibiting some solicitude, Warden Prunty noted that a special wire had been installed at the bottom of the fence to prevent rats and other small animals from climbing up and dying. Significantly, he did not justify the lethal fence on the basis that the prison contained particularly violent offenders (Calipatria was a "medium"-security institution). Rather, he characterized it as a *management* decision. "This is simply a way to keep that same level of security while saving money," he said. "The fence doesn't get distracted, it doesn't look away for a moment and it doesn't get tired." Twenty more California prisons were slated to receive their own electrified fences in the coming months.

A 1993 summary report of the "Bureau of Justice Statistics – Princeton Project" provides an interesting example of how the well-managed dispensation of pain has come to supersede all other correctional goals. Those contributing to the report included UCLA's James Q. Wilson, the Brookings Institution's John DiIulio, the Rand Corporation's Joan Petersilia, the Kennedy School of Government's Mark H. Moore, and penologist Charles Logan. They concluded that the prison system should not be saddled with problems of "outcome" (e.g., lower rates of recidivism). Rather, the central problem facing American penology is that of efficient management. DiIulio saw the challenge as one similar to those which once faced the fast-food industry. As he put it:

McDonald's Corporation . . . measured performance not simply by the conventional bottom line of profits, but by a dozen or so measures that roving teams of inspectors apply – Are the floors clean? Are the salt shakers full? Are the cashiers greeting customers and wearing their uniforms correctly? and so on. McDonald's recognized that the profits made by their stores were conditioned by economic and other factors over which their franchisees had little or no direct control. But the store owners, managers, and staff could be and are held strictly accountable for other factors that might affect business.[15]

Commenting that prisons have an "intrinsic . . . not just instrumental value," Logan defined the mission of the prison "to keep prisoners in, keep them safe, keep them in line, keep them healthy, and keep them busy – and to do it with fairness, without undue suffering, and as efficiently as possible."[16] It all sounded relatively reasonable. He proposed a standard of *"Care – keep them healthy."* Conceding that a well-run prison should try to prevent suicide, malnutrition, exposure to the elements and the spread of contagious diseases, he qualified his standard of *"Care – keep them healthy"* with the comment that "convicts are entitled only to a very basic minimal level of personal care."[17] When it came to *"Conditions – without undue suffering,"* it became clearer where this philosophy of prison management was headed. Logan included such basic considerations as "population density, food, clothing, bedding, noise, light, air circulation and quality, temperature, sanitation, recreation, visitation, and communications with the outside." He noted, however, that the dimensions of these conditions should be "curved." "Differences imply improvements at the lower end," he said, "but have declining or even negative merit ('too good for them') above some higher point."[18]

In February 1995, one got a glimpse of how Logan's approach might play out in legislation. Congressman Dick Zimmer of New Jersey filed a "no frills prisons" bill that would eliminate television sets, computers, and musical instruments, in pursuit of "the least amount of amenities and personal comforts consistent with Constitutional requirements."[19] In fact, Logan's standards could equally be applied to a well-run chicken farm, a dog kennel, or an abattoir. His tone echoes criminologist Ernest Van Den Haag who, when asked whether sentencing individuals to life in prison without parole might not turn prisons into geriatric wards, replied: "Hardly. Criminals usually die young."[20] And, indeed, some do. Consider the treatment of inmates in the terminal stages of AIDS in New York's prisons.

Dying with Dignity

A "medical-parole" program was enacted by the New York State Legislature to allow those inmates with AIDS who were near death to be released to die at home. About 8,000 of the 65,000 inmates in that state's prisons in 1994 were infected with HIV, with 4,000 having full-blown AIDS. Corrections officials interpreted the law to mean that no one would be considered for medical parole if he or she could still walk. Speaking to a reporter from the *New York Times*, a social worker cited the case of a 29-year-old inmate with AIDS thrush, an AIDS-related cancer, hepatitis B, and a tumor on his neck. However, he could still walk. Over a period of months he had applied for medical parole three times but died eight days after he was denied a third time. Another inmate with AIDS, while in prison, had suffered a seizure and heart attack that left him comatose and weighing 70 pounds. The family's request for medical parole was denied and he died alone two weeks later. In the first two years of the medical-parole program, corrections administrators had allowed only 30 of the 447 applicants to go home to die. At the time of the report, 110 of the remaining 417 applicants had already died in prison while awaiting approval. Judged by the criteria of modern penology, however, the medical-parole program was a resounding success. As the corrections commissioner put it: "Everybody says it's inefficient, but it's doing exactly what the legislators wanted it to do. No one has gotten embarrassed by it and everyone is happy."[21]

The New York example is not unusual or rare. Take these cases from a county jail that I recently monitored for a federal court.

A Child Molester. A 58-year-old male was being held in jail on charges of sexual involvement with two adolescent boys. He was a lifelong resident of the county, and his inappropriate relationships with the boys had gone undetected and unreported over a period of many years. The incidents came to light when one of the victims, then in his early twenties, mentioned his involvement with the man a number of years earlier. Although the man clearly had a history of sexual abuse of juveniles, there were no allegations of violence or physical coercion. He was well known and respected locally, and in fact had known some of the jail nurses socially. He had been in psychiatric treatment for a severe depression for six years before his earlier sexual activities came to light and he was arrested. The defendant was arrested in June 1989. He was still in the local jail two years later, and his case had not yet gone to trial. His aberrant sexual activities having been discovered a number of years after the fact, with no indication that he was continuing to engage in them, the man presented no risk to anyone.

Meanwhile, his long-standing severe heart condition had deteriorated and, in addition to prostate cancer, he had developed an inoperable brain cancer. He couldn't talk or write. While in jail, he frequently had to be transported to a local hospital for emergency treatment to save his life. After each trip he was returned to his jail cell. Following an acute deterioration in his condition, he was rushed to the hospital. He appeared to be dying and in fact was clinically dead upon reaching the emergency room and had to be resuscitated. After being revived, he was again returned to isolation at the jail. As the nurse's note read: "Inmate returned from hospital in terminal stage. Placed in administrative confinement for close medical observation." The man expired in an isolation room in the jail the next day. There was no reason why this man could not have been at home, monitored in a nursing facility, or dealt with humanely in his last days, if not his last hours.

A Recidivist Drug Dealer. L.U., an elderly woman accused of writing prescriptions for Dilaudid and selling some of her prescribed drugs, had been arrested on a new charge while awaiting trial and was therefore labeled by the state's attorney as a "recidivist," and was jailed. However, in addition to being a repeat offender, at the time of her arrest she was also in the terminal stages of cancer, incontinent, suffering from parkinsonism, forced to wear a colostomy bag, and unable to move from room to bathroom or to complete toilet functions without assistance.

Because she had been labeled a "recidivist," the rules allowed no alternative arrangements for monitoring or supervision. The jail nursing staff asked me to prevail upon the state's attorney to allow the woman to be transferred to a nursing home or hospice. I requested this. However, responding to the demands of a young female assistant prosecutor, the state's attorney was adamant that the woman be kept in the jail because of her history of selling drugs. At the time of my last visit to the jail, the woman was near death.

A Drunk with AIDS. One afternoon, upon entering the isolation unit of the jail, I came upon a young man in his late teens stripped nude, pacing back and forth on the cement floor. The isolation cell was also an "observation" cell – the door and front being made of nonbreakable glass – affording him no privacy from administrators, guards, detectives, staff, and other visitors who might walk past. A large hand-lettered sign read "AIDS." He had been arrested for drinking in public. His bond was $203. He was unable to come up with that amount. When brought to the jail, he stated that he had HIV and AIDS. He had open sores that were exuding liquid. The nurse's note said that he also had a "staph and an ear infection." He was running a fever. Orders were written to wear rubber gloves when treating him, though there was no note of his having been seen medically beyond a cursory exam at the time of admission.

Seven days after being booked into the jail, the young man had still not gone to court on his drunk charge, nor had he been assigned a lawyer. He remained in the strip cell. He asked my assistance in getting released. A check of his record confirmed his statement that he had been arrested for drinking in public. His bond was still $203 and his hearing was not scheduled for another week. He was suddenly released two days later. I could find no record as to why, or what had happened.

Supermax

No better example of modern correctional management in the service of pain can be found than the emergence in recent years of the so-called new-generation "supermax" facilities in both the federal and state prison systems. These prisons use computer technology to exile and control inmates by keeping them in around-the-clock isolation from virtually all human contact. The prisons are generally clean, well-manicured, and in good repair. Inmates are invisible. They are allowed no programs or contact with other inmates. They are fed through slots in a door and are usually kept in their cells 23 hours a day. Security systems are discreetly concealed, including electronic sensors buried in the ground that trigger alarms at the touch of a human foot. Harvard psychiatrist Stuart Grassian described the Pelican Bay supermax in California as dehumanizing and "driving some inmates mad."[22] In a number of the facilities, guards were accused of routinely meting out sadistic treatment, including such actions as hogtieing inmates, shackling them to toilets, shooting them with electric-shock "Taser" guns, scalding, and beating them. Inmates in an underground Oklahoma supermax prison (condemned by Amnesty International) likened their situation to being locked in a tomb.[23]

Ironically, the purpose of these prisons is not to contain those who have committed the most egregious crimes on the street. Rather, the supermax is a simple management tool, a tangible threat for keeping potentially disruptive inmates in less secure facilities under control. Beyond that, as a former warden at the first of the supermax prisons (in Marion, Illinois) put it in congressional testimony, "The purpose of the Marion Control Unit is to control revolutionary attitudes in the prison system and in the society at large."[24] The disproportionate percentage of black men in the general prison populations is outstripped by the much greater percentages of black men housed in supermax prisons.

In his assessment of Maryland's supermax prison in Baltimore, for example, criminologist William Chambliss found that of the 288 inmates confined there on a day in 1993, 283 (98%) were African-Americans. Inmates are placed in this facility not because of the heinousness of their crimes but by prison administrators who judge them to be a management problem of some sort in another prison and in need of being "taught a lesson."[25] Inmates are sentenced to the supermax for a minimum of 13 months, from which there is no possible reduction. Should an inmate commit an infraction of the rules (e.g. speak to a guard in an unapproved way), he must begin his 13-month confinement over again.

Each cell has a metal toilet, a washbowl, and a thin mattress. There are two 4″ × 12″ windows covered by thick steel mesh. The cell door is solid steel except for a 3″ × 6″ glazed opening. In Maryland's supermax, inmates are confined to individual 8′ × 12′ cells. For the first four months inmates are confined to their cells 23 hours per day. If, by their fifth month they have not been written up by a guard, they are kept in their cells 22 hours per day.

When an inmate is to leave his cell, he must first strip naked and hand his clothes through a small slot in the wall, which guards can open but inmates cannot. While the guard examines the clothes, the inmate stands naked and must turn in a 360-degree circle so the guard can inspect his body. The clothing is then returned to the inmate and he puts it on in front of the guard. The inmate is then ordered to stand with his back to the wall and again place his arms through the slot. The guard then handcuffs the inmate's wrists behind his back. Time outside the cell consists of running around in circles in a 20′ × 20′ steel mesh-enclosed cage.[26]

The "Crime Control-Industrial Complex"

American criminal justice in the 21st century was sketched out by the *Wall Street Journal* under the complex headline "Making Crime Pay: Triangle of Interests Creates Infrastructure to Fight Lawlessness; Cities See Jobs; Politicians Sense a Popular Issue – and Businesses Cash In: The Cold War of the '90s." According to the *Journal*, the nation's fear of crime had fueled the creation of "a new version of the old 'military-industrial complex' – an infrastructure born amid political rhetoric and a shower of federal, state and local dollars . . . these mutually reinforcing interests are forging a formidable new 'iron triangle' similar to the triangle that arms makers, military services and lawmakers formed three decades ago."[27]

In 1993, Daniel Feldman, chair of the New York State Assembly's Committee on Correction, commented that prison expansion in that state was increasingly being fed by a combination of "political pork and bad economics."[28] Noting that New York's incarceration policies had already carried the state in the direction of bankruptcy, he concluded that something other than "law and order" was afoot. "I was surprised," he said, "when my 1987 appointment as chair of the Assembly's correction committee produced a stream of letters, telegrams, and resolutions to my office, from numerous upstate rural communities enthusiastically requesting prisons in their districts."[29]

Feldman found that "low-density Republican districts accounted for 89% of state prison employees, housed over 89% of state inmates, and accounted for over 89% of Department of Corrections expenditures although Republicans accounted for only 57% of the membership of the Senate." He concluded that "When Republican legislators cry 'Lock 'em up!' they often mean 'Lock 'em up in my district.' "[30] (See Table 8.) Indeed, the so-called NIMBY ("not in my backyard") syndrome does not exist when it comes to prison building in most states. Filled with inner-city black men, they are usually sited in all-white rural communities, which routinely vie for them. Researchers from the University of Georgia's Carl Vinson Institute of Government found that local leaders around the country recognized the economic benefits of having a prison in their community, particularly when the community had experienced an erosion of its tax base or had suffered job losses.[31]

A 1994 Washington conference on Law Enforcement Technology in the 21st Century made the point well. Cosponsored by the Justice Department, the National Defense Preparedness Association (which seeks new markets for the defense industry), and a

Table 8. *New York Senate Prison Data by District and Party, 1992*

Senate district	Party	Number of DOC employees	Number of inmates	Prison expenditures
14	D.	282	924	$13,246,000
24	R.D.L.	490	830	19,978,000
28	D.L.	317	599	13,004,000
29	D.L.	147	267	5,911,000
31	R.C.	149	407	6,583,000
37	R.C.	1,830	2,990	74,381,000
38	R.C.	454	778	20,166,000
39	R.C.	397	630	15,928,000
40	R.C.	3,854	7,105	172,909,000
41	R.C.	3,128	5,798	135,667,000
42	R.C.	257	0	8,829,000
44	R.C.	610	1,046	22,003,000
45	R.C.L.	5,050	10,359	199,190,000
46	R.C.	1,134	2,025	39,566,000
47	R.C.	1,112	2,398	48,112,000
48	D.I.	1,430	2,572	55,515,000
50	R.C.	1,237	2,848	54,169,000
52	R.C.	1,333	2,816	56,532,000
5	R.C.	246	454	7,931,000
54	D.	19	60	841,000
56	R.	536	998	20,342,000
57	D.C.	583	1,104	25,214,000
58	D.L.	19	60	841,000
49	R.C.	3,124	6,812	122,202,000
61	R.	740	1,937	22,372,000

Note: D = Democrat; R = Republican; L = Liberal; C = Conservative

Source: Daniel L. Feldman, "20 Years of Prison Expansion: A Failing National Strategy," *Public Administration Review* 53, no. 6 (November/December 1993).

group with the acronym SPIES, conferees were called together to find ways of "dual use and conversion" of defense technology in the war on crime – particularly in the inner city. Among the technologies displayed were those concerned with sophisticated eavesdropping and night vision, sensing devices, disabling weapons that temporarily blind or deafen, and a host of computerized models relative to such matters as fingerprinting, criminal records, and intelligence gathering. A "second annual" conference was scheduled for May of 1995, to be chaired by Judge William Webster, former director of the CIA and the FBI, with keynoters a mixture of liberals and conservatives: Vice President Albert Gore, Attorney General Janet Reno, Representative Patricia Schroeder (D-CO), Representative Bill McCollum (R-FL), and Representative Henry Hyde (R-IL). Noting that "there continues to be an extraordinary window of opportunity," the conference brochure stated: "Justice, Defense and Industry partnerships are crucial elements in effectively addressing investment shortfalls in law enforcement research, development, and commercialization." A half-day was "dedicated to industry presentations on the business of technology" and another half-day on "creative funding mechanisms."[32]

The state of Texas provides another glimpse of what is in store. A 1994 program audit of the Texas prison system by the state comptroller warned the legislature that a powerful "prison-industrial complex" was already in place and could be expected to fight efforts to bring costs down. The auditors noted that this new political entity had "spawned its own self-perpetuating interest groups, complete with consultants, lobbyists, burgeoning state bureaucracies and a rising private corrections industry," and concluded that, like any special-interest group, "the correctional industry is in business to *keep its empire growing*" (emphasis in original).[33]

Seventy-six thousand new prison beds were projected for the Texas system in 1995–1996 alone, with 206,000 beds needed within five years. Commenting that only eight Texas cities had populations that large, the auditors noted with some irony that "billions of tax dollars change hands; bulldozers kick up dust; walls and bars are mortared in place. It certainly looks like progress." The corrections department had become the kind of unresponsive and unaccountable bureaucracy one might expect of a keeper–captive independent state. In some prison shower areas, 30 to 60 shower heads had to be turned on simultaneously in order for one inmate to take a shower. The department owned 2,450 vehicles, some units having more cars than employees authorized to drive them. Although 12,000 community-based alternative drug-treatment beds had been authorized by the legislature for nonviolent offenders, the new slots turned out not to be "community-based" at all. They were set up as adjuncts to the main prison system. Aside from the ins and outs of how to conduct an execution properly, the manual of regulations contained a full six pages on how to purchase postage stamps.

A sense of the level of discussion that drives the industry can be gleaned from the debate over whether steel jail cells are preferable to concrete. The spokesperson for Mark Correctional Systems, a steel cell manufacturer, noted that his company's cells are "more conducive to human dignity" than concrete cells. The head of Rotondo Cos., a rival manufacturer of prefabricated concrete cells, replied that concrete cells are every bit as dignifying as steel cells. Prison architects were of two minds. One opined that concrete is more porous than steel (and therefore likely to retain the stench of bodily excretions), while another said he found no differences. The vice president for sales at Mark Correctional Systems countered that he had visited hundreds of prisons and, except for those with steel cells, had "never found one that didn't stink of urine."[34]

This is the mind-set that motivates the Florida Department of Corrections to entitle its 1992–1993 annual report, *Corrections as a Business*. Reading like a corporate brochure, the report notes that, as prisons go, "it doesn't get any better than this." Amidst the statistics, profiles of typical inmates, and listing of "Additions and Removals from Death Row," one is reassured that all is right with the world in Florida's correctional industry. As the report concludes, "A Clean Prison Is a Happy Prison."[35]

From "Nothing Works" to "Who Cares?"

The "nothing works" school of criminology having run its course, we are ready for a new slogan: "They're not worth the effort." Ivan Hannaford has observed that as we near the end of the 20th century we seem to have moved closer to the views of Herbert Spencer, who in the mid-19th century wrote: "The belief . . . that by due skill an ill working humanity may be framed into well-working institutions . . . is a delusion. The defective natures of citizens will show themselves in the bad acting of whatever social structure they are arranged into. There is no political alchemy by which you can get golden conduct out of leaden instincts."[36] Spencer's comments probably pretty well describe the feelings of a significant segment of the white population in the United States when it comes to black crime and criminals.

For now, we shall probably continue our reliance on imprisonment as our major anticrime strategy, making sentences longer and the conditions of incarceration more willfully brutal. As the costs of this strategy mount and the percentage of African-Americans in our prisons exceeds 60%, we will move to create less expensive holding facilities – a tactic that surfaced when the Cold War wound down and the prospect of closing military bases was first introduced. My guess is that this policy will be a natural outgrowth of the hundreds of so-called boot camps that have sprung up across the country as we enter the last decade of the 1990s. As these facilities fail at their rehabilitative tasks, we can expect them to be gradually transformed into simple internment camps.[37]

Some have already picked up on that theme. In announcing his formal entry into the 1996 presidential race, Texas Senator Phil Gramm outlined his anticrime strategy in this way: "I know how to fix that," he said, "and if I have to string barbed wire on every closed military base in America, I'm willing to do it."[38] Similarly, the Speaker of the House of Representatives, Newt Gingrich (R-GA), is a strong proponent of converting military bases into "stockades" to be filled with what he called "violent criminals."[39] As we have seen in recent years, the term *violent criminal* can cover a wide spectrum. Under federal law, for example, stealing a car radio on federal property is a "violent" crime. In many states, possession of drugs or burglary of an unoccupied structure is a "violent" crime, as are verbal threats. Even of "crimes against persons," three-fourths involve no physical violence of any kind.

For the time being, however, we will continue to arrest more citizens, mete out longer sentences, build more prisons, try more juveniles as adults, and execute more offenders. As these measures reach extremes and we further cut an already shredded safety net, we can expect more violent explosions in some inner cities, though this may be somewhat moderated by the fact that the United States will have such a large percentage of its young black men confined to prisons and camps that they will not be in the community to rebel. In that event, one can expect isolated prison riots, which will be quickly put down with the overwhelming technology of lethal and disabling nonlethal force now available to the correctional industry. Meanwhile, the inner cities will teem with single women and children until such time as they, too, can be removed to resocialization facilities or faux orphanages.

With prison populations likely to reach three to five million within the next decade, we can anticipate more emphasis upon identifying and dealing with the "predisposed" criminal – a typology created to rationalize the national embarrassment over having become a gulag society with the majority of young American men of color in prisons or camps.[40] It will have played out as a variation on the theme for crime control advanced by E. A. Hooton, an American physical anthropologist of the 1930s (also resurrected by Wilson and Herrnstein).[41] As Hooton put it: "The elimination of crime can be effected only by the extirpation of the physically, mentally, and morally unfit, or by their complete segregation in a socially aseptic environment."[42]

As we end the century, some very old "from-the-gut" anticrime paradigms have resurfaced. It is probably only a matter of time before the unspoken racial premises that sustain our national anticrime strategies will be articulated – namely, that African-American males overpopulate the nation's jails and prisons because they are temperamentally and constitutionally crime-prone.[43] In the present climate, we cannot rule out the reappearance of the preventive and deterrent proposals that overwhelmed progressive thought earlier in the century. Herrnstein's "voluntary" reproductive eugenics proposals to offer financial and other incentives to the underclass not to reproduce are likely to gain political viability. The "voluntary" aspects will then give way to the coercive modalities integral to criminal justice procedure whenever it has been brought to bear on the economic, social, and personal problems of minorities.

Options

When I finished the first draft of this book, I dutifully sent it off to my editor for his comments and suggestions. Most things passed muster relatively untouched. However, he took exception to the final chapter. It was too pessimistic. I offered too few recommendations for how the problems might be addressed. "If you don't have any suggestions for future policy," he said, "why write the book?" He was, of course, right. The truth is, I don't have many suggestions – and those I do have, aren't likely to be taken. That will perhaps explain why this last chapter is the shortest and, with apologies, the gloomiest.

It's not that I don't know or couldn't propose effective options. They've always been there for the taking. In thirty years' association with corrections, for example, I've watched alternative programs come and go with the wind: many worked; some didn't. The point is, it really didn't matter. That element of the justice system was there to fulfill other purposes – some symbolic, some venal. As University of Michigan sociologist Robert Vinter found in his studies of juvenile correctional programs a quarter-century ago, whether or not a rehabilitative program gained official sanction was unrelated to its efficacy. Successful programs regularly disappeared from state and local budgets. Indeed, when it came to programs like state-run reform schools, the less successful they were, the greater the likelihood they would be made permanent fixtures of the juvenile justice bureaucracy.[44]

The idea that a system which claims to "treat" a social malady might intensify it instead is not new. It is the premise of conservative theorizing about welfare. However, when it comes to criminal justice that possibility is militantly ignored. The major actors in the criminal justice system seem at times to revel in their capacity to devise and sustain programs that are demonstrably harmful. The social iatrogenesis doesn't end there. Even those relatively few successful rehabilitative programs which do survive for a while are eventually undone by the criminal justice paradigm which insists that "treatment" be retributive and "help" alienating. It's an old story – "alternatives" eventually turn out not to be alternatives at all.

Are there humane and decent ways to address crime? Surely there are. We have never had to sell off our humanity to buy public safety. However, in recent years even those more classically "liberal" groups and professions which, in the past, might have supported reasonable changes in public policy are themselves caught up in the scent of the hunt. The "crime war" mentality of the past two decades has birthed a generation of policy planners, social workers, counselors, child-care workers, probation officers, psychiatrists, and psychologists willing to trash confidentiality, as well as clients, in the service of the "sheep from the goats" sorting the criminal justice model demands – and which, though now primarily racially driven, carries ominous implications for all citizens.

The country is now in the throes of feeding a powerful crime-control industry. Placing Moynihan's fear of "defining down" deviance in a more authentic context, the Norwegian criminologist Nils Christie observes that "the old defences against committing unwanted acts are gone, while new technical forms of control have been created. God and neighbors have been replaced by the mechanical efficiency of modern forms of surveillance. . . . *This new situation, with an unlimited reservoir of acts which can be defined as crimes, also creates unlimited possibilities for warfare against all sorts of unwanted acts*" (emphasis in original).[45]

The blunt truth has not changed that much. If we were being reasonable, we would return to the tasks outlined by James Vorenberg and begin to wrestle seriously with "root causes," a search for which would be self-evident were the subjects of our fear primarily white. The work to be done in the cities will require massive infusions of funding to rebuild the infrastructure, programs directed at Head Start, family support systems, nutrition, improved education, employment opportunities, housing, and adequate family income. Rather than withdrawing aid from single mothers, we should increase it, tying it to support services that encourage and support fathers to stay in the home, as is done in Sweden – a country with a significantly higher rate of single-mother births than the United States and with little crime and violence to show for it.

We need a new language, a different framework within which to consider those events which the Dutch criminologist Louk Hulsman characterizes as potentially "criminalizable." It is his view (one I share) that, rather than studying the criminal justice response to these incidents, we need to study the process whereby *most* such incidents are handled outside the criminal justice or juvenile justice systems. Hulsman suggests that in the Netherlands, for example, only about 1% to 2% of such events are formally handled in the criminal justice system. Indeed, most victims do not even regard these problematic situations as being firstly and foremost "criminal." Hulsman does not see this as "defining down" or ignoring deviance. Most such events, being "problematic," are to be dealt with in some way. He notes that among the alternative ways of viewing such incidents are other models of social control – for example, punishment, compensation, therapy, education, and the civil legal arena.

Hulsman suggests, however, that these models can only be used where a certain set of values exists – values based in:

- Respect for diversity
- A secular rather than religiously fundamentalist public sector
- A system in which the clients have significant influence over the professionals who claim to serve them
- A recognition that the kinds of reductions of reality demanded by the criminal justice model are simple *reconstructions*, not the reality itself. As Hulsman puts it: "the menu is not the meal, nor is the map the territory."[46]

For example, one could not look to the therapeutic model to deal with a problematic event if the client had no influence over the judgment and actions of the professional who ostensibly provides this service. In an intriguing experiment in Holland, threats made to women by former husbands or boyfriends (and which often involved other criminalizable events such as breaking and entering or simple assault) were handled civilly rather than in criminal court. Later research revealed that the civil procedure was more satisfying to the women involved, while the men came to better understand the power relationship with their wives or girlfriends as being one of equality. Significantly, the judges began considering these incidents within a framework of *relationships* rather than one of criminal justice. As a result, there was less need to label and force complex human behavior and motivations to fit the narrow confines of the criminal justice model. As a result, the potential for individualization and respecting diversity was greatly enhanced.

My proposals, therefore, rest on a "least harm" premise. They are presented, not as a blueprint or plan, but as a means of chipping away at the edges of the fictitious entities the criminal justice system produces in abundance and upon which current national policy is based. Having in mind the observations of Graham Greene (noted in Chapter 4), I make these modest proposals in the hope that they might divert us from our present disastrous course – while fueling a minimal "sense of guilt" and rekindling some slight "indecision of mind" among a majority grown smugly indignant – particularly when it comes to those whom we label "criminal."

The most effective response to crime in our inner cities would begin with dismantling much of the massive, counterproductive criminal justice machinery that produces multiple problems for every one it solves. In this effort, we would:

- Report crime on the basis of convictions rather than arrests.
- Halt all "sting" operations in the inner city. They are as likely to entice economically vulnerable individuals into crime as they are to deter others.
- Stop recruiting "snitches" and informants as the central tactic of the drug war in the inner city. This single tactic is probably more responsible for the increased violence in many inner cities in the late 1980s and early 1990s than any other single factor. Its long-term effects are devastating to the social bonds upon which social control rests.
- Mitigate the endemic opportunism that characterizes American prosecutorial practice by appointing, not electing, local prosecutors and by barring both state and (appointed) federal prosecutors from running for any political office after having served in that capacity.
- Bring a sense of narrative to criminal justice processing by reshaping criminal justice procedure in adult courts to resemble the juvenile court in its original conception, with the introduction of heretofore "extraneous" facts and information (e.g., family history, medical history, personal history, community history).
- Scrap the "just deserts" models, so enthusiastically embraced by liberals and conservatives alike in the 1980s, which have fallen even more disproportionately upon African-Americans than any presumed disparities in

the earlier "indeterminate" sentencing models. We would, in the words of one federal judge, "face the possibility that the basic premise of [current sentencing 'guidelines'] – that the human element should be wiped away from the sentencing process and replaced by the clean, sharp edges of a sentencing slide rule – is itself highly questionable."[47]

- Divert as many young offenders from criminal justice handling as possible, stressing individualized programming and alternative supervision (much as has traditionally been done for youths from upper-middle-class families in most courts of the nation).

- Support juvenile courts willing to experiment with approaches that were implicit in the original intent of creating the juvenile court, thereby bringing into the court arena for discussion those conditions, agencies, and pertinent individuals that may have influenced or otherwise bear upon an offender's illegal actions.

- Rethink the idea of confidentiality in the juvenile courts. If records of previous offense history are to be made public by prosecutors, complete records of psychiatric exams, psychological tests, medical records, family histories, child placements, and child-welfare involvements should also be made public simultaneously.

- Close all state-run reform schools (variously called "learning centers," "training schools," "youth development centers," and "industrial schools"). Transfer the institutional monies retrieved in the closings to the purchase of alternative care and supervision of each youngster for the length of time he or she would have otherwise been institutionalized.

- Shift fiscal priorities from construction of prisons and jails to funding prevention, treatment, and alternative supervision and care – including job training and employment programs for inner-city young men through "Civilian Conservation Corps"–type programs directed at environmental and infrastructural problems.

- Tailor criminal sentences to the strengths and weaknesses of the offender as well as to vicissitudes of the crime. In a word, begin treating the average inner-city offender with the same caution and care we would insist upon were he or she one of "us."

- Establish "whole truth in sentencing" legislation whereby the cost to the taxpayers of each prison sentence is announced at the time of sentencing. For example, an individual sentenced to five years for a $300 theft costs taxpayers approximately $125,000 in most states.

- Return probation officers to their original role as unashamed *advocates* for criminal defendants, not agents of the court or aides to the prosecutor. Probation officers should sit with the defense at sentencing and be required to find, develop, and aggressively pursue the "least restrictive" alternative as an alternative to incarceration. Let the prosecutor argue the opposite. In the process, we would disband that silly new breed of "attack" probation and parole officers who arm themselves and play at being 19th-century bounty hunters.
- Demand greater accountability of publicly funded human-service professionals (e.g., those involved in mental health services, substance abuse clinics, family services, school counseling, and child-welfare agencies) who routinely dump their clientele into the criminal justice system. Publicly run human-service agencies and publicly funded private agencies should keep police-type hours – open and staffed 24 hours a day – and be ready to respond to human emergencies associated with drug use, alcoholism, public order, and domestic violence, all of which make up the bulk of arrests in this country and are usually exacerbated by formal criminal justice handling.
- Make it much more difficult for teachers, psychologists, social workers, school counselors, child-protective workers, and other human-service professionals to involve the police or fall back on the criminal justice system for assistance with difficult clientele. If they are unwilling to put themselves at minimal risk, we should seek to fund others who are.
- Reassess the mechanisms of "affirmative action" in staffing the criminal justice system. It is not a question of whether more men and women of minorities are needed; they are. However, the criminal justice system (particularly the prosecution, police, and corrections) tend to screen and train prospective minority staff in such a way as to validate practices that further victimize minorities. In the tradition of "identifying with the aggressor," minority police and corrections officers can assume the worst attitudes and mimic the worst behaviors of the white staff in dealing with minority citizens from the underclass who are caught up in the various stages of the criminal justice system.
- In light of the various "wars" against crime we have waged in the inner city, we might consider a "G.I. Bill" of sorts for the young veterans of these wars. We might remind ourselves that the purpose of war – to

paraphrase former Chairman of the Joint Chiefs of Staff, General Colin Powell – is to kill people and break things. A postwar "G.I. Bill" could take the form of guaranteeing funding for a college education or job training for surviving youngsters from the inner cities who are motivated to further their education, skills, and employability. The costs would be considerably less than the POW camps we are about to build.

• Finally, we would reject the "triage" philosophy of crime control that drives current correctional philosophy and professional practice – and is racist to its core – which assumes that certain individuals and groups are disposable. We would talk less about "lost generations," "new breeds," "animals," "savages," and "genes," and begin investing each person's life and experience with value. We would eschew the language of a recent drug czar who toyed with the idea of beheading offenders. We might even allow such forbidden words as *decency* and *respect* to enter our vocabulary and deliberations about offenders.

Without major political changes in the nation, none of this is likely to happen.[48] Having put in place the conditions to ensure a violent self-fulfilling prophecy on crime control, we are poised to move from disciplining an incorrigible population to controlling a disposable one. Clearly, this too familiar venture avoids confronting the murkiness of "root causes" while offering a more comforting analysis to the majority.

Notes

PREFACE

1. Jacques Barzun, *A Stroll with William James* (New York: Harper & Row, 1983), p. 28.

INTRODUCTION

1. E. J. Dionne, *Why Americans Hate Politics* (New York, 1992), p. 96. As Dionne put it, "If Murray's argument were right, the trends he rightly deplores should have reversed themselves. 'When the relative advantage of work over welfare increased sharply.' They did not. In fact, the problems of youth unemployment and family breakdown grew worse in the 1970s and 1980s. That suggests that simply cutting welfare programs, though appealing from the point of view of conservative ideology, would do nothing to improve matters – and would very likely make things much worse." By the summer of 1994, the drop in welfare benefits was continuing a slide that began in 1972. The average monthly cash grant was $380 and had not kept pace with inflation. Welfare alone combined with food stamps continued their decline. "Welfare as We've Known It: (The Shrinking Welfare Check)," *New York Times,* June 19, 1994, p. 4E.
2. Patrick Murphy, "Keeping Score: The Frailties of the Federal Drug Budget," *Rand Drug Policy Research Center: Issue Paper,* January 1994, p. 5;

"Welfare as We've Known It: (The Price Tag)," *New York Times*, June 19, 1994, p. 4E.

3. A 1993 University of Michigan Institute for Social Research study (Greg J. Duncan et al., *Journal of Population Economics* [August 1993]) noted that among those who escaped poverty in the 1980s, the situation of U.S. blacks was decidedly worse than that of most of the industrialized world. Challenging the idea that welfare is a disincentive to escaping poverty, the researchers found that the chances of escaping poverty in those countries with more generous welfare benefits was much greater than in the U.S.A. For example, when comparing the ability of poor families (those with a median income of less than 50% of the country's median income) to escape poverty, there were gross differences among countries. The highest rates of escape from poverty were shown in those countries with relatively liberal welfare benefits: Finland, Sweden, France, Luxembourg, and West Germany. The lowest rate of escape from poverty registered was among U.S. blacks.

4. Scott Boggess and John Bounds, *Comparison Study of Uniform Crime Report, National Crime Survey and Imprisonment Rates* (National Bureau of Economic Research, University of Michigan, 1993). In reanalyzing the major sources of crime statistics, the authors concluded that the rate of index (serious) crime as measured by UCR data actually fell by 2% between 1979 and 1991, while the NCS registered a 27% drop in crimes against persons and a 31% drop in property crimes during the same period.

5. U.S. Department of Justice, Bureau of Justice Statistics, *Justice Expenditure and Employment, 1990*, Bulletin NCLJ-135777 (Washington, D.C: August 1992), p. 1. These figures are generally grossly understated in that indirect costs are not included, nor is capital outlay or service on the debt.

6. For example, a "Jail Expo" sponsored by the American Jail Association in the spring of 1994 announced that county and local jails alone represented a $58 billion "market" to prospective vendors and builders.

7. Herbert Blumer, "Social Problems as Collective Behavior," *Social Problems*, 18 (Winter 1971): 298.

8. Joel Best, ed., *Images of Issues: Typifying Contemporary Social Problems*, (New York: Aldine De Gruyter, 1989), p. xvii.

9. "Poll Finds a Lack of Faith in Police," *New York Times*, June 19, 1994, p. 30.

10. Paul Lieberman, "40% of Riot Suspects Found to Have Criminal Records," *Los Angeles Times*, May 19, 1992, p. B4. A later *L.A. Times* survey of 700 people convicted of riot-related felonies (more than 90%, of "looting") found that 60% had been previously arrested. *Los Angeles Times*, May 2, 1993, p. A34.

11. James Austin and Donald Irie, "Los Angeles County Sheriff's Department Jail Population Analysis and Policy Simulations: Briefing Report," National Council on Crime and Delinquency, August 21, 1992.

12. A similar study of the Cook County Jail in Illinois showed that 29% of all black men ages 20–29 were jailed in 1990 for an average of at least 32 days. "1990–2009 Briefing Report," Cook County Department of Corrections, prepared by James Austin for the National Council on Crime and Delinquency, 1990.

13. "40% of Riot Suspects," *Los Angeles Times*, May 19, 1992, p. B4.

14. Alfred Blumstein, "Systems Analysis and the Criminal Justice System," *Annals of the American Academy of Political and Social Science*, 374 (November 1967), p. 99.

15. Marvin Wolfgang, Robert Figlio, and Thorsten Sellin, *Delinquency in a Birth Cohort* (Chicago: University of Chicago Press, 1972).

16. Alfred Blumstein and Elizabeth Graddy, "Prevalence and Recidivism in Index Arrests: A Feedback Model," *Law and Society Review* 16, no. 2 (1981–1982), pp. 265–290. The cities surveyed were: Birmingham, Phoenix, Tucson, Oakland, Long Beach, Los Angeles, Sacramento, San Diego, San Francisco, San Jose, Denver, Washington, D.C., Miami, Jacksonville, Tampa, Atlanta, Chicago, Indianapolis, Wichita, Louisville, New Orleans, Baltimore, Boston, Detroit, Minneapolis, St. Paul, Kansas City, St. Louis, Omaha, Newark, Jersey City, Albuquerque, Buffalo, Rochester, New York, Charlotte, Cincinnati, Cleveland, Columbus, Toledo, Oklahoma City, Tulsa, Portland, Philadelphia, Pittsburgh, Memphis, Dallas, Houston, San Antonio, El Paso, Fort Worth, Austin, Norfolk, Seattle, Milwaukee, and Honolulu.

17. Ibid., pp. 279–280.

18. Robert Tillman, "The Size of the 'Criminal Population': The Prevalence and Incidence of Adult Arrests," *Criminology* 25, no. 3 (Fall 1987).

19. Peter Reuter, Robert MacCoun, Patrick Murphy, et al., *Money from Crime: A Study of the Economics of Drug Dealing in Washington, D.C.*, The Rand Corporation, June 1990.

20. Blumstein had discovered that a disproportionate percentage of arrests over the lifetime of African-American males occur in the juvenile years (before age 18). Blumstein and Graddy, p. 287.

21. Mark Mauer, *Young Black Men and the Criminal Justice System: A Growing National Problem*, The Sentencing Project, Washington, D.C., 1990.

22. *Hobbling a Generation: African-American Males in the District of Columbia's Criminal Justice System*, National Center on Institutions and Alternatives, March 1992.

23. *Hobbling a Generation II African-American Males in Baltimore, Maryland's Criminal Justice System*, National Center on Institutions and Alternatives, September 1992. Washington, D.C.

24. Sonia Nazario, "Odds Grim for Black Men in California," *Washington Post*, December 12, 1993, p. A9.

25. A study of arrests and admissions to local jails in 1993 revealed that of the 8,084,344 admissions to local jails, 5,979,000 were new. Allowing for those who might have had previous arrests (and records) in other jurisdictions, it seems likely that at least four to five million additional citizens acquire a criminal record each year (Census of Jails and Annual Survey of Jails and Jail Inmates 1993–94, April 1995, NCJ-151651, Table 20, p. 13).

1. IS IT VIOLENT CRIME?

1. A few simple administrative procedures could have appreciably lowered the "failure to appear" rates without resort to arrest. It was the practice in Duval County to require arrestees who had been released from jail on bond or recognizance to call the court clerk's office the following day in order to find out the date of their court hearing. Though about 90% did, a small percentage did not. Given the somewhat disorganized lives of many of those who were being routinely jailed, this should not have come as any surprise. Most of those who did not show up for their court hearing had not "jumped" bail. It was more likely to be a matter of negligence, forgetfulness, inability to schedule one's life, losing a paper that instructed them to call back – perhaps hoping the authorities would be equally forgetful. Some jurisdictions (e.g., Alexandria, Virginia) have found that giving the defendant a definite date for his or her court appearance at the time the person is released from jail cut the "failure to appear" substantially. Similarly, a reminder mailed or phoned to the defendant a few days before the court date appreciably lowers the rates of "failure to appear." A 1982 national study concluded that willful failures to appear (where the defendant absconded or had to be returned by force) did not exceed 4% of all released defendants, including both felons and misdemeanants. (Donald E. Pryor and Walter F. Smith, "Significant Research Findings concerning Pretrial Release," *Pretrial Issues*, Washington, D.C.: Pretrial Services Resource Center, Feb. 1982, 4.1.) A 1990 study revealed that as many as 24% of all released felony defendants failed to make their scheduled court appearances, though only about 8% remained fugitives. More interesting, those charged with the putatively lesser felonies

(released on "recognizance" or "unsecured bond") had the highest rates of "failure to appear." Persons charged with violent offenses were more likely to appear for their scheduled court hearings. *Felony Defendants in Large Urban Counties, 1990,* NCJ-141872 (Washington, D.C.: U.S. Department of Justice, Bureau of Justice Statistics, 1993), p. 11.

2. Peter McWilliams, *Ain't Nobody's Business If You Do: The Absurdity of Consensual Crimes in a Free Society* (Los Angeles: Prelude Press, 1993), p. 1.

3. Dawn Day, "Drug Arrests: Are Blacks Being Targeted?" (excerpted from forthcoming book), in *Newsbriefs,* April 1995 (Washington, D.C.: The Criminal Justice Policy Foundation).

4. Richard Posner, *Overcoming Law* (Cambridge, Mass.: Harvard University Press, 1995).

5. Edwin M. Schur, *The Americanization of Sex* (Philadelphia: Temple University Press, 1988); idem, *Crimes without Victims: Deviant Behavior and Public Policy* (Englewood Cliffs, N.J.: Prentice-Hall, 1965); and Hugo Adam Bedau, *Victimless Crimes: Two Sides of a Controversy* (Englewood Cliffs, N.J.: Prentice-Hall, 1974).

6. Randall Sheldon and William Brown, "Correlates of Jail Overcrowding: A Case Study of a County Detention Center," *Crime and Delinquency* 37, no. 3 (July 1991).

7. U.S. Department of Justice, FBI, *Crime in the United States, 1991* (Washington, D.C: USGPO, 1992), p. 213.

8. "Census of Jails and Annual Survey of Jails: Jails and Jail Inmates 1993–94," Bureau of Justice Statistics Bulletin, April 1995, NCJ-151651, p. 13, Table 20.

9. U. S. Department of Justice, FBI, *Crime in the United States, 1991,* p. 213.

10. Research and Evaluation Division, Michigan Council on Crime and Delinquency, *Trends in the Michigan Criminal Justice System: From Crisis to Chaos,* March 1993, Lansing, Mich., p. 26.

11. Ibid., pp. 23–24.

12. Darrell Steffensmeier, "Incarceration and Crime: Facing Fiscal Realities in Pennsylvania," Pennsylvania Commission on Sentencing, September 1992.

13. D. Gilliard, "Prisoners in 1992," Bureau of Justice Statistics, May 1993, NCJ-141874, Appendix, Table 1, p. 10. The percentage of new court commitments for violent offenses to state prisons has generally fallen over the past decade and a half. For example, 42% of new commitments to state prisons were violent in 1977, whereas that figure had fallen to about 27% by the early 1990s.

14. Ibid., p. 10.

15. U.S. Department of Justice, Bureau of Justice Statistics, *Correctional Populations in the United States, 1991*, NCJ-142729 (Washington, D.C.: USGPO, 1993), Table 4.3.

16. U.S. Justice Department, Felony Sentences in State Courts, 1990.

17. Theodore G. Chiricos and William Bales, "Unemployment and Punishment: An Empirical Analysis," *Criminology* 29, no. 4 (November 1991).

18. During my tenure, I found a number of individuals who had been jailed for walking dogs without leashes. I thought this was probably attributable to a peculiarly fervent "law and order" attitude on the part of local police. However, I was wrong. Two years after filing my Duval County Jail Report, I read in the *Los Angeles Times* a somewhat lengthy article on a local 52-year-old equipment courier who had been jailed for four days for failing to get a license for his eight-year-old dog, Samantha, after she had chased a cat, prompting a complaint.

19. Todd R. Clear, Patricia M. Harris, and S. Christopher Baird, "Probationer Violations and Officer Response," *Journal of Criminal Justice* 20 (1992), p. 1.

20. Report to Monroe County Bar Association Board of Trustees, *Justice in Jeopardy*, May 1992.

21. James Austin, *Los Angeles County Sheriff's Department Jail Population Analysis and Policy Simulations*, National Council on Crime and Delinquency, San Francisco, Calif., Aug. 21, 1992. In this study, the NCCD researchers found that of the 168,400 bookings into the Los Angeles County Jail in 1991, the most frequent offense was "Motor Vehicle Violation" (22%), followed by drug "Possession" (19%), "Driving under the Influence" (8%), "Theft" (7%), and "Assault" (5%).

22. H. Donaldson, "The Negro Migration of 1916–1918," *The Journal of Negro History*, 383 (1921), pp. 415–416.

23. Shirley Ann Vining Brown, "Race as a Factor in the Intra-Prison Outcomes of Youthful First Offenders," Ph.D. diss., University of Michigan, 1975.

24. Mark T. Carlton, *Politics and Punishment* (Baton Rouge: Louisiana State University Press, 1971).

25. Abraham Epstein, *The Negro Migrant in Pittsburgh* (N.Y.: Arno Press, and the *New York Times*, 1969), pp. 46–54.

26. F. D. Tyson, *Negro Migration in 1916–17*, Report of U.S. Department of Labor (Washington, D.C.: GPO, 1919), p. 141.

27. Brown, "Race as a Factor in the Intra-Prison Outcomes of Youthful First Offenders," p. 11.

28. FBI, *Crime in the U.S.: Uniform Crime Reports, 1989* (Washington, D.C.: U.S. Department of Justice, 1990), p. 2.

29. Occasionally, these practices fall out of the station-house closet. For example, in April 1994 the *New York Times* obtained a draft report prepared for the Mollen Commission investigating police corruption in New York City. It stated that New York City police often made false arrests, tampered with evidence, and committed perjury. As the *Times* stated: "The practice – by officers either legitimately interested in clearing the streets of criminals or simply eager to inflate statistics – has at times been condoned by superiors . . . it is prevalent enough in the department that it has its own nickname: 'testifying.' . . . Perjury is perhaps the most widespread form of police wrongdoing facing today's criminal justice system" (*New York Times*, April 22, 1994, p. A1).

30. For a discussion on the differences, validity, and reliability of the UCR versus the NCS, see Alfred Blumstein, Jacqueline Cohen, and Richard Rosenfeld, "Trend and Deviation in Crime Rates: A Comparison of UCR and NCS data for Burglary and Robbery," *Criminology* 29 (1991): 237–263; Scott Menard, "Residual Gains, Reliability, and the UCR–NCS Relationship: A Comment on Blumstein, Cohen, and Rosenfeld," *Criminology*, 30 (1992), 105–113; David MacDowall and Colin Loftin, "Comparing the UCR and NCS Over Time," *Criminology*, 30 (1992): 125–132; Alfred Blumstein, Jacqueline Cohen, and Richard Rosenfeld, "The UCR–NCS Relationship Revisited: A Reply to Menard," *Criminology* 30 (1992): 115–124; and Scott Boggess and John Bounds, *Comparison Study of UCR, NCS, and Imprisonment Rates*, National Bureau of Economic Research, University of Michigan, Ann Arbor, 1993.

31. U.S. Department of Justice, Office of Justice Programs, *The Prosecution of Felony Arrests, 1987.*

32. Albert J. Reiss and Jeffrey A. Roth, eds., *Understanding and Preventing Violence* (Washington, D.C.: National Academy Press, 1993), pp. 413–414.

33. Christopher Jencks, "Is the Underclass Growing?" in Christopher Jencks and P. Peterson, eds., *The Urban Underclass* (Washington, D.C.: Brookings Institute, 1991).

34. William J. Chambliss, "Moral Panics and Racial Oppression," unpublished manuscript, 1993, p. 36.

35. Boggess and Bounds, *Comparison Study of UCR, NCS, and Imprisonment Rates*, p. 24.

36. Charles Murray, "The Legacy of the '60s," *Commentary*, July 1992, p. 27.

37. James Q. Wilson and John DiIulio, Jr., "Crackdown," *The New Republic*, July 10, 1989, p. 21.

38. Michael Levi, "Violent Crime," in *The Oxford Handbook of Criminology*, ed.

M. Maguire, R. Morgan, and R. Reiner (Oxford: Clarendon Press, 1994), p. 319.

39. David H. Fischer, *Albion's Way: Four British Folkways in America* (New York: Oxford University Press, 1989). Fischer teased out empirical indicators for each group's specific ideas, practices, and rules regarding speech, building, family, marriage, gender, sex, naming, child rearing, age, death, religion, magic, learning, literacy, food, dress, sport, work, time, wealth, inheritance, rank, association, order, power, and freedom. Fischer's thesis continues to hold. For example, a study of 1992 homicide rates based on data compiled by the National Center for Health Statistics and the FBI's Uniform Crime Report revealed that 7 of the 10 states with the highest per capita murder rates were in the South. Louisiana led all states, with 18.5 murders per 100,000 people, followed closely by Mississippi, Texas, Alabama, Georgia, and South Carolina. Homicide rates were generally lowest across the northern tier of the nation. Homicide Study, Population Reference Bureau Inc. (PRB), Washington, D.C., 1995.

40. Ibid., p. 889.

41. Ibid., p. 890.

42. Ibid., p. 892.

43. Richard Harwood, "300 Years of Crime," *Washington Post*, Dec. 20, 1993, p. A15.

44. Robert M. Morgenthau, "What Prosecutors Won't Tell You," Op-Ed, *New York Times*, Feb. 7, 1995, p. A25.

45. Joseph E. Kett, *Rites of Passage: Adolescence in America 1790 to the Present* (New York: Basic Books, 1977). For example, Kett noted that New York City had 8 major and 10 minor riots between 1834 and 1871. During the Draft Riots of 1863, mobs "virtually seized control of the city for 3 days, terrorizing the police and yielding only before the massed artillery and bayonets of regular soldiers." Kett noted that casual street violence was rife at all times (p. 80).

46. Figures obtained from Officer Robert Fitzer, San Francisco Police Department Historian.

47. Lewis Lapham, "Reactionary Chic: How the Nineties Right Recycles the Bombast of the Sixties Left," *Harper's Magazine*, March 1995, p. 41.

48. U.S. Department of Justice, Office of Justice Programs, Bureau of Justice Statistics, *Criminal Victimization in the United States, 1991*, National Crime Victimization Survey Report, NCJ-139563, December 1992, p. 91.

49. Ibid., p. 91.

50. *Sourcebook of Criminal Justice Statistics, 1993*, U.S. Department of Justice, NCJ 148211, 1994, pp. 247, 385.

51. Howard N. Snyder and Melissa Sickmund, *Juvenile Offenders and Victims: A Focus on Violence – Statistics Summary*, National Center for Juvenile Justice, May 1995, U.S. Justice Department, OJJDP, pp. 15, 17.

52. U.S. Department of Justice, Office of Justice Programs, Bureau of Justice Statistics, "The Prosecution of Felony Arrests, 1987."

53. California State Attorney General's Statistical Report on Law Enforcement Practice, "Dispositions of Adult Felony Arrests, 1990: Type of Disposition By Race/Ethnic Group – San Francisco County," p. 45.

54. U.S. Department of Justice, Bureau of Justice Statistics, *Tracking Offenders, 1988*, Bulletin NCJ-129861, June 1991, p. 2, table 2.

55. U.S. Department of Justice, Bureau of Justice Statistics, Patrick Langan and John M. Dawson, *Felony Sentences in State Courts, 1990*, NCJ-1441872, March 1993, p. 5.

56. U.S. Department of Justice, Office of Justice Programs, Bureau of Justice Statistics, Pheny Z. Smith, *Felony Defendants in Large Urban Counties, 1990*, NCJ-1441872, May 1993, p. 13.

57. Michael Tonry, *Malign Neglect: Race, Crime, and Punishment in America* (New York: Oxford University Press, 1995), p. 22.

58. Jerome Miller, *The Duval County Jail Report*, submitted to the Honorable Howell W. Melton, U.S. District Judge, Middle District of Florida, Jacksonville, Florida, June 1, 1993.

59. Ibid., p. 97.

60. U.S. Department of Justice, Bureau of Justice Statistics, *Federal Criminal Case Processing, 1982–1991, with Preliminary Data for 1992*, NCJCJ-136945, November 1993, 1992, p. 5.

61. Ibid., p. 12.

62. California State Attorney General's Statistical Report on Law Enforcement Practice, "Dispositions of Adult Felony Arrests, 1990: Type of Disposition By Race/Ethnic Group – San Francisco County," p. 45.

63. Lola E. Odubekun, *The Vera Institute Atlas of Crime and Justice in New York City*, Vera Institute, New York City, 1993, pp. 26–27.

64. Take, for example, the comment of one of the leaders in the victims' movement in California in support of a statewide referendum on a "three strikes and you're out" bill that would mandate "life without parole" for a third-time felony offender (violent and nonviolent). As he put it: "When bad guys are killing bad guys, that's one thing. But when they start killing regular people, that's where you draw the line in the sand." Jane Gross, "Drive to Keep Repeat Felons in Prison Gains in California," *New York Times*, Dec. 26, 1993, pp. A1, A22.

65. *Los Angeles Times*, December 26, 1993 (reported in the *Washington Post*, Dec. 26, 1993, p. A19).

66. John M. Dawson, *Murder in Large Urban Counties, 1988*, U.S. Department of Justice, Bureau of Justice Statistics, NCJ-130614, May 1993, p. 4.

67. Patrick Langan, *Murder in Families*, Bureau of Justice Statistics, U.S. Dept. of Justice, July 1994.

68. U.S. Department of Justice, Bureau of Justice Statistics, Catherine J. Whitaker, and Lisa Bastian, "Teenage Victims: A National Crime Survey Report," NCJ-128129, May 1991, p. 11.

69. James Alan Fox, "Teenage Males Are Committing Murder at an Increasing Rate" (Office of Juvenile Justice and Delinquency Prevention, U.S. Justice Department, 1994) prepared for the National Center for Juvenile Justice, revised, April 18, 1993, p. 2.

70. M. Wolfgang, R. Figlio, and T. Sellin, *Delinquency in a Birth Cohort* (Chicago: University of Chicago Press, 1972).

71. Donna Hamparian, Richard Schuster, Simon Dinitz, and John Conrad, *The Violent Few: A Study of Dangerous Juvenile Offenders* (Lexington, Mass.: D. C. Heath, Lexington Books, 1978), p. 86.

72. Martin Gold and David J. Reimer, "Changing Patterns of Delinquent Behavior among Americans 13 through 16 Years Old: 1967–1972," *Crime and Delinquency*, vol. 7, no. 4 (December 1975): 483–517.

73. Jeffrey A. Butts and D. J. Connors, "The Juvenile Court's Response to Violent Offenders: 1985–1989," U.S. Department of Justice, *OJJDP Update on Statistics*, April 1993. The states surveyed were AL, AZ, CA, MD, MS, NE, OH, PA, UT, VA.

74. Howard N. Snyder, Jeffrey Butts, et al., *Juvenile Court Statistics 1990* (prepared by National Center for Juvenile Justice, Office of Juvenile Justice and Delinquency Prevention, U.S. Justice Department, November, 1993, Washington, D.C.), p. 10.

75. David M. Altschuler, *The State of the Region: Youth Crime and Juvenile Justice in Maryland and Baltimore* (Baltimore: The Johns Hopkins University Institute for Policy Studies, Fall 1992), p. 12.

76. Ibid., pp. 13–14. As the Johns Hopkins researchers put it: "While persons under age 18 accounted for 20.1 percent of *arrests* for serious violent crime in 1990, they accounted for only 11 percent of the violent offenses *cleared*. Similarly, while youths accounted for 31 percent of serious property crime *arrests*, they accounted for only 21 percent of serious property crime offenses *cleared*." Among serious violent crimes, the largest disparity was for homicides, in which the percentage cleared by juvenile arrests was about one-

third of the juvenile arrest percentages (5 percent versus 14 percent). Juvenile clearances for robbery, forcible rape and felonious assault were each about half of that indicated by the corresponding juvenile arrest percentages.

77. Ibid., pp. 13–14.

78. Franklin E. Zimring, "Measuring Juvenile Participation in Violent Crime: Problems and Research Opportunities," unpublished paper, University of California Law School, Berkeley, 1995, p. 3.

79. Jeffrey A. Butts, Howard Snyder, Terrence Finnegan et al., *Juvenile Court Statistics, 1991,* prepared by the National Center for Juvenile Justice, Pittsburgh, Pa., May 1994, p. 120.

80. Ibid. The states included were AL, AZ, CA, MD, MS, MT, NE, NJ, OH, PA, UT, WV.

81. A 1981 survey of victims of juvenile offenders indicated that 72% of the cases listed as violent involved no physical injury. In 93% of those offenses in which an injury did occur, it was not serious enough to require formal medical attention. McDermott and Hindelang, *Juvenile Criminal Behavior in the United States,* research monograph prepared for the U.S. National Institute for Juvenile Justice and Delinquency Prevention, Criminal Justice Research Center, Albany, N.Y., 1981, p. 27.

82. Donna Hamparian et al., *The Violent Few,* p. 86.

83. Donald Russell, M.D., and G. P. Harper, M.D., "Who Are Our Assaultive Juveniles? A Study of 100 Cases," *Journal of Forensic Sciences* 18 (October 1973): 385–397.

84. Zimring, p. 22.

85. Delbert Elliott, "Youth Violence: An Overview," Center for Study of Youth Policy, the University of Pennsylvania, December 1994, p. 3.

2. TRACKING RACIAL BIAS

1. Jerome G. Miller, *Duval County Jail Report,* submitted to the Honorable Howell W. Melton, U.S. District Judge, Middle District of Florida, Jacksonville, June 1, 1993, pp. 82–83.

2. Jacksonville Community Council, Inc., "Young Black Males Study: A Report to the Citizens of Jacksonville," summer 1992.

3. Alfred Blumstein, "Systems Analysis on the Criminal Justice System," (1967), p. 99 (Intro., n. 14).

4. Clifford R. Shaw, *The Jack-Roller: A Delinquent Boy's Own Story* (Chicago: University of Chicago Press, 1930), p. 36.

5. Peter Reuter, Robert MacCoun, Patrick Murphy et al., *Money from Crime: A Study of the Economics of Drug Dealing in Washington, D.C.* (Santa Monica, Calif.: The Rand Corporation, June 1990).

6. This particular area of the city, known as "Back of the Yards," was bounded by Halsted Street on the east, Western Avenue on the west, 39th Street on the north, and 47th Street on the south (Shaw, p. 36).

7. Shaw, p. 35.

8. Ibid., p. 36.

9. Roger Lane, *Violent Death in the City: Suicide, Accident and Murder in 19th Century Philadelphia* (Cambridge, Mass.: Harvard University Press, 1979); Eric Monkkonen, "Diverging Homicide Rates: England and the United States, 1850–1875," in T. R. Gurr, ed., *Violence in America*, vol. 1: *The History of Crime* (Newbury Park, Calif.: Sage Publications, 1989).

10. Shaw, p. 137.

11. Shirley Ann Vining-Brown, (chap. 1, n. 23), pp. 18–19.

12. *Negro Population: 1790–1915*, Department of Commerce; Bureau of the Census, Sam L. Rogers, Director (Washington D.C.: GPO, 1918), p. 438.

13. This was a particularly interesting figure in view of the fact that these patterns no longer prevail. There is now a much greater overrepresentation of minorities among those detained or sentenced on misdemeanors and lesser felonies. For example, a Florida study found that young unemployed black men held on so-called public-order charges (mostly misdemeanors) were three times more likely to be kept in jail than unemployed white arrestees, and almost seven times more likely to be held in jail than white arrestees. Theodore G. Chiricos and William D. Bales, "Unemployment and Punishment: An Empirical Analysis," *Criminology* 29, no. 4 (November 1991).

14. Ibid., p. 438.

15. NAACP, *Thirty Years of Lynching in the United States, 1889–1918* (April 1919; rpt. New York: Arno Press and *New York Times*, 1969), p. 7.

16. Ibid.

17. Richard Maxwell Brown, *Strain of Violence: Historical Studies of American Violence and Vigilantism* (New York: Oxford University Press, 1975), p. 217.

18. Ibid., pp. 217–218.

19. Gunner Myrdal, *An American Dilemma*, 2d ed. (New York: Harper and Row Publishers, 1962).

20. M. Tonry, "Racial Disproportion in U.S. Prisons," *British Journal of Criminology*, February 15, 1993, pp. 13–14. In his cross-national study, Tonry concludes that, although the overall incarceration rates may differ from country to country, the white–black ratios of incarceration are more similar than

different in Australia, Canada, England, Wales, and the United States. He concludes: "The overriding problem turns out not to be a unique American problem of over-reliance on incarceration but a general problem in English-speaking white dominant countries that minority citizens are locked up grossly out of proportion to their numbers in the population." Tonry notes that "patterns of differential incarceration by race in Australia, Canada, England and Wales, and the United States are much more similar than differences in their gross incarceration rates suggest . . . the ratio of black to white incarceration rates in England and Wales is 7.10:1, slightly higher than America's 6.44:1. Differential incarceration of Aboriginal people in Australia makes these patterns appear modes. The Royal Commission into Aboriginal Deaths in Custody (1990) found that for Australia as a whole, adult Aboriginal people are 15.1 times more likely than adult non-Aboriginal people to be in prison, but they are only 8.3 times more likely to be serving non-custodial correctional orders."

21. Shirley Ann Vining Brown, "Race as a Factor in the Intra-Prison Outcomes of Youthful First Offenders," Ph.D. diss., University of Michigan, 1975, pp. 11–17. Brown cites a series of studies spanning the years 1915 through 1969 which found racial bias at every step of the criminal justice process: from biased attitudes of police, to racially biased arrest practices, conviction rates, sentencing practices, and parole decisions.

22. Haywood Burns, "Can a Black Man Get a Fair Trial in this Country?" *New York Times Sunday Magazine*, July 12, 1970.

23. Bureau of Justice Statistics Bulletin, *Prisoners in 1993*, p. 9, Tables 14 and 15, U.S. Justice Department, June, 1994.

24. James Q. Wilson and Richard Herrnstein, *Crime and Human Nature* (New York: Simon & Schuster, 1985), pp. 468–472.

25. George Lakoff and Mark Johnson, *Metaphors We Live By* (Chicago: University of Chicago Press, 1980), p. 157.

26. Clifford Shaw, *The Jack Roller* (Chicago: University of Chicago Press, 1945), pp. 1–2.

27. W. I. Thomas and Dorothy S. Thomas, *The Child in America* (New York: Alfred A. Knopf, 1928), pp. 571–572.

28. Interview in *New York Times*, February 20, 1995, pp. C9, 16.

29. John Hagan, "Review Essay: A Great Truth in the Study of Crime," *Journal of Criminology* 25, no. 2 (1987): 426–427.

30. A. Blumstein, "On the Racial Disproportionality of United States Prison Populations," *Journal of Criminal Law and Criminology* 73 (Fall 1983): 1259–1281.

31. William Julius Wilson, *The Truly Disadvantaged: The Inner City, the Underclass, and Public Policy* (Chicago: University of Chicago Press, 1987); Christopher Jencks, *Rethinking Social Policy: Race, Poverty, and the Underclass* (Cambridge, Mass.: Harvard University Press, 1992), pp. 110–111.

32. Michael Tonry, "Racial Disparities Getting Worse in U.S. Prisons and Jails," *The IARCA Journal on Community Corrections* 6, no. 3 (June 1994): 24–25.

33. Joan Petersilia, *Racial Disparities in the Criminal Justice System* (Santa Monica, Calif.: The Rand Corporation, 1983); S. Klein, J. Petersilia, and S. Turner, "Race and Imprisonment Decisions in California," *Science* 247:812–816.

34. Patrick Langan, "Racism on Trial: New Evidence to Explain the Racial Composition of Prisons in the United States," *Journal of Criminal Law and Criminology* 776 (1985): 666–683.

35. *USA Today*, January 6, 1994, p. 2A.

36. Study commissioned by New Jersey State Supreme Court, "Task Force on Minority Concerns," Trenton, N.J., 1989.

37. Associated Press, "U.S. Judge, Citing Racism, Gives Black Defendant Lesser Sentence," *New York Times*, February 20, 1993.

38. Robert D. Crutchfield, George S. Bridges, and Susan R. Pitchford, "Analytical and Aggregation Biases in Analyses of Imprisonment: Reconciling Discrepancies in Studies of Racial Disparity," *Journal of Research in Crime and Delinquency* 31, no. 2 (May 1994): 166–182.

39. Ibid., p. 177

40. Ibid., p. 167.

41. Ibid., p. 181.

42. Judge Gerald W. Heaney, *American Criminal Law Review*, Fall 1991.

43. U.S. Sentencing Commission Study on Mandatory Sentencing and Race, August 1991.

44. Theodore Chiricos and William D. Bales, "Unemployment and Punishment: An Empirical Analysis," *Criminology* 29, no. 4 (November 1991).

45. Ibid., p. 718. One of the more interesting findings of the Chiricos and Bales study was that young unemployed black men jailed on so-called public-order charges (mostly misdemeanors) were found to be three times more likely to be kept in jail than unemployed white arrestees held on the same charges. This speaks to the establishment of informal rites of passage for young African-American males in the unnecessary and repeated involvement in the criminal justice system at deeper levels than the charge probably warrants (p. 718).

46. Florida House Criminal Justice Committee, Chr. Elvin Martinez, chairman, "Report on Habitual Offender Law," Tallahassee, Florida, September 1992.

47. Investigative Series, *San Jose Mercury News*, December 8, 1991.

48. James D. Unnever and Larry A. Hembroff, "The Prediction of Racial/ Ethnic Sentencing Disparities: An Expectation States Approach," *Journal of Research in Crime and Delinquency* 25, no 1 (February 1988): 54.

49. Ibid., p. 55.

50. Ibid., p. 56.

51. *Los Angeles Times*, "Trouble in Anti-Crime Paradise: As Implementation of 'three strikes' law begins, the statute's defects are ever more obvious" (editorial), July 15, 1994.

52. Carl E. Pope and William Feyerherm, *Minorities and the Juvenile Justice System*, Office of Juvenile Justice and Delinquency Prevention, U.S. Department of Justice, 1992, pp. 73–74.

53. Ibid., pp. 2–3.

54. Ibid., pp. 73–74.

55. Ibid., p. 10.

56. *Criminal Justice Newsletter*, April 18, 1994, p. 9.

57. Ibid., p. 11.

58. Kimberly L. Kempf, *The Role of Race in Juvenile Justice Processing in Pennsylvania*, Study Grant #89–90/J/01/3615, Pennsylvania Commission on Crime and Delinquency, August 1992. Kempf specified this further: "The most consistent finding related to process since the mid-1980's is that the impact of race on disposition may be obscured by previous detention. . . . Seriousness of offense also may itself, be the result of racial disparity . . . black youths are more often charged with the felony when [the] offense could be considered a misdemeanor; this discretion over number and type of charges complicates the interpretation of disparities" (pp. 7–8).

59. Carl E. Pope and William Feyerherm, *Minorities and the Juvenile Justice System: Research Summary*, December 1993.

60. Kimberly Kempf, *The Role of Race*, August 1992 (Abstract, p. 1.) Kempf specifies this further: "Biased outcomes appear most clearly at early stages of the process. Cases referred to court are judged as in need of formal processing more often when minority youths are involved. Minorities also are more often detained than white youths in similar situations, except among minor offenses when the reverse is true. At the disposition stage only white youths with the most offensive cases remain for intervention. These white youths receive placement dispositions more often than comparable Latino or African-American youths. Their placements, however, most often involve group home settings or drug treatment while placements for minorities more typically are public residential facilities, including those in the state which

provide the most restrictive confinement. Considering that serious drug offending was virtually absent among cases involving white youths and that juvenile justice personnel rated the quality and treatment provided by public residential programs less favorably than other placement options, these findings suggest that the best interests of minority youths are not being met adequately in Pennsylvania."

61. Edmund F. McGarrell, "Trends in Racial Disproportionality in Juvenile Court Processing: 1985–1989," *Crime and Delinquency* 39, no. 1 (January 1993): 29–48. McGarrell's findings touched all the familiar bases: ". . . the increasing over-representation of minorities in detention centers and training schools has been a growing concern of policymakers and researchers. The court data analyzed herein further document this cause for concern. Indeed, given the relatively short time frame (1985–1989), the trends are quite pronounced. Referrals of non-Whites to juvenile courts have increased dramatically, causing increased numbers of non-White cases to be detained, petitioned, and placed outside the home. Further, the increases in non-White detentions, petitions, and placements exceed those expected by the increase in referrals. At the same time, White cases have remained relatively stable. The consequence of these trends is increased over-representation of minorities in the juvenile justice system. . . . although a small proportion of the increase can be attributed to the increase in the non-White youth population at large, the data on rates of non-White cases clearly show that the increased volume of cases goes well beyond that anticipated due to demographic shifts. The increased formality in the handling of drug offenses has had a differential effect on non-White as opposed to White youths. Both the volume of non-White drug offenses and the severity in the disposition of drug offenses increased dramatically from 1985 to 1989. For Whites, on the other hand, the increased formality in handling of drug offenses was largely offset by the decrease in the number of White youths referred for drug offenses. Given the proactive nature of drug enforcement, these findings raise fundamental questions about the targets of investigation and apprehension under the recent war on drugs."

62. David Huizinga and Delbert Elliott, "Juvenile Offenders: Prevalence, Offender Incidence and Arrest Rates by Race," paper presented at Meeting on Race and the Incarceration of Juveniles, Racine, Wisconsin, December 1986, University of Colorado, Boulder, Institute of Behavioral Science, National Youth Survey.

63. Ibid., p. 1.

64. On the matter of the reliability of self-reporting as an accurate measure of

delinquent behavior, the authors comment, "While there is some question about whether people will be honest and report violations they have committed, the evidence indicates that they will report such behaviors as long as their answers are protected by anonymity and confidentiality . . . offenses recorded in police records are usually reported in self-report surveys." (M. J. Hindelang, T. Hirschi, and J. G. Wies, *Measuring Delinquency* [Beverly Hills, Calif.: Sage, 1981]; D. Huizinga, D. and D. S. Elliott, *Self-Reported Measures of Delinquency and Crime: Methodological Issues and Comparative Findings* [Boulder, Colo.: Behavioral Research Institute, 1986], p. 6.) Predictably, Wilson and Herrnstein suggest there is evidence that black youths are perhaps not as likely to report their delinquencies as white juveniles (*Crime and Human Nature*, p. 463). Huizinga and Elliott apparently found no such tendencies.

65. Huizinga and Elliott, p. 14.
66. Ibid., p. 16.
67. Ibid., p. 17.
68. Delbert S. Elliott, "Longitudinal Research in Criminology: Promise and Practice," in *Cross-National Longitudinal Research on Human Development and Criminal Behavior*, ed. E. G. Weitekamp and K. Hans-Jurgen (London: Kluwer, 1992).
69. W. McCord and J. Sanchez, "Curing Criminal Negligence," *Psychology Today*, April 1982.
70. Katherine Hunt Federle and Meda Chesney-Lind, "Special Issues in Juvenile Justice: Gender, Race, and Ethnicity," in *Juvenile Justice and Public Policy: Toward a National Agenda*, ed. Ira Schwartz (New York: Lexington Books/New York and Oxford: Maxwell Macmillian Int., 1992), pp. 179–180.
71. M. Wordes, T. Bynum, and C. Corley, "Locking Up Youth: The Impact of Race on Detention Decisions," *Journal of Research in Crime and Delinquency* 31, no. 2 (May 1994): p. 164.
72. Katherine Hunt Federle and Meda Chesney-Lind, "Special Issues in Juvenile Justice," pp. 179–180.
73. Huizinga and Elliott, "Juvenile Offenders," p. 14 (n. 62 above).
74. Federle and Chesney-Lind, "Special Issues in Juvenile Justice," p. 190.
75. *U.S. News & World Report*, "Is Nature to Blame for Careers of Crime?" February 10, 1986, p. 67.
76. In 1984, Harvard law professor and psychiatrist Alan Stone warned his professions about the "invidious aspect" of the diagnosis of the so-called sociopath as defined by the official Diagnostic and Statistical Manual (III) of

the American Psychiatric Association. Stone suggested that the wide-ranging criteria for this label could in effect be applied to a large percentage of inner-city black males. The defining "symptoms" of sociopathy include truancy, delinquency, running away from home, theft, vandalism, school grades below expected, and repeated sexual intercourse in casual relationships. Only three of these factors need to exist before age 15 to establish the disorder in this age group. If the male is over age 18 and unemployed, defined as not being a responsible parent, refuses to accept social norms, fails to maintain attachments to a sexual partner, fails to meet financial obligations, does not plan ahead, and shows disregard for the truth or exhibits "recklessness," he is to be diagnosed as a sociopath. As Stone concluded, "whatever scientific value the diagnosis of sociopath may have, there can be little question that the urban poor and racial minorities will be swept into this diagnostic category." He then added, "the DSM-III may well introduce . . . racism." Stone's reservations notwithstanding, quasi-medical labels attached to offenders have been firmly enshrined in state laws and in some cases carry life or death implications. For example, a diagnosis of "sociopath" or "antisocial personality" in Texas is an "aggravating" factor to be weighed by the jury in deciding whether a murder defendant deserves the death penalty. Indeed, a middle-aged white physician employed by prosecutors throughout the state earned the title of "Dr. Death" for his down-home manner in convincing juries that certain defendants were sociopaths and thereby suitable for execution. On occasion, he rendered his diagnosis without ever having met or interviewed the accused, relying instead on his observation of the defendant's demeanor in the courtroom during the trial. (Alan A. Stone, *Law, Psychiatry and Morality: Essays and Analysis* (Washington, D.C.: American Psychiatric Press, 1984).

77. Clarence Lusane, *Pipe Dream Blues* (Boston: South End Press, 1990).

78. U.S. Department of Health and Human Services, Public Health Service, *Preliminary Estimates from the 1992 National Household Survey on Drug Abuse,* Advance Report No. 3, June 1993, Substance Abuse and Mental Health Services Administration, Office of Applied Studies (OAS internal draft version 7, 6/14/93, p. 8).

79. Ibid., p. 12.

80. *Los Angeles Times,* "Blacks Feel Brunt of Drug War," April 22, 1990.

81. Report of National Center on Institutions and Alternatives, "Hobbling a Generation II," 1992 (Alexandria, Virginia).

82. Sam Vincent Meddis, "Is the Drug War Racist?" *USA Today,* July 23–25, 1993, p. 2A.

83. J. G. Miller, *Duval Jail Report*, filed with Middle District Court of Florida, Jacksonville, Fla., June 1993.

84. "Does the Punishment Fit the Crime? Drug Users and Drunk Drivers, Questions of Race and Class," *The Sentencing Project*, Washington D.C., 1993.

85. In August 1993, Federal Judge Lyle E. Strom in Omaha, Nebraska, became the first in the nation to rule that sentences could not be more severe for those who deal in crack cocaine than those who deal in powder cocaine. Judge Strom departed from federal sentencing guidelines. He commented that even were the disparate penalties inherently constitutional, when applied to blacks their impact was "disproportionately severe." He also noted that more than 90% of the persons prosecuted for dealing crack were African-American ("Federal Judge Attacks Disparity in Sentencing for Cocaine Cases," *Wall Street Journal*, August 3, 1993). In March 1995, the federal sentencing commission announced their intention to adjust the guidelines for those caught with crack cocaine versus powder cocaine to bring the recommended sentences into conformity. The Clinton administration refused to support the Commission's reforms and they died in Congress.

86. Criminal Justice Policy Council, *Sentencing Dynamics Study*, Texas Punishment Standards Commission, 1992.

87. Report to Monroe County Bar Association Board of Trustees, "Justice in Jeopardy," Monroe County Bar Association, May 1992.

88. In a 1992 conversation with the author.

89. *Pittsburgh Post-Gazette*, January 22, 1994, Sec. B, p. A1.

90. Howard Snyder, Ph.D., "Arrests of Youth 1990," National Center for Juvenile Justice (Research Branch of National Council of Juvenile and Family Court Judges), Pittsburgh, Pa.

91. National Center on Institutions and Alternatives, "Hobbling a Generation II," p. 3.

92. D. Altschuler, *The State of the Region: Youth Crime and Juvenile Justice in Maryland and Baltimore* (Baltimore: The Johns Hopkins Institute for Policy Studies, Fall 1992), p. vi.

93. H. Snyder, T. A. Finnegan, E. H. Nimick, M. H. Sickmund, D. P. Sullivan, and N. J. Tierney (1990). *Juvenile Court Statistics, 1988*. National Center for Juvenile Justice, Pittsburgh, Pa.

94. Ibid., p. 4.

95. Duster notes that the War on Drugs of the 1980s amplified these differences even more. In Florida, admissions to state prisons tripled from 1983 to 1989. In 1983 in Virginia, 63% of prison commitments for drugs were white, 37% minority. By 1989, the pattern had reversed, with 34% of the new commit-

ments being white and 65% minority. "Yet, in this very period we find a significant increase in scientific journal articles and scholarly books (Mednick et al. 1984; Wilson and Herrnstein 1985) suggesting a greater role for biological explanations of crime" (Troy Duster, "Genetics, Race, and Crime, etc.," pp. 133–135).

3. UNANTICIPATED CONSEQUENCES

1. G. H. Mead, "The Psychology of Punitive Justice," *American Journal of Sociology* 23 (1917): 577–602.
2. In re Gault, 387 U.S. 1 (1967).
3. Robert K. Merton, *Social Theory and Social Structure*, rev. ed. (Glencoe, Ill. 1957), pp. 64–65. Originally published 1949.
4. Mead, "Psychology of Punitive Justice"; Emile Durkheim, *The Division of Labor in Society* (Glencoe, Ill.: Free Press, 1947); W. G. Sumner, *Folkway* (Boston: Ginn & Co. 1906); Albert G. Keller, *Social Evolution* (New York: Macmillan, 1927); R. M. MacIver, *Social Causation* (Boston: Ginn & Co. 1942); W. I. Thomas and F. Znaniecki, *The Polish Peasant in Europe and America*, 2 vols. (New York: Knopf, 1927. Originally published in 5 vols., 1918).
5. Dane Archer and Rosemary Gartner, *Violence and Crime in Cross-National Perspective* (New Haven: Yale University Press, 1984), p. 35. See also the comprehensive historical study of the death penalty by William J. Bowers with G. Pierce and J. McDevitt, *Legal Homicide: Death as Punishment in America, 1864–1982* (Boston: Northeastern University Press, 1984). These researchers concluded not only that the death penalty deters crime no more than does a life sentence, but that imposition of the death penalty (particularly when publicized) actually increases the homicide rate. They theorize that executions inspire some potential murderers to identify with the state, assuming the role of angels of vengeance to those they see as deserving punishment. They also suggest that some suicidal persons are drawn to homicide as a means of ensuring their own deaths.
6. Mike Tidwell, *In the Shadow of the White House: Drugs, Death, and Redemption on the Streets of the Nation's Capital* (Rocklin, Calif.: Prima Publishing, 1992), p. 189.
7. Paul Gendreau, Francis T. Cullen, and James Bonta, "Intensive Rehabilitation Supervision: The Next Generation in Community Corrections?" *Federal Probation* 58 (March 1994): 72–78. Among a series of published narrative

reviews and meta-analyses of the offender-treatment outcome literature, Gendreau et al. list : D. A. Andrews and J. Bonta, *The Psychology of Criminal Conduct* (Cincinnati, Ohio: Anderson Publishers, 1994); D. A. Andrews, J. Bonta, and R. D. Hoge, "Classification for Effective Rehabilitation: Rediscovering Psychology," *Criminal Justice and Behavior* 17 (1990): 19–52; F. T. Cullen and P. Gendreau, "The Effectiveness of Correctional Rehabilitation: Reconsidering the 'Nothing Works' Debate, in L. Goodstein and D. Mac-Kenzie, eds., *American Prisons: Issues in Research and Policy* (New York: Plenum, 1989), pp. 23–44; C. J. Garrett, "Effects of Residential Treatment on Adjudicated Delinquents: A Meta-analysis," *Journal of Research in Crime and Delinquency*, 22 (1985): 287–308; P. Gendreau and D. A. Andrews, "Tertiary Prevention: What the Meta-analysis of the Offender Treatment Literature Tells Us about 'What Works,' " *Canadian Journal of Criminology* 32 (1990): 173–184; R. Izzo and R. R. Ross, "Meta-analysis of Rehabilitation Programs for Juvenile Delinquents: A Brief Report," *Criminal Justice and Behavior* 17 (1990): 134–142; M. W. Lipsey, "Juvenile Delinquency Treatment: A Meta-analytic Inquiry into the Variability of Effects," in T. D. Cook, H. Cooper, D. S. Cordray, H. Hartmann, L. V. Hedges, R. J. Light, T. A. Louis, and F. Mosteller, eds., *Meta-analysis for Explanation* (New York: Russell Sage Foundation, 1992), pp. 83–127; F. Losel, "Evaluating Psychosocial Interventions in Prison and Other Contexts," paper presented at the Twentieth Criminological Conference, Strasbourg, Germany, November 1993; and T. Palmer, *The Re-emergence of Correctional Intervention* (Newbury Park, Calif.: Sage Publications, 1992).

8. Robert J. MacCoun, "Drugs and the Law: A Psychological Analysis of Drug Prohibition," *Psychological Bulletin* 113, no. 3 (1993): 508.

9. Ibid., p. 508. H. G. Grasmick, E. Davenport, M. B. Chamlin, and R. J. Bursik, "Protestant Fundamentalism and the Retributive Doctrine of Punishment," *Criminology* 30 (1992): 21–45; S. Jacoby, *Wild Justice: The Evolution of Revenge* (New York: Harper & Row, 1983); R. M. Bohm, L. J. Clark, and A. F. Aveni, "Knowledge and Death Penalty Opinions: A Test of the Marshall Hypothesis," *Journal of Research in Crime and Delinquency* 28 (1991): 360–387; P. C. Ellsworth and L. Ross, "Public Opinion and Capital Punishment: A Close Examination of the Views of Abolitionists and Retentionists," *Crime and Delinquency* 29 (1983): 116–169; T. R. Tyler and R. Weber, "Support for the Death Penalty: Instrumental Response to Crime or Symbolic Attitude?" *Law and Society Review* 17 (1982): 21–44.

10. Elijah Anderson, "The Code of the Streets," *The Atlantic Monthly* 273, no 3., (1995): 82.

11. Ibid., p. 92.

12. Ibid., p. 94.

13. William Chambliss, "Moral Panics and Racial Oppression," manuscript prepared for Darney Hawkins, ed., *Ethnicity, Race and Crime* (unpublished manuscript, 1993), p. 4.

14. *The Nation*, June 1, 1992, p. 744.

15. Richard Posner, *Overcoming Law* (Cambridge, Mass.: Harvard University Press), p. 485.

16. "The Dreaded 'Encounter' with Police," *Washington Post*, January 18, 1994, Metro Section, p. 1.

17. "Police Teach Getting Arrested Safely 101," *Wall Street Journal*, June 16, 1994, pp. B1, 16.

18. *Washington Post*, Metro section, May 8, 1994, p. B6.

19. "Secret Threat to Justice," *The National Law Journal*, February 20, 1995, pp. 1, 28.

20. *United States v. Shepherd*, 857 F. Supp. 105 (D. D.C. 1994).

21. Donald Koblitz, "Germany's Poison Chalice," Op-Ed, *New York Times*, January 21, 1994.

22. *Washington Post*, January 12, 1993, p. D1.

23. Roger Morris, *The Devil's Butcher Shop: The New Mexico Prison Uprising*, (New York, London, Toronto, Sydney: Franklin Watts, 1983), p. 87.

24. Gresham Sykes, *The Society of Captives* (Princeton, N.J.: Princeton University Press, 1958), pp. 78–79.

25. Kevin Thomas, " 'Fire This Time': Light on L.A. Riots," *Los Angeles Times*, April 29, 1994.

26. *Washington Times*, February 27, 1995, p. C15.

27. Debriefing interviews conducted with juveniles removed from the Camp Hill adult correctional facility (Harrisburg, Pa.: The Camp Hill Project, 1977).

28. U.S. Department of Justice, FBI, *Crime in the United States, 1992* (Washington, D.C.: USGPO, 1993), p. 217.

29. In February 1993, the American Civil Liberties Union of Maryland filed a federal lawsuit challenging the practice of stopping motorists on the basis of a profile. The suit charged that state troopers target black men driving expensive cars. The profile was described as focusing on a young black man or men wearing expensive jewelry, driving expensive cars such as sports cars, wearing beepers, and carrying lists of telephone numbers. The lead plaintiff in the suit was Robert L. Wilkins, a 29-year-old Harvard Law School graduate who worked as a public defender in Washington, D.C., and was stopped

for speeding. As the *Baltimore Sun* summarized the incident: "It was about 6 A.M., and Mr. Wilkins' aunt and uncle were asleep in the back seat of the car, a rental Cadillac. . . . The trooper went back to his cruiser and returned to the vehicle to ask [the driver] to sign a release form consenting to a search. Mr. Wilkins identified himself as a lawyer, who had a case in a Washington court that day, and told [the trooper] that he had no right to search the car unless he was arresting [the driver]. The trooper asked if they had 'nothing to hide, then what was the problem?'

"Another trooper arrived, and detained the car for a half hour while a narcotics-sniffing German shepherd was brought to the scene by an Allegany sheriff's deputy. . . . The plaintiffs were ordered out of the car. They refused at first, noting that it was raining, but got out because they were afraid of being attacked by the dog. The dog sniffed the car without visible reaction. The episode lasted about 45 minutes" (*Baltimore Sun*, February 13, 1993, p. 1).

30. H. Donaldson, "The Negro Migration of 1916–18," *The Journal of Negro History* 383 (1921): 415–416.

31. National Association of Criminal Defense Lawyers, *The Champion*, September/October 1993, p. 28.

32. Dianan Jean Schemo, "Anger over List Divides Blacks and College Town," *New York Times*, September 27, 1992, p. 40.

33. Dirk Johnson, "2 Out of 3 Young Black Men in Denver Are on Police List of Gang Suspects," *New York Times*, December 10, 1993.

34. Ibid.

35. In the 1980s, the U.S. Justice Department assisted localities in developing computerized lists of juveniles labeled as "shodi" youths – those labeled by police as "serious or habitual offenders." Those so identified are then targeted by the prosecution for more punitive sanctions. The question as to what a "serious" or "habitual" offender is, is open to wide interpretation locally. In Duval County, the list of almost 1,000 mostly black youth contained names of a large percentage of lesser and nuisance offenders.

36. U.S. Department of Justice, Bureau of Justice Statistics, *Survey of Criminal History Information Systems, 1993*, NCJ-148951, January 1995, pp. 5–6.

37. U.S. Department of Justice, Bureau of Justice Statistics, *Use and Management of Criminal History Record Information: A Comprehensive Report*, NCJ-143501, November 1993, p. 25.

38. U.S. Department of Justice, Bureau of Justice Statistics, *Use and Management of Criminal History Record Information: A Comprehensive Report*, NCJ-143501, November 1993, p. 24.

39. *Computerized Criminal History System Audit, 1992,* Illinois Criminal Justice Information Authority, Chicago, Illinois, 1993.

40. U.S. Department of Justice, Bureau of Justice Statistics, Survey of Criminal History Information Systems, NCJ-125620, March 1991, pp. 1–3.

41. Jeffrey Fagan, "Disclosure of Juvenile Arrests Has High Price," *New York Times,* letter to editor, July 14, 1992.

42. For a summary review of psychological labeling theory, the reader is referred to D. Archer, "Social Deviance," in G. Lindzey and E. Aronson, eds., *The Handbook of Social Psychology,* 3d ed. (New York: Random House, 1985), 2: 743–804.

43. David P. Farrington, "The Effects of Public Labeling," *British Journal of Criminology* 17 (1977): 112–125.

44. R. J. Hart, "Crime and Punishment in the Army," *Journal of Personality and Social Psychology* 36 (1978): 1456–1471.

45. C. R. Tittle, "Deterrents or Labeling?" *Social Forces* 53 (1974): 399–410.

46. MacCoun, "Drugs and the Law," p. 505.

47. J. Braithwaite, *Crime, Shame and Reintegration* (Cambridge: Cambridge University Press, 1989).

48. MacCoun, p. 506.

49. John Hagan and Alberto Palloni, "The Social Reproduction of a Criminal Class in Working-Class London circa 1950–1980," *American Journal of Sociology* 96, no. 2 (September 1990).

50. Donald West and David Farrington, *The Delinquent Way of Life* (New York: Crane Russak, 1977), p. 161.

51. Hagan and Palloni. Hagan developed the implications of these findings in "The Social Embeddedness of Crime and Unemployment," a paper presented at the February 1993 meeting of the American Association for the Advancement of Science in Boston, Massachusetts.

52. John H. Laub and Robert J. Sampson, "The Long Term Effect of Punitive Discipline" (February 1993), revised version of paper presented at the Life History Research Society Meeting, May 6, 1992.

53. Sheldon Glueck and Eleanor Glueck, *Unraveling Juvenile Delinquency* (New York: The Commonwealth Fund, 1950).

54. Laub and Sampson, p. 9.

55. Ibid., p. 16.

56. Ibid., p. 16.

57. Ibid., pp. 17–18. Laub and Sampson do a great service in calling our attention to the theories on cumulative continuity and state dependence. It is this phenomenon of the *cumulative* effect of criminal justice intrusion on later

adjustment which has been lacking in many of the static criminological studies on the career or repetitive criminal. For an interesting analysis of this perspective, see Daniel Nagin and Raymond Paternoster, "On the Relationship of Past and Future Participation in Delinquency," *Criminology* 29(1991): 163–190.

58. Daniel Goleman, "75 Years Later, Study Still Tracking Geniuses," *New York Times*, March 7, 1995, p. C9.

59. John Hagan, "The Poverty of a Classless Criminology," *Journal of Criminology* 30, no. 1 (February 1992): 10.

60. John Hagan, "The Social Embeddedness of Crime and Unemployment" (University of Toronto; research funded by the Social Sciences and Humanities Research Council of Canada and a Killam Research Fellowship from the Canada Council, 1994). Here, Hagan relies heavily on the work of M. Granovetter, *Getting a Job: A Study of Contacts and Careers* (Cambridge, Mass.: Harvard Univ. Press, 1974), and idem, "Economic Action and Social Structure: The Problem of Embeddedness," *American Journal of Sociology* 91(1985): 481–510.

61. Hogan, "The Social Embeddedness of Crime and Unemployment," p. 32.

62. Ibid., p. 29.

63. Richard D. Schwartz and Jerome H. Skolnick, "Two Legal Studies of Legal Stigma," paper read at Annual Meeting of American Sociological Association, August 1960.

64. Dane Archer and Rosemary Gartner, *Violence and Crime in Cross-National Perspective* (New Haven: Yale University Press, 1984).

65. Ibid., p.

66. Marvin E. Wolfgang, Robert M. Figlio, and Thorsten Sellin, *Delinquency in a Birth Cohort* (Chicago: University of Chicago Press, 1972), p. 25.

67. D. M. Hamparian, R. Schuster, S. Dinitz, and J. P. Conrad, *The Violent Few: A Study of Dangerous Juvenile Offenders* (Boston: Lexington Books, D.C. Heath and Company, 1978), p. 119.

68. Lyle W. Shannon, *Assessing the Relationship of Adult Criminal Careers to Juvenile Careers: A Summary* (Washington, D.C.: U.S. Office of Juvenile Justice and Delinquency Prevention, 1982), p. 10.

69. Stevens H. Clarke and Anita L. Harrison, *Recidivism of Criminal Offenders Assigned to Community Correctional Programs or Released from Prison in North Carolina in 1989*, study prepared for the North Carolina Sentencing and Policy Advisory Commission, 1992, pp. 29–30.

70. Ibid., p. 30.

71. M. W. Lipsey, "Juvenile Delinquency Treatment: A Meta-analytic Inquiry

into the Variability of Effect" (Claremont, Calif.: Claremont Graduate School, 1990).

72. Paul Gendreau, "The Principles of Effective Intervention with Offenders," American Association of Probation and Parole, 1994, p. 22.

73. Theodore N. Ferdinand, "Juvenile Delinquency or Juvenile Justice: Which Came First?" *Criminology* 27, no. 1 (1989).

74. Stanley Cohen, *Visions of Social Control* (Cambridge: Polity Press, 1985).

75. T. Ferdinand, "Juvenile Delinquency or Juvenile Justice" (1989), p. 79.

76. Charles Murray and Louis Cox, *Beyond Probation: Juvenile Corrections and the Chronic Offender* (Beverly Hills, Calif.: Sage Publications, 1979).

77. Elliott Currie, *Confronting Crime: An American Challenge* (New York: Pantheon Books, 1985), pp. 74–75. Currie added: "Furthermore, the data revealed an important finding that Murray and Cox passed over so quickly that it was easy to miss altogether. Many of the delinquents sent to at-home placements remained in them for three months or less; but receiving these at-home services for a year or more brought the suppression effect of the 'least' and the 'most' drastic alternatives so close together that it is difficult to grant much significance to the remaining differences (the year-long at-home placements 'suppressed' future arrests by 61 percent, imprisonment by 68 percent). These findings, indeed, generally affirm the underlying logic behind (community-based alternative) programs: not that every serious delinquent can be handled equally well with less drastic forms of treatment, but that a range of carefully designed placements can be an effective – as well as humane and fiscally appealing – alternative to conventional youth prisons."

78. Robert B. Coates, Alden D. Miller, and Lloyd E. Ohlin, "Juvenile Detention and Its Consequences," *Center for Criminal Justice* (Cambridge, Mass.: Harvard Law School, 1975).

79. E. J. Dionne, *Why Americans Hate Politics* (New York: Simon and Schuster, 1992).

80. *New York Times*, April 29, 1992.

81. Andrew Clymer, "A G.O.P. Leader Aims at 'Welfare State' Values," *New York Times*, January 4, 1990.

82. Peter Reuter, "Have the Hawks of Drug Policy Gone Too Far?" *Rand Research Review* no. 2 (Fall 1992): 3. Reuter argues for an "owlish" rather than a "hawkish" approach to drug control. He advocates a "less ideological, more pragmatic approach to the problem that favors minimizing the harm that results not only from drug use, but from drug control." Writing in *Daedalus* (Summer 1992), he summarized his findings in this way: "To an extraordinary degree, the hawks have taken control of drug policy and given it a

distinctly punitive hue. . . . I believe that we might well be better off if we simply punished drug dealers less aggressively; I believe that matters would be still further improved if some of the money saved by reduced punishment were spent on better quality treatment of the drug dependent."

83. Jonathan Marshall and Peter Dale Scott, *Cocaine Politics: Drugs, Armies and the CIA in Central America* (Berkeley and Los Angeles: University of California Press, 1991).

84. B. Gellman and S. Horwitz, "Letter Stirs Debate after Acquittal: Writer Says Jurors Bowed to Racial Issue in D.C. Murder Case," *Washington Post,* March 29, 1990, p. A1.

85. According to nationally syndicated columnist Samuel Francis, black jurors in Smith County, Texas, who deadlocked in a trial of a black man admitted that they were influenced by the failure of an all-white grand jury to indict a white policeman who had shot a bedridden black woman during a drug raid. Similar decisions involving black defendants were made in Georgia, and a number of federal criminal cases ended in mistrials over racially divided juries in which black jurors refused to convict black defendants. Samuel Francis, "Criminal Justice Hues and Cries," *The Washington Times,* Sept. 4, 1994.

86. Benjamin A. Holden, "Harsh Judgment: Many Well-Off Blacks See Injustice at Work in King, Denny Cases," *Wall Street Journal,* August 10, 1993, p. A1.

87. *A Call to Reject the Federal Weed and Seed Program in Los Angeles* (Van Nuys, Calif.: Urban Strategies Group of the Labor/Community Strategies Center, 1992).

88. P. M. Harris, T. R. Clear, and S. C. Baird, "Have Community Service Officers Changed Their Attitude Toward Their Work?" *Justice Quarterly* 6, no. 2 (1993): 233–246.

89. U. S. Department of Justice, National Institute of Justice, *Research in Brief,* May 1995, p. 7.

90. Paul W. Brown, "Guns and Probation Officers: The Unspoken Reality," *Federal Probation,* June 1990, pp. 21–26.

91. W. Dickey, "Reflections of a Former Corrections Director: Are Offenders Tougher Today?" *Federal Probation* 56 no. 2 (June 1992): 43.

92. Barry J. Nidorf, " 'Nothing Works' Revisited," Guest Editorial, *Perspectives* (American Probation and Parole Association, Summer 1991), pp. 12–13.

93. In Alabama, for example, approximately 70% of those "technically violated" and returned to prison were cited for the following violations: Failure to Report, Failure to Pay Court Costs and/or Supervision Fees, Positive Uri-

nalysis for Drug Use, Changing Residence and/or Leaving State without Permission, and Failure to Maintain Employment. Timothy Roche, *Technical Probation and Parole Violators within the Alabama Department of Corrections* (Alexandria, Va.: NCIA, September 1992), p. 2.

94. In the summer of 1993, I was asked to give a training session to supervisors and administrators of so-called Pre-Trial Service staff from programs across Florida and the South. I was followed by a special agent of the Florida Department of Law Enforcement who trained these assorted social workers and counselors in "Kinesic Interviewing Techniques" of clientele. The course outline included the following: "*Interview Settings* – Use 2-man in beginning. Use him in rear behind subject. *Statements* – Written statement – have them corrected, initialed, and signed. Make mistake deliberately for correction purposes. *Good Interview Format* – Include asking about weaknesses from other investigators who may have previously interviewed same subject. *Voice Pitch* – These 'No' answers are generally seen as indicators of deception: Five-second 'No'; 'No' followed by crossing of arms or legs; Late 'No' when other answers are on time; 'No' followed by closing of eyes; saying 'No' more than once; 'No' by swearing to God. *Body Language* – Lip Behavior under Stress, Upper Teeth 'Upper teeth smile only – showing deception,' etc. *Eyes of the Guilty* – Watch for the person who looks at the ceiling for the first time, and starts blinking slowly. A shrewd or cunning person is more likely to look you in the eye than an honest person. *Beware of the Following Person:* Attacks trivial details; Attacks the agency; Overly Polite, Brings up things in the Past. *When You Accuse Look For:* Pleasure, defiantly challenging – usually guilty, Defiance – legs crossed, protecting genital area (except Blacks), arms crossed: Acceptance on face, sad facial look, drop head and eyes – usually guilty," etc. (Wayne D. Porter, Special Agent, *Kinesic Interviewing Techniques,* Florida Department of Law Enforcement, Division of Criminal Investigation, July 1, 1993).

95. *Perspectives,* American Probation and Parole Association, Summer 1991, pp. 6, 14, 27, 37.

96. Andrew Rutherford, in book review of Nils Christie, *Crime Control as Industry: Towards Gulags, Western Style?* (London: Routledge, 1993); Anderson, in *British Journal of Criminology* (Fall, 1993).

97. Observed by a staff member of the National Center on Institutions and Alternatives, 1991.

98. The practice of "violating" probationers and parolees for technical reasons is not, of course, confined to California. It is common practice in most states and contributes a significant proportion to most state prison populations. A

study of over 7,000 persons terminated from probation – a fourth of whom had violated conditions of their probation – revealed that applying the more severe sanctions (i.e., return to prison) "was no more likely to affect the seriousness of chronic violators' subsequent misbehaviors than application of more lenient ones." Todd R. Clear, Patricia M. Harris, and S. Christopher Baird, "Probationer Violations and Officer Response," *Journal of Criminal Justice* 20 (1992): 1.

99. *New York Times*, January 21, 1994, p. A7.

100. Advertisement appearing in *Corrections Today* (1993), magazine of the American Correctional Association.

101. Ira Glasser, "Prisoners of Benevolence: Power versus Liberty in the Welfare State," in Willard Gaylin et al., *Doing Good: The Limits of Benevolence* (New York: Pantheon Books, 1978), p. 124.

102. Edmund Leach, *A Runaway World: The BBC Reith Lectures*, London, British Broadcasting Corporation, 1967.

103. A. Nehamas, "The Examined Life of Michel Foucault: Subject and Abject," *The New Republic*, February 15, 1993, pp. 30–31.

104. Gerald M. Caplan, "Abscam Wasn't Worth It," *Washington Post*, May 5, 1981 (Op-Ed).

105. In a recent article on 25 common offenses committed by the average citizen, two staff reporters for the *Wall Street Journal* admitted to having committed at least 16 crimes carrying maximum jail terms of 15 years and fines as much as $30,000, including "gambling illegally," "drinking in public," "engaging in prohibited sex acts," "speeding," "buying stolen goods," "lying on an application," "patronizing a prostitute," and "possessing marijuana." Steven Adler and Wade Lambert, "Common Criminals: Just About Everyone Violates Some Laws, Even Model Citizens – Many Often View Legal Rules as Foolish or Intrusive, but Careers Can Be Hurt," *Wall Street Journal*, March 12, 1993, pp. A1, A4.

106. Though this many outstanding arrest warrants might appear startling, they are not an anomaly. For example, in April of 1994, the San Diego County Marshal's Office had a backlog of 622,000 unserved misdemeanor warrants. "Failure to Punish Misdemeanors Fuels Violence, St. Louis Officials Say, " *Washington Post*, April 10, 1994, p. A8.

107. Most licenses had been suspended for nonpayment of traffic fines or for such matters as not notifying the Department of Transportation of a change of address. Jerome G. Miller, *The Duval County Jail Report*, submitted to the Honorable Howell W. Melton, United States District Judge, Middle District of Florida, Jacksonville, Florida, June 1, 1993.

4. THE POLITICS OF CRIME

1. Graham Greene, *Reflections,* selected by Judith Adamson (New York: Reinhardt Books, 1991).
2. Jock Young, "Recent Paradigms in Criminology," in *Oxford Handbook of Criminology,* ed. M. Maguire, R. Morgan, and R. Reiner (Oxford: Clarendon Press, 1994), p. 118.
3. Among the most influential were sociologists Lloyd Ohlin of Harvard University's Law School's Center for Criminal Justice and Richard Cloward of Columbia University's School of Social Work. Cloward and Ohlin's treatise on crime, *Delinquency and Opportunity,* an early classic in the field, tied crime and delinquency to economics and opportunity structures (or lack thereof) for black youth.
4. Judith Wilks, and Robert Martinson, "Is the Treatment of Criminal Offenders Really Necessary?" *Federal Probation* 40 (March 1976): 4.
5. In his book *The Rise of the Counter-Establishment: From Conservative Ideology to Political Power,* Sydney Blumenthal provided a fascinating account of how right-wing supporters developed a marketing plan for Murray's book *Losing Ground* before it was written and its findings gathered.
6. James Traub, "Intellectual Stock Picking," *The New Yorker,* February 7, 1994, pp. 27–28. Upon William Hammett's unexpected departure from the Manhattan Institute, the *New York Observer* commented: "Without his marketing ability, it is doubtful that some of the key conservative books of the past decade or so would have seen the light of day, let alone found their ideas written in law by Newt Gingrich. The House speaker has been waving around copies of such institute-sponsored publications as Charles Murray's book on welfare, *Losing Ground,* and Myron Magnet's more recent volume, *The Dream and the Nightmare,* on the corrosive impact of 60s morality." *The New York Observer,* March 20, 1995, p. 7.
7. I happened to be on Governor of Pennsylvania Milton Shapp's staff when Wilson's *Thinking About Crime* appeared. It was purchased by the Republican leadership and distributed free of charge to all Republican members of the Pennsylvania Legislature for their use in planning state criminal justice policies.
8. E. J. Dionne, *Why Americans Hate Politics* (New York: Simon and Schuster, 1991), p. 65.
9. Ibid., p. 66.
10. Private conversation with Kenneth Feinberg, then chief administrative aide to Senator Kennedy.

11. David Frum, "The Conservative Cave-In," *Harper's Magazine*, July 1994, p. 13. (Adapted from *Dead Right* [New York: Basic Books, 1994].)

12. James Q. Wilson, "Redefining Equality: The Liberation of Mickey Kaus," *The Public Interest*, no. 109 (Fall 1992), p. 103.

13. Charles Booth, *Life and Labour of the People of London* (1892), 1:10–11; quoted in Pauline V. Young, *Scientific Surveys and Research* (New York: Prentice-Hall, 1939), p. 13.

14. James R. Kincaid, *Child-Loving: The Erotic Child and Victorian Culture* (New York and London: Routledge, 1992).

15. Ibid., pp. 20–21.

16. *Newsweek*, February 3, 1992, p. 55.

17. Kincaid, p. 27.

18. Ibid.

19. For example, in October 1992 the director of Rand's criminal justice programs wrote an Op-Ed piece for the *Los Angeles Times* entitled "Building More Jails Will Not Make Us Safer" (*Los Angeles Times*, October 4, 1995, p. M6).

20. There were of course exceptions like Gunnar Myrdal's classic *An American Dilemma: The Negro Problem and Modern Democracy* (New York: Harper & Row, 1940), and Elliott Liebow's *Tally's Corner*.

21. Gresham M. Sykes, and David Matza, "Techniques of Neutralization: A Theory of Delinquency," *American Sociological Review* 22 (December 1957): 664 – 678; Edwin H. Sutherland, "Development of a Theory," in Albert K. Cohen et al., eds., *The Sutherland Papers* (Bloomington: Indiana University Press, 1956), pp. 20–31; Sheldon Glueck and Eleanor Sheldon, *Unraveling Juvenile Delinquency* (Cambridge, Mass.: Harvard University Press, 1950); David Matza, *Delinquency and Drift* (New York: John Wiley & Sons Publishers, 1964).

22. William I. Thomas and Florian Znaniecki, *The Polish Peasant in Europe and America, II* (New York: Knopf, 1927), pp. 1832–1834.

23. Jerome Bruner, *Acts of Meaning* (Cambridge, Mass.: Harvard University Press, 1990), p. 4.

24. Charles R. Morris, "It's *Not* the Economy, Stupid," *The Atlantic* 272, no. 1 (July 1993): 50–51.

25. Groups like the Rand Corporation, American Institutes of Research, Abt Associates, and Arthur D. Little all began doing research on crime and delinquency. Carnegie Mellon University researcher Alfred Blumstein, before his interest in criminology, had previously been a member of the Research Staff of the Research and Engineering Support Division of the Institute for Defense Analyses during the 1960s.

26. Richard B. Abell, "Beyond Willie Horton: The Battle of the Prison Bulge," *Policy Review* (Spring 1989), p. 34.

27. Phil Gramm, "Don't Let Judges Set Crooks Free," *New York Times*, Op-Ed, July 8, 1993.

28. Michael Tonry, "General Barr's Last Stand," *Overcrowded Times* 4, no. 1 (February 1993): 2–3. Published for the Edna McConnell Clark Foundation by Castine Research Corporation, Castine, Maine.

29. Kathleen Maguire, Ann Pastore, and T. Flanagan, *Bureau of Justice Statistics Sourcebook of Criminal Justice Statistics – 1992*, Hindelang Criminal Justice Research Center, 1992. (See, in particular, sections 5.61, 6.2, and 6.112.) Projecting from the 1990 figures published in this report, I estimated that there were approximately three million on probation and another half-million on parole on an average day in 1993. In addition, approximately 70% of the 14 million arrestees are released on some sort of money or recognizance bond. As many as one-fourth of these (mostly misdemeanor arrestees) repeat within the same year. On this basis, I estimated that at least three million individuals are out on bond or being sought on warrants on any given day.

30. Ibid., p. 3.

31. Quentin Skinner, *The Return of Grand Theory in Human Sciences* (Cambridge: Cambridge University Press, 1985), p. 8.

32. Lani Guinier, "Clinton Spoke the Truth on Race," *New York Times*, Op-Ed, October 19, 1993, p. A29.

33. Shirley Brown, *Race as a Factor in the Intra-Prison Outcomes of Youthful First Offenders*, unpublished Ph.D. thesis, University of Michigan, Ann Arbor, pp. 18–19.

34. Walter Goodman, *Critic's Notebook*, "Crime and Black Images in TV News," *New York Times*, December 23, 1993.

35. Herbert Blumer, "Social Problems as Collective Behavior," *Social Problems* 18 (Winter 1971): p. 300.

36. Ibid., p. 298.

37. Ibid., p. 302.

38. Ibid., p. 302. Recently there has been more recognition among sociologists of the importance of this area for inquiry. Sociologist William Chambliss has been addressing it for a number of years. More recently, those who espouse the so-called constructionist perspective have also focused on how various mixes of social conditions become "social problems." Cf. comments on "constructionist" theory in the introduction to this book.

39. Barry O'Neill, "The History of a Hoax," *New York Times Magazine*, March 6, 1994, p. 46.

40. Ibid., p. 48.
41. Goldwater, quoted in Thomas E. Cronin, Tania Cronin, and Michael Milakovich, *United States Crime in the Streets* (Bloomington: Indiana University Press, 1981).
42. *New York Times*, September 4, 1964, p. 13.
43. William Chambliss, "Moral Panics and Racial Oppression," in Hawkins, ed., *Ethnicity, Race and Crime*, p. 22.
44. Ibid., p. 26.
45. *New York Times*, January 23, 1994, p. 16.
46. Mark Fishman, "Crime Waves as Ideology," *Social Problems*, June 1978.
47. Ibid., p. 11.
48. Ibid., p. 14.
49. Richard Morin, "Crime Time: The Fear, the Facts: How Sensationalism Got Ahead of the Stats," *Washington Post*, January 30, 1994, "Outlook Section," p. C1.
50. Ibid.
51. Ibid., p. C2.
52. Ellen Edwards, "Networks Make Crime Top Story: Survey Says Coverage Fanned Public's Fear," *Washington Post*, March 3, 1994, pp. C1, C8.
53. *New York Times*, December 1993, p. B6.
54. In January 1991, the Florida Fourth District Appeals Court ordered Broward County Sheriff Nick Navarro to cease producing crack cocaine, holding that in so doing he was acting illegally (*Associated Press*, January 4, 1991, in *New York Times*, January 5, 1991).
55. As quoted by Peter McWilliams in *Ain't Nobody's Business If You Do: The Absurdity of Consensual Crimes in a Free Society* (Los Angeles: Prelude Press, 1993), p. 37.
56. "Leading the Charge and Loving the Lights: Westchester Prosecutor Courts a TV Jury," *New York Times*, February 21, 1995, p. B1.
57. The reader is reminded that the term *crocodile tears* means more than simply playacting one's grief; it is a predatory exercise arising out of the myth that the crocodile cries as it devours its victim.
58. Janet Maslin, "In Dirty Laundryland: A Day with Jenny, Phil, Sally, Maury, Oprah et al.," *New York Times*, October 10, 1993, sec. 9, p. 7.
59. "News from Lake Wobegon," on National Public Radio's *Prairie Home Companion*, December 1993.
60. Milan Kundera, *The Unbearable Lightness of Being* (New York: Harper Collins 1984), p. 251.
61. Jacques Barzun, *A Stroll with William James* (New York: Harper & Row, 1983), p. 68.

62. For an inside look at how prime-time "reality-based" cop shows "effortlessly smooth out the indiscretions of the lumpen detectives and make them into heroes rushing across the screen . . . because this is what the viewers and advertisers have come to expect," see an intriguing article by Debra Seagal, former "story analyst" for the American Broadcasting Company's *American Detective* (Debra Seagal, "Tales from the Cutting-Room Floor: The Reality of 'Reality-Based Television," *Harper's,* November 1993, pp. 54–55).

63. Wendy Kaminar, "Crime and Community," *The Atlantic Monthly,* May 1994, vol. 273, no. 5, p. 114.

64. U.S. Department of Labor, Bureau of Labor Statistics, Tracy A. Jack and Mark J. Zak, "Results from the First national Census of Fatal Occupational Injuries, 1992," *Compensation and Working Conditions,* December 1993, table 5.

65. U.S. Department of Justice, FBI, *Law Enforcement Officers Killed and Assaulted: 1990,* p. 17; 1992, p. 29; FBI Uniform Crime Reports (Washington, DC: USGPO).

66. Victor Kappeler, Mark Blumberg, and Gary Potter, *The Mythology of Crime and Criminal Justice* (Prospect Heights, Ill.: Waveland Press, 1993), p. 131.

67. Adam Walinsky, "The Crisis of Public Order," *The Atlantic Monthly,* July 1995, p. 52.

68. Ronald H. Brown, "Republican Baloney on Crime," *Washington Post,* 1992.

69. Barney H. Frank, "Race and Crime: Let's Talk Sense," *New York Times,* January 13, 1992, Op-Ed, p. A15.

70. Susan Roberts, "A Critical Evaluation of the City Life Cycle Idea," *Urban Geography* 12, no. 5 (1991): 431–449.

71. Ibid., p. 440.

72. P. E. Peterson, *City Limits* (Chicago: University of Chicago Press, 1981), p. 214.

73. Roger Starr, "Making New York Smaller," *New York Times Magazine,* November 14, 1976, p. 32.

74. Marvin Stone, "Let Big Cities Die?" *U.S. News & World Report,* August 8, 1977, p. 80.

75. "Where Do We Go Next? A Survey of New York City," *Economist,* March 25, 1978, p. 10.

76. Malcolm Gladwell, "Outlook," *Washington Post,* March 19, 1995, p. C1.

77. Joseph Goulden, *The Nation,* November 23, 1970.

78. James Vorenberg, "The War on Crime: The First Five Years," *Atlantic,* February 1971.

79. I was on the Massachusetts committee that oversaw the distribution of

LEAA funds in that state. As Vorenberg (who was also on the committee) left a meeting the week his critical *Atlantic* article appeared, he mentioned that he had to leave early to stem an attempt to cut the funding to the Center for Criminal Justice on the part of the administrators at LEAA, who were unhappy with his comments.

80. Daniel P. Moynihan, "Defining Deviancy Down," *The American Scholar,* Winter 1993, pp. 17–30.

81. James Q. Wilson, *The Moral Sense* (New York: The Free Press, 1993), p. 137. Among the obscure findings Wilson managed to work into this book is one by psychologists Allison Rosenberg and Jerome Kagan, which suggests that "most very inhibited Caucasian children have blue eyes while most very uninhibited ones have brown eyes. . . ." Wilson uses this finding to bolster his views on the genetic and temperamental foundations of human morality. In any other context, the Rosenberg and Kagan finding would be simply interesting or unremarkable. However, in the context of some of Wilson's other writings on race and IQ, and by implication race and crime, this finding takes on the more ominous potential for misinterpretation.

82. Daniel Patrick Moynihan, "Toward a New Intolerance," *The Public Interest,* no. 112, Summer 1993, p. 121.

83. Albert J. Reiss, Jr., and Jeffrey A. Roth, *Understanding and Preventing Violence* (Washington, D.C.: National Academy Press, 1993), p. 50. (The authors update the earlier trends outlined by Holinger, cf. n. 85 below.) For an interesting discussion on the validity of recorded homicide rates as the most reliable crime indicator, see Dane Archer and Rosemary Gartner's reference summary of worldwide data on crime. As to the validity of recorded homicide rates, they comment: "The finding that serious offenses are relatively immune to under-reporting has particular significance for the offense of homicide . . . evidence on this question appears to be consistent and persuasive: homicide is the most valid of offense indicators in that official statistics on this offense are immune to under-reporting." Dane Archer, and Rosemary Gartner, *Violence and Crime in Cross-National Perspective* (New Haven: Yale University Press, 1984), p. 35.

84. Reiss and Roth, p. 51 (see figure 2–1).

85. Paul C. Holinger, *Violent Deaths in the United States: An Epidemiologic Study of Suicide, Homicide, and Accidents* (New York and London: The Guilford Press, 1987), pp. 209–210.

86. Emile Durkheim, *The Rules of Sociological Method* (Glencoe, Ill.: The Free Press/London: Collier-Macmillan Ltd., 1946; orig. pub. in 1885), pp. 68–69.

87. The fact that there is virtually no credible research to suggest that this type of handling "reforms" delinquents is beside the point. It is a matter of looking "tough" on crime. It meets the majority's criteria for the proper political image of crime, no less than the unshaven face of Willie Horton met the same need. The military learned long ago that the boot camp was not likely to rehabilitate a young offender, despite the folk myths to the contrary. That is the major reason the military stopped admitting anyone with even the most minor record of criminal behavior. However, one might be tempted to support boot camps for young inner-city youths were they authentic – i.e., were they, as in the military, followed by intensive training in a trade or occupation, with guaranteed employment with full benefits, including retirement at age 38, followed by a pension.

88. Ron Suskind, "Islands in a Storm: As Urban Woes Grow, 'PLUs' Are Seeking Psychological Suburbia," *Wall Street Journal*, vol. 219, no. 96, p. 1.

89. Michel McQueen, "Political Paradox: People with the Least to Fear from Crime Drive the Crime Issue," *Wall Street Journal*, August 12, 1992, p. A12.

90. John Dawson and Barbara Boland, "Murder in Large Urban Counties, 1988," Bureau of Justice Statistics Special Report, May 1993, pp. 1, 3.

91. McQueen, p. A14.

92. Ibid., p. A12.

93. Barry Meier, "Reality and Anxiety: Crime and the Fear of It," *New York Times*, February 18, 1993, p. A14.

5. RACE, "APPLIED SCIENCE," AND PUBLIC POLICY

1. Richard Herrnstein and Charles Murray, *The Bell Curve: Intelligence and Class Structure in American Life* (New York: Free Press, 1994).

2. Indeed, among those sources cited by Herrnstein and Murray were well-known champions of apartheid and opponents of desegregation, published in a journal that at one time had a leading Nazi race scientist and a mentor of Joseph Mengele serving on its editorial board. Charles Lane, "The Tainted Sources of 'The Bell Curve,' " *New York Review of Books*, vol. 41, no. 20, Dec. 1, 1994, p. 14.

3. *The New Yorker*, Jan. 16, 1995, "The Talk of The Town," p. 28.

4. Troy Duster, *Backdoor to Eugenics* (New York and London: Routledge, Chapman, and Hall, Inc., 1990), p. 93.

5. Luca Cavalli-Sforza, Paolo Menozzi, and Alberto Piazza, *The History and*

Geography of Human Genes (Princeton, N.J.: Princeton University Press, 1994).

6. *Baltimore Sun*, February 21, 1995, p. 11A.

7. Stephen Jay Gould, "Curveball," *The New Yorker*, November 28, 1994.

8. Sydney Blumenthal, *The Rise of the Counter-Establishment: From Conservative Ideology to Political Power* (New York: Times Books, 1986), p. 294. Blumenthal described the process of creating Murray's earlier best-seller, *Losing Ground*, in this way: "Only two years before Murray's book and Murray himself became celebrated, he was toiling in Iowa as an obscure policy wonk . . . his principal claim to fame was a pamphlet authored for the Heritage Foundation, 'Safety Nets and the Truly Needy,' which argued that welfare fostered poverty. By now Murray had befriended Michael Horowitz, the general counsel at the Office of Management and Budget [in the Reagan administration], a neoconservative talent scout. [Murray] was invited to a luncheon at the Manhattan Institute, the Counter-Establishment think tank . . . William Hammett, the institute's president, appraised Murray as a 'nobody' who could be somebody [and] decided to take 'a flier' on Murray. In short order, $125,000 was raised to support him while he turned his idea into a book. . . . Once Murray completed his manuscript . . . [a] big chunk of the money was earmarked for promotion. 'Events of the past six months demonstrate that the Manhattan Institute has indeed become a noticeable force in American political ideas and we offer the following summary for our supporters' evaluation,' Hammett wrote in a private memorandum on December 26, 1984. In it he described 'THE MAKING OF A CLASSIC'. 'Losing Ground' could 'alter the terms of debate over what is perhaps the most compelling political issue of our time: the modern welfare state.' "

Blumenthal went on to show that a highly sophisticated marketing strategy was created, beginning with an institute-funded two-day conference of leading conservative and liberal scholars "along with some of the best writers on the subject" to discuss Murray's thesis. Murray was then sent on a nationwide "victory tour" of personal appearances and television and radio interviews. All cash on hand at the Manhattan Institute was set aside for the tour, which extended over a number of months, and during which, as Blumenthal noted, "Murray was transformed from 'a nobody' into an intellectual star."

9. Lewis Lapham, "Reactionary Chic: How the Nineties Right Recycles the Bombast of the Sixties Left," *Harper's Magazine*, March 1995, p. 18.

10. Ibid., p. 9.

11. Quentin Skinner, *The Return of Grand Theory in Human Sciences* (Cambridge: Cambridge University Press, 1985), p. 8.

12. As Skinner put it: "To perceive all human behaviour in law-like, causal terms – as R. D. Laing and his associates have especially protested – presupposes that the question to ask about abnormal behaviour must always be what malfunction is promoting it. But this is to overlook the possibility that the behaviour in question may be strategic, a way of trying to cope with the world. And this oversight, Laing has argued, has the effect of reducing the agents involved to objects of manipulation when they deserve to be treated as subjects of consciousness" (p. 9). (Nowhere is this more obvious than in the writings of Wilson, Murray, and Herrnstein. The closest one gets to a person is as an object of manipulation.)

13. Ibid., p. 9.

14. Stefan Kuhl, *The Nazi Connection: Eugenics, American Racism, and German National Socialism* (New York/Oxford: Oxford University Press, 1994), p. 66.

15. Gould, "Curveball," *The New Yorker,* November 28, 1994.

16. Jacques Barzun, *Darwin, Marx, Wagner: Critique of a Heritage* (New York: Doubleday Anchor Books, 1958), p. 26.

17. Ysabel Rennie, *The Search for Criminal Man: A Conceptual History of the Dangerous Offender* (Lexington, Mass. and Toronto: Lexington Books/D. C. Heath and Co. 1978), p. 63. Rennie cites Loren Eiseley's *Darwin's Century: Evolution and the Men Who Discovered It* (New York: Doubleday Anchor Books, 1961), pp. 264, 268.

18. Chicago forensic psychiatrist Helen L. Morrison (quoted on "Soundprints," produced by The Johns Hopkins University for National Public Radio, 1994). As Eugene H. Methwin, senior editor at *Reader's Digest,* commented in an article on serial murderers, "Dr. Morrison hopes her research will lead to techniques allowing earlier recognition and apprehension of these beasts in human form." E. Methvin, "Psycho Killer, *Qu'est-ce que c'est?:* The Face of Evil," *The National Review,* January 23, 1995, p. 42.

19. Ibid., p. 93. Duster makes note of the fact that, between 1983 and 1988, articles in professional journals attributing crime to genes increased fourfold over the previous decade.

20. James Q. Wilson and Richard Herrnstein, *Crime and Human Nature* (New York: Simon and Schuster, 1985).

21. In 1911, as he was British Home Secretary and responsible for the nation's prisons, Winston Churchill wrote: "The mood and temper of the public in regard to the treatment of crime and criminals is one of the most unfailing tests of the civilization of any country. A calm dispassionate recognition of the rights of the accused and even of the convicted criminal against the State; a constant heart-searching of all charged with the deed of punish-

ment; tireless efforts toward the discovery of regenerative processes; unfailing faith that there is a treasure, if you can find it, in the heart of every man. These are the symbols which in the treatment of crime and criminals make and measure the stored-up strength of a nation and are sign and proof of the living virtue in it."

22. As Wilson and Herrnstein summarize the research: "Psychopaths are not impervious to conditioning, but the autonomic nervous system that mediates emotional responses, quite sensitive in nonpsychopaths, is insensitive in them, especially (but not exclusively) when conditioning involves anticipating a punishing stimulus like an electric shock. . . ." (*Crime and Human Nature*, p. 203). And when it came to crime and IQ: "There are two . . . constitutional factors that could also contribute to higher black crime rates, intelligence and temperament" (ibid., p. 466).

23. Havelock Ellis, *The Criminal*, 3d ed. (London: The Walter Scott Publishing Co., Ltd.; New York: Charles Scribner's Sons, 1903), pp. 123–124. When studies appeared to contradict this view, other explanations were at the ready. Ellis mentions, for example, that in a study of 52 youthful offenders, one researcher found that only a small proportion of the boys showed less sensitivity to pain than normal children, while greater sensitivity to pain was noted in 92% of the delinquents. This difference was attributed to "the neurotic character of many of the delinquents, and the fact that their general health was below the normal standard" (p. 135).

24. This quote is taken from the previously untranslated first Italian edition of Lombroso's *L'uomo delinquente* (1899) and did not appear in the later English edition (*Crime: Its Causes and Remedies*, 1918). The translation was provided to Pier Beirne by Professor Leonard Savitz and appears in Beirne's *Inventing Criminology: Essays on the Rise of 'Homo Criminalis' "* (State University of New York Press, 1993), p. 178.

25. Samuel A. Cartwright, "Slavery in the Light of Ethnology," in E. N. Elliott, ed., *Cotton Is King, and Pro-Slavery Arguments* (Augusta, Ga., 1860), pp. 689–728; cited in Robert Proctor, *Racial Hygiene* (Cambridge, Mass.: Harvard University Press, 1988), p. 13.

26. Daniel Pick, *Faces of Degeneration: A European Disorder 1848–c. 1918* (New York: Cambridge University Press, 1989).

27. A. J. McKelway, "Three Prison Systems of the Southern States of America," in *Penal and Reformatory Institutions*, ed. Charles Henderson (New York: Russell Sage Foundation, Charities Publication Committee, 1910), p. 88.

28. Pick, pp. 155–175.

29. Cesare Lombroso, *L'uomo bianco e l'uomo di colore: Letture sull'origine e le*

varietà delle razze umane (Padua, 1871), pp. 222–223; cited in Pick, *Faces of Degeneration,* p. 126.

30. Ibid., p. 165. In his analysis of Jekyll and Hyde, Pick notes that: "The riddle of atavism is only solved in Jekyll's final statement, delivered posthumously into the hand of his lawyer. We learn how an early recognition of the 'thorough and primitive duality of man' had led him to transgress the bounds of chemistry, to experiment with the alchemy in a fabulous dream of separating good from evil . . . instead of the dream of transcending an animal history Jekyll discovers tragically that Hyde's 'ape-like spite' is overpowering. Ever larger quantities of the antidote are needed to suppress the fiend, for as the drug wears off, 'the animal within me' is once again 'licking the chops of memory.' Sleep itself becomes the catalyst of Hyde's liberation. Jekyll awakes to find his hands 'corded' and hairy" (pp. 165–166).

31. Pick, p. 171. Pick adds that: "Stoker's novel refers to Max Nordau and Cesare Lombroso, to a whole realm of investigation into degeneration and atavism which itself wavered between a taxonomy of visible stigmata and the horror of invisible maladies. There was an unresolved contradiction between the desired image of a specific, identifiable criminal type (marked out by ancestry) and the wider representation of a society in crisis, threatened by waves of degenerate blood and moral contagion." Pick adds that *Dracula*'s Jonathan Harker, like Lombroso and Morel, "journeys from specific images of deformity (goitre in particular: 'Here and there we passed Czechs and Slovaks, all in picturesque attire, but I noticed that goitre was painfully prevalent'), towards the citadel of full-blown degeneracy. From that early work on cretinism and goitre, a medicopsychiatric theory had emerged in which, . . . the degenerate was cast as a kind of social vampire who preyed on the nation and desired, in Lombroso's words, 'not only to extinguish life in the victim, but to mutilate the corpse, tear its flesh and drink its blood.' "

32. Quoted in *The Baltimore Sun,* February 2, 1986.

33. Sam Roberts, "Metro Matters," *New York Times,* March 2, 1992.

34. Carl N. Degler, *In Search of Human Nature: The Decline and Revival of Darwinism in American Social Thought* (Oxford: Oxford University Press, 1991), p. 43.

35. Mark H. Haller, *Eugenics: Hereditarian Attitudes in American Thought* (New Brunswick, N.J.: Rutgers University Press, 1963), p. 47.

36. Martin W. Barr, *Mental Defectives: Their History, Treatment and Training* (Philadelphia: P. Blakiston's Sons & Co., 1904), p. 190; cited by Haller in *Eugenics,* p. 48.

37. "Castration" refers to surgical removal of the testes of males and the ovaries of females.

38. Haller, *Eugenics*, p. 48.

39. Ibid., p. 48.

40. Degler, *In Search of Human Nature*, p. 45.

41. Haller, p. 50.

42. Lawrence Friedman, *Crime and Punishment in American History* (New York: Basic Books, 1993), p. 336.

43. Richard Maxwell Brown, *Strain of Violence: Historical Studies of American Violence and Vigilantism* (New York: Oxford University Press, 1975), p. 210.

44. Jesse Ewell, M.D., in *Virginia Medical Semi-Monthly* 11 (January 11, 1907): 464; cited in Haller, *Eugenics*, p. 209.

45. Haller, p. 47. Haller (p. 209) cites Hunter McGuire and G. Frank Lydston, "Sexual Crimes among Southern Negroes," *Virginia Medical Monthly* 20 (May 1893): 122. Others who recommended similar measures were Robert Boal, "Emasculation and Ovariotomy as a Penalty for Crime and Reformation of Criminals," *Transactions of the Illinois State Medical Society* (1894), p. 535; and Dr. William A. Hammond, "Castration Recommended as a Substitute for Capital Punishment," *Journal of the American Medical Association* 18 (April 16, 1892): 499-500.

46. Haller, p. 46.

47. Friedman, *Crime and Punishment in American History*, p. 336.

48. Max G. Schlapp and Edward H. Smith, *The New Criminology: A Consideration of the Chemical Causation of Abnormal Behavior* (New York: Boni & Liveright, 1928).

49. Friedman, p. 338.

50. Tony Platt and Paul Takagi, "Biosocial Criminology: A Critique," in F. Marsh and Janet Katz, *Biology, Crime and Ethics* (Cincinnati: Anderson Publishing Co., 1984), p. 61.

51. Margaret Canovan, *G. K. Chesterton: Radical Populist* (New York and London: Harcourt Brace Jovanovich, 1977), p. 70. Canovan cites Chesterton's book of essays, *Eugenics and Other Evils* (London: Cassell, 1922), p. 164.

52. *Los Angeles Times*, Jan. 13, 1995, pp. B1, B4.

53. Peter Breggin, "Psychosurgery for Political Purposes," *Duquesne Law Review* 13, no. 841 (1973): 853.

54. Ibid., p. 14.

55. Ibid., p. 13.

56. E. Rodin, "A Neurological Appraisal of Some Episodic Behavioral Disturbances with Special Emphasis on Aggressive Outbursts," Exhibit 3 for the American Orthopsychiatric Association, *Kaimowitz v. Dept. of Mental Health*,

Civil No. 73–19, 434-AW (Cir. Ct. Wayne Co., Mich., July 19, 1973); cited in Breggin.

57. James Q. Wilson, "Uncommon Sense about the IQ Debate," *Fortune*, January 11, 1993, p. 99.

58. Letter to Editor, *Journal of the American Medical Association* 201 (1967): 895.

59. Vernon H. Mark, and Frank Ervin, *Violence and the Brain* (New York: Harper & Row, 1970), p. 65. None of these suggestions came without a certain amount of political and personal baggage. In the late 1980s, Dr. Mark also led the movement in Philadelphia calling for a total quarantine of persons with AIDS. The ubiquitous image of the criminal as "monster" merges with other apparently primal fears.

60. "Killer's brain causes clash," *USA Today*, April 20, 1993, p. 1.

61. Moriz Benedikt, *Anatomical Studies upon Brains of Criminals*, trans. E. P. Fowler (New York: William Wood and Co., 1881).

62. Friedman, *Crime and Punishment in American History*, p. 3398.

63. Richard Herrnstein, *IQ and the Meritocracy* (Boston: Little, Brown, 1973), p. 221.

64. Richard M. Lerner, *Final Solutions: Biology, Prejudice, and Genocide* (University Park, Pa.: The Pennsylvania State University Press, 1992), p. 184.

65. Christopher Lasch, *The Revolt of the Elites and the Betrayal of Democracy* (New York: W. W. Norton, 1995), p. 34.

66. Stephen Jay Gould, "Curveball," *The New Yorker*, November 28, 1994. As Gould put it, "The authors omit facts, misuse statistical methods, and seem unwilling to admit the consequences of their own words."

67. Leon Kamin, Review of *Crime and Human Nature* in *The Scientific American*, February 1986, p. 24.

68. Leon Kamin, "Reply," *The Scientific American*, May 1986, p. 7.

69. Ed Koch, "The Mugger and His Genes," *Policy Review*, Winter 1986.

70. Joseph Hunt, "Rapists Have Big Ears: Genetic Screening in Massachusetts," *The Real Paper*, July 4, 1973, p. 4.

71. Juan B. Cortes, *Delinquency and Crime: A Biophysical Approach* (New York: Seminar Press, 1972).

72. Graeme Newman, *Understanding Violence* (New York: J. B. Lippincott, 1979).

73. Anthony Platt and Paul Takagi, "Biosocial Criminology: A Critique," *Crime and Social Justice* 11 (Spring/Summer 1979): 8.

74. Correspondence in *Science*, vol. 225, March 1, 1985, pp. 983–989. In 1983, Mednick submitted a research proposal to the federal Office of Juvenile Justice and Delinquency Prevention (OJJDP) to conduct another study of genetic influences on delinquency. He planned to identify 2,000

nine- to twelve-year-old boys for the experiment, musing that though it would be better to pick six-year-olds, there might be political problems in applying the various tests. Mednick wanted to administer electroencephalograms (to identify psychomotor epilepsy); measure with skin galvanometers, the electrical properties of skin response on the palms and soles of feet to boys exposed to "artificially induced stress" (by shooting a gun off without warning behind each boy); measure testosterone levels (though Mednick admitted that hockey players might have the same levels); identify laterality (on the theory that left-handers are more prone to delinquency); and search for physical anomalies such as malformed ears, low-set ears, asymmetrical ears, soft pliable ears, high palates, furrowed tongues, curved fingers, and a third toe longer than second. (The reference to third toes was reminiscent of Lombroso's view of the atavistic criminal with "prehensile" feet.) Mednick also planned to administer IQ tests. Significantly, when it came to looking at social, economic, and familial issues, Mednick proposed conducting a 30-minute interview that would theoretically cover such issues as "family interaction," "situational factors," "attitudes toward the law," and "relationships with peers." Mednick's proposal was positively received by Alfred Regnery, the Reagan-appointed administrator of the Office of Juvenile Justice and Delinquency Prevention. As a result of congressional pressure and concerns of some OJJDP staff that the research might violate a congressionally imposed ban on human experimentation, however, the project was not funded.

75. Albert J. Reiss, Jr., and Jeffrey A. Roth, eds., *Understanding and Preventing Violence* (Washington D.C.: National Academy Press, 1993).

76. Allen Beck, *Survey of Youth in Custody, 1987* (September 1988), NCJ-11365; *Profile of Jail Inmates, 1989* (April 1991), NCJ-129097.

77. Robert Tillman, "The Size of the 'Criminal Population': The Prevalence and Incidence of Adult Arrests," *Criminology* 25, no. 3 (Fall 1987); Peter Reuter, Robert MacCoun, Patrick Murphy, et al., *Money from Crime: A Study of the Economics of Drug Dealing in Washington, D.C.* (Santa Monica, Calif.: The Rand Corporation, June 1990); Mark Mauer, *Young Black Men and the Criminal Justice System: A Growing National Problem* (Washington, D.C.: The Sentencing Project, 1990); *Hobbling a Generation: African American Males in the District of Columbia's Criminal Justice System* (Washington, D.C.: The National Center on Institutions and Alternatives, March 1992); *Hobbling a Generation II: African American Males in Baltimore's Criminal Justice System* (Washington, D.C.: The National Center on Institutions and Alternatives, June 1992); Jerome Miller, *The Duval County Jail Report*, submitted to the

Honorable Howell W. Melton, U.S. District Judge, Middle District of Florida, June 1, 1993, p. 139.

78. Anne C. Case and Lawrence F. Katz, "The Company You Keep: The Effects of Family and Neighborhood on Disadvantaged Youths," NBER Boston Youth Survey, funded by Russell Sage Foundation and National Science Foundation (Cambridge, Mass.: Bell Associates, May 1991).

79. Joan McCord, "Research Perspectives on Criminal Behavior," paper presented at the American Association for the Advancement of Science symposium on "Controversy over Crime and Heredity: An Exploration," Feb. 15, 1993.

80. Hans G. Brunner, et al. *Science*, November 1993.

81. Natalie Angier, "Study Finds a Genetic Flaw That May Explain Some Male Violence," *New York Times*, October 22, 1993.

82. Brunner, et al.

83. *New York Times*, Oct. 22, 1993.

84. Ibid.

85. Ibid.

86. Ibid.

87. Jerome Kagan, quoted in "Seeking the Roots of Violence," *Time*, April 19, 1993, p. 53.

88. Ibid.

89. As Kagan commented: "Most youth or adults who commit a violent crime will not commit a second. . . . The group we are concerned with are the recidivists – those who have been arrested many times. This is the group for whom there might be some biological contribution" (in "Seeking the Roots of Violence," *Time*, April 19, 1993, p. 53).

90. Private conversations with authors. The Scandinavian studies upon which most current theories of genetic influences on criminal behavior are based seem more likely to apply, if at all, to a rural or suburban white middle-class American adolescent than to the inner-city African-American juvenile subject to overwhelmingly debilitating environmental and social conditions.

91. As Amherst University sociologist Richard Moran put it: "a brief look at penal history reveals that it was under the banner of humanitarian concerns that involuntary sterilization of the mentally ill, mentally defective, the epileptic, sex offenders, 'degenerates', syphilitics, and the so-called hereditary criminal were undertaken. Lobotomy, electrical shock, and preventive incarceration of the 'dangerous classes' were likewise practiced as preferable penal substitutes." Richard Moran, "Biomedical Research and the Politics of Crime Control," *Contemporary Crises* vol. 2 (1979): 337.

92. Graeme Newman, *Just and Painful: A Case for the Corporal Punishment of Criminals* (London: Harrow and Heston/Macmillan, 1983), pp. 69–70.

93. Canovan, *G. K. Chesterton*, p. 70.

94. James Q. Wilson and Richard Herrnstein, *Crime and Human Nature* (New York: Simon and Schuster, 1985), p. 505.

95. Ibid.

96. H. L. A. Hart, *Punishment and Responsibility*, rev. ed. (Oxford: Oxford University Press, 1978).

97. *The Baltimore Sun*, April 3, 1995, p. D1.

98. Daniel Seligman, *A Question of Intelligence: The IQ Debate in America* (New York: Birch Lane Press, 1992). Seligman saw Michael Young's 1950s science-fiction novel, *The Rise of the Meritocracy*, as foretelling *The Bell Curve*. "For many low-IQ workers, it is easy enough to specify the basis of their unhappiness," writes Seligman. "Young asks, 'Are they not bound to recognize that they have an inferior status – not, as in the past, because they were denied opportunity; but because they *are* inferior? For the first time in human history, the inferior man has no ready buttress for his self-regard.' Tough to take eh?" concluded Seligman.

99. Richard J. Herrnstein, "Subversive Intelligence," *National Review*, October 19, 1992.

100. In *Darwinism, Medical Progress and Eugenics*, quoted in Semmel, *Imperialism and Social Reform* (London: Allen and Unwin, 1975), p. 48.

101. Margaret Canovan, *G. K. Chesterton: Radical Populist*, p. 67.

102. Ibid.

103. Charles Wickstead Armstrong, *The Survival of the Unfittest* (London: Daniel, 1931), p. 93.

104. Piers Beirne, *Inventing Criminology* (Albany: State University of New York, 1993), pp. 221–223.

105. Carl N. Degler, *In Search of Human Nature: The Decline and Revival of Darwinism in American Social Thought* (New York: Oxford University Press, 1991), p. 47.

106. Philip Reilly, *Genetics, Law, and the Social Policy* (Cambridge, Mass.: Harvard University Press, 1991).

107. Stefan Kuhl, *The Nazi Connection: Eugenics, American Racism, and German National Socialism* (New York and Oxford: Oxford University Press, 1994).

108. Troy Duster, *Genetics, Race and Crime: Genetic Identification and Criminal Justice* (New Jersey: Cold Spring Harbor Laboratory Press), 0–87969–379–7/92, p. 132.

109. Ingo Muller, *Hitler's Justice: The Courts of the Third Reich*, trans. by Deborah

Lucas Schneider (Cambridge, Mass.: Harvard University Press, 1991), p. 123.

110. R. Moran, p. 337.

111. Rennie, *The Search for Criminal Man* (1978), p. 88.

112. Christopher Winship, "Lessons Beyond 'The Bell Curve,'" *New York Times,* Op-Ed, November 15, 1994, p. A29.

113. John Hogan, "Genes and Crime: A U.S. Plan to Reduce Violence Rekindles an Old Controversy," *Scientific American,* February 1993, pp. 24–29.

114. Jerome Kagan, *Unstable Ideas: Temperament, Cognition, and Self* (Cambridge, Mass.: Harvard University Press, 1989), p. 28.

115. Nathan Glazer, "Race and IQ," *The New Republic,* October 31, 1994, p. 16.

116. Svend Ranulf, *Moral Indignation and Middle Class Psychology* (New York: Schocken Books, 1964), p. 54. Regarding Weber's warning, in a classic example of Nordic understatement, Ranulf, a sociologist living in a country soon to be invaded by Germany, commented in 1938, "We believe that these words have their full validity today."

117. W. Sombart, *Die Juden und das Wirtschaftsleben* (Leipzig, 1911), p. 296; quoted by Ranulf, p. 54.

118. "*g*" refers to the "general factor" of intelligence, first so-named by British psychologist Charles Spearman in 1904. Gould noted that nothing in *The Bell Curve* angered him more than Herrnstein and Murray's unjustified reliance on "that number known as *g*. . . . [they] simply declare that the issue has been decided – it is by now beyond much technical dispute that there is such a thing as a general factor of cognitive ability on which human beings differ and that this general factor is measured reasonably well by a variety of standardized tests, best of all by IQ tests designed for that purpose.'" Gould comments, "Such a statement represents extraordinary obfuscation, achievable only if one takes 'expert' to mean that group of psychometricians working the tradition of *g* and its avatar IQ."

119. Christopher Jencks, *Rethinking Social Policy: Race, Poverty, and the Underclass* (Cambridge, Mass.: Harvard University Press, 1992), pp. 110–111.

120. Ibid.

121. Mickey Kaus, *The End of Equality* (New York: Basic Books, 1992). Wilson, in his review of Kaus's book, while criticizing its hope for social equality, upbraided Kaus's liberal critics for not accepting (as, implicitly, Kaus does) what is essentially Herrnstein's view of genetics and the meritocracy. Wilson leaves no doubt as to where he stands. As he wrote: "Robert Kuttner, writing in the *New Republic,* suggests that Kaus may have become a 'convert to conservative fantasies of market meritocracy or unfounded genetic theo-

ries of intelligence.' Robert Scheer, writing in the *Los Angeles Times Book Review*, displays an impressive command of old-left venom. He describes the book as a self-indulgent rant of a kind one expects to find in an erotic novel and calls Kaus' proposals 'harebrained' and 'bizarre.' Kuttner here displays an ignorance of the evidence on the heritability of intelligence that is truly remarkable. I wonder if he thinks that he is as smart as he is – and he is very smart, indeed – simply because his parents sent him to the best schools." James Q. Wilson, "Redefining Equality: The Liberalism of Mickey Kaus," in *The Public Interest*, no. 109 (Fall 1992), p. 104.

122. Wilson, p. 102.

123. G. K. Chesterton, *Eugenics and Other Evils* (London: Cassell, 1922), p. 12.

124. The Tuskegee Study was run as a public health service by the Centers for Disease Control to study the "natural course" of syphilis. A total of 412 infected black men and a control group of another 200 were selected. The infected men were not told they had syphilis, nor were they treated. Even when penicillin was discovered in the early 1940s, the Tuskegee subjects were not treated. In order to prevent the possibility of treatment "contaminating" the study, the disease was allowed to run its course for 40 years, killing, maiming, and permanently impairing the subjects – even after the effects of antibiotics in stopping the course of the disease had been clearly demonstrated (James H. Jones, *Bad Blood*, 1981). In 1993, previously secret documents of the Atomic Energy Commission (AEC) revealed that at least 1,000 people had been exposed to potentially harmful doses of radiation for research purposes. Among them were 19 mentally retarded teenaged boys from poor families placed at the Fernald state institution in Massachusetts. They were exposed to radioactive iron and calcium in their breakfast cereal. (The study was funded in part by the Quaker Oats Company.) In Tennessee, 18 institutionalized patients were injected with plutonium and seven newborn boys (six of them black) were injected with radioactive iron, causing a biologist at the AEC to comment that the experiments had a "a little of the Buchenwald touch."

Similarly, between 1949 and 1957 the Medical College of Virginia (MCV) ran a secret laboratory designed to assess the potential for massive nuclear casualties. About 100 African-American burn patients were subjected to radiation or antibiotic treatment annually for "investigational purposes." Among the experiments were those in which dogs and burn patients were matched. The dogs were burnt and then irradiated. It was found that dogs subjected to "insignificant" (i.e., nonlethal) doses of radiation died at five times the rate as those not so irradiated. In the "Special Burn" Units established at two Virginia "colored" hospitals, burn patients were injected with radioactive isotopes to observe their rates of recovery or death. As Honicker put it: "The problem was that the radioisotopes, being highly energetic, could have contributed to the further destruction of red blood cells – cells in patients who were already on the brink of life and death." "Burning Secrets: In a Virginia Hospital, A Cold War Time of Strange Experiments," *Washington Post*, "Outlook," June 19, 1995, p. C 4.

125. David Rothman, "Shiny Happy People: The Problem with 'Cosmetic Psychopharmacology,' " *The New Republic*, February 14, 1994. p. 34.

126. Robert Wright, "Brave New World Dept.: The Biology of Violence," *The New Yorker*, March 13, 1995, pp. 68–77.

127. David C. Rowe, "An Adaptive Strategy Theory of Crime and Delinquency," forthcoming in J. David Hawkins, ed., *Some Current Theories of Delinquency and Crime* (New York: Cambridge University Press, 1994).

128. Speech delivered to an invited audience in London, July 1994. Wilson later summarized his rationale for massive long-term incarceration in this way: "There are one million people in prison. We are not going to change them. . . . We have boys on the streets; we can't change them" (*New York Times*, December 30, 1994, p. A24).

129. James Q. Wilson, "A New Approach to Welfare Reform: Humility," *Wall Street Journal*, December 29, 1994, p. A10.

6. THE FUTURE

1. Nils Christie, *Crime Control as Industry: Towards Gulags Western Style?* (London and New York: Routledge), p. 165.

2. Ivan Hannaford, "The Idiocy of Race," *The Wilson Quarterly*, Spring 1994, p. 28.

3. Svend Ranulf, *Moral Indignation and Middle-Class Psychology: A Sociological Study* (New York: Schocken Books, 1964), pp. 1–2; first published by Levin & Munksgaard, Ejnar Munksgaard, Copenhagen, 1938.

4. Ibid., pp. 10–11.

5. *Washington Post*, August 2, 1994.

6. Of an evening recently, I tuned into "The David Brudnoy Show" on WBZ, Boston's clear-channel 50,000-watt station, to hear a talk-show host with a Ph.D., touted as an intellectual and featured in *The New York Times Magazine*, call for 20,000 executions annually as a means of deterring violence.

7. *New York Times*, September 17, 1994, pp. A1, 11.

8. HR 667, Title Vf, Sections 401 and 501.
9. DiIulio, John, "Let 'em Rot," *The Wall Street Journal*, January 26, 1994.
10. Newman, G., p. 69.
11. Rorie Sherman, " 'Dr. Death' Visits the Condemned," *The National Law Journal*, November 8, 1993, p. 11. *The National Law Journal* reported that "Suicide advocate Dr. Jack Kevorkian . . . and his attorney announced that Texas officials agreed to allow 32-year-old convicted murderer Jonathan Wayne Nobles to donate one of his kidneys before being executed. . . . Ms. Nobles' attorney, Sandra L. Babcock of the Texas Appellate Practice and Educational Resource Center in Austin, [said] her client is incompetent to make decisions about such a donation. Mr. Nobles has a history of mental illness, including numerous suicide attempts, the first when he was 5, [said] Ms. Babcock, adding: 'It seems exploitative to solicit organs from prisoners 'especially from death row population, because so many of them are mentally ill'."
12. *Corrections Digest*, November 27, 1991.
13. *New York Times*, May 5, 1995, p. A10.
14. Associated Press, "California Prisons Turn on Electrified Fence," *The Atlanta Journal/Constitution*, November 21, 1993, p. E5.
15. DiIulio, John J., G. Alpert, M. Moore, G. Cole, J. Petersilia, C. Logan, and J.Q. Wilson, *Performance Measures for the Criminal Justice System* (Discussion Papers from the BJS-Princeton Project, October 1993 NCJ-143505).
16. Ibid., p. 29.
17. Ibid., p. 28.
18. Ensuring that "care" for prison inmates is minimal has been a hallmark of modern penal management. It is the same kind of thinking which caused the American eugenicist Harry Laughlin to see virtually any kind of caring institutions as less than helpful for dealing with the underclass. In 1936, he presented the English version of the Nazi propaganda film, *Erbkrank* ("Hereditary Defective") to the Carnegie Institution. The film found an enthusiastic response from the American audience. The director of the Racial Policy Office of the Nazi party opened the film with this comment: "A people that builds palaces for the descendants of drunks, criminals, and idiots, and which at the same time houses its workers and farmers in miserable huts, is on the way to rapid self-destruction." Laughlin noted that the Nazi film "contrasts the squalid living conditions of normal children in certain German city slums with the finer and costly modern custodial institutions built for the care of handicapped persons produced by the socially inadequate and degenerate . . ." The better remedy was to be found in eugenics. (Kuhl, S., op. cit. pp. 48, 49.)

19. "Close The Door on Federal 'Glamour Slammers,'" Press Release, Congressman Dick Zimmer, Washington, D.C. ,February 9, 1995.

20. Van Den Haag, Ernest, "How to Cut Crime," *The National Review*, May 30, 1994, p. 34.

21. Ian Fisher, "Weighing Caution Against Compassion," the *New York Times*, Metro sec., March 7, 1994, p. B3.

22. *Los Angeles Times*, September 7, 1993, p. B3 (East Coast Edition).

23. Twice-convicted murderer Thomas Grasso, whose case fueled the death penalty debate in the 1994 election campaign between Mario Cuomo and George Pataki, was returned to Oklahoma by newly elected Governor Pataki where he was executed on March 20, 1995. At the time of his execution Grasso remarked that after spending some time in the Oklahoma facility, he much preferred dying. (Associated Press, *Washington Times*, p. A4, March 21, 1995.)

24. "The Nature of Imprisonment in the U.S.," Committee to End the Marion Lockdown, Spring 1994 (Chicago, Il.) p. 5.

25. William J. Chambliss, "Moral Panics and Racial Oppression," in *Ethnicity, Race, and Crime*, ed. by Darney Hawkins (SUNY Press, from author's 1993 unpublished manuscript), pp. 7–8.

26. Ibid.

27. *Wall Street Journal*, May 12, 1994, p. A1.

28. Daniel L. Feldman, "20 Years of Prison Expansion: A Failing National Strategy," *Public Administration Review* 53, no. 6 (November/December 1993): 561.

29. Ibid.

30. Ibid., p. 562.

31. David Ammons, Richard Campbell, and Sandra Somoze, "Selecting Prison Sites: State Processes, Site-Selection Criteria, and Local Initiatives," University of Georgia, Carl Vinson Institute of Government, 1993.

32. "Law Enforcement Technology for the 21st Century, May 15–17, 1995," conference brochure, National Institute of Justice, American Defense Preparedness Association, Washington, D.C.

33. "Audit of Texas Department of Corrections," Comptroller of Public Accounts (John Sharp), State of Texas, Austin, 1994.

34. *Wall Street Journal*, June 18, 1993.

35. Florida Department of Corrections, 1992/93 Annual Report, *Corrections as a Business: Making Public Dollars Go Further*, Harry Singletary, Secretary, Tallahassee, Florida, September 14, 1993, pp. 21–22.

36. Ivan Hannaford, "The Idiocy of Race," *The Wilson Quarterly*, Spring 1994, p. 28.

37. The obsession with "boot camps" has been particularly curious from the start in that there was virtually no research that showed they lowered either recidivism or prison populations. Indeed, some research suggested that boot camps might indirectly raise prison populations as a result of the fact that the bulk of inmates sent to them would not otherwise go to prison but would be placed on probation. When sending the person to boot camp, the judge tells the young recruit that if he fails there, he will be sent to prison. Depending upon the camp, 40% to 70% of the inmates do fail or are dismissed from the program. To make good its threat, the court must send these inmates to prison. Had they not been offered boot camp, they probably would have successfully completed a period of probation.

38. As announced on National Public Radio (report by NPR correspondent John Burnette, "All Things Considered," February 24, 1995).

39. National Public Radio, "All Things Considered," January 25, 1994.

40. The speed with which this is occurring goes unacknowledged. For example, conservative criminologist John DiIulio predicted in February 1994 that the number of inmates, probationers, or parolees in the national corrections systems could surpass four million by the year 2000 (quoted in *The Congressional Quarterly Researcher*, February 4, 1994, p. 115). However, by the end of 1994, more than 5.1 million Americans were in jail, prison, on probation, or on parole (U.S. Department of Justice, Bureau of Justice Statistics, NCJ0156432, August 1995).

41. While criticizing Hooton for his "circularity" in hypothesizing that "physical correlates of crime reflect biological inferiority," Wilson and Herrnstein bemoaned the "rough treatment" Hooton's work "suffered [at the hands of] the criminological community, especially the sociologists who were bound to resent its skimpy treatment of sociological variables." In fact, Hooton did deal with some sociological variables, mentioning in particular the criminalizing effects of imprisonment on blacks. However, his anticrime prescriptions deserved the critical reviews they received.

42. Earnest Albert Hooton, *Crime and the Man* (Cambridge, Mass.: Harvard University Press, 1939).

43. Indeed, these days we hardly need depend upon dubious genetics alone to prove extraordinary things. For example, in 1992 a group of sociologists from the University of New Mexico concluded that such advantages as "economic well-being," "educational attainment," and "family stability" have precisely the opposite effect on African-Americans that they do on whites. The better off, more educated, and more stable the African-American family, the more prone its members are to murder, rob, and burglarize others. As the authors

summarized their findings: "for blacks, higher family income and educational attainment are generally associated with *higher* crime rates; conversely, increases in unemployment and percentage of female-headed families are associated with *declining* crime rates. . . . White crime rates declined as family income and educational attainment increased, and increased as the consumer price index and criminal exposure increased . . . black crime rates increased with higher family income and educational attainment, and decreased as the percentage of female-headed families increased." The writers concluded, "it appears that common assumption[s] about legitimate opportunity and crime . . . was largely justified for whites, but not for blacks." Gary La Free, Kriss Drass, and Patrick O'Day, "Race and Crime in Postwar America: Determinants of African American and White Rates, 1957–1988," *Criminology* 30, no. 2 (1992): 173–177.

44. Robert Vinter, Theodore Newcomb, and Rhea Kish, eds., *Time Out: A National Study of Juvenile Correctional Programs,* National Assessment of Juvenile Corrections, the University of Michigan, Ann Arbor, June 1976.

45. Nils Christie, *Crime Control as Industry: Towards Gulags Western Style?* (London and New York: Routledge, 1993), pp. 21–22.

46. In an unpublished presentation to the International Conference on Imprisonment, Academy of Science, Oslo, Norway, April 28, 1995.

47. Judge Jose Cabranes, quoted in *New York Times,* April 12, 1992.

48. One could envision a change in these trends were a new national leadership to emerge that was sensitive to the racial issues involved and charismatic enough to be able to refocus the national debate on crime. However, such a prospect seems unlikely at this writing.

Index